THE CURRICULUM

A Comparative Perspective

THE CURRICULUM

A Comparative Perspective

BRIAN HOLMES

Emeritus Professor of Comparative Education,
University of London

MARTIN McLEAN

Lecturer in Comparative Education,
University of London Institute of Education

The College of Preceptors

London
UNWIN HYMAN
Boston   Sydney   Wellington

Published by the Academic Division of
Unwin Hyman Ltd
15/17 Broadwick Street, London W1V 1FP, UK

Unwin Hyman Inc.,
8 Winchester Place, Winchester, Mass. 01890, USA

Allen & Unwin (Australia) Ltd,
8 Napier Street, North Sydney, NSW 2060, Australia

Allen & Unwin (New Zealand) Ltd in association with the
Port Nicholson Press Ltd,
Compusales Building, 75 Ghuznee Street, Wellington 1, New Zealand

First published in 1989

British Library Cataloguing in Publication Data
Holmes, Brian
    The curriculum: a comparative perspective.
1. Educational institutions.   Curriculum.
Development.   Objectives
I. Title   II. McLean, Martin
375.'001
ISBN 0–04–375002–8
ISBN 0–04–375003–6   pbk

Library of Congress Cataloging-in-Publication Data
Holmes, Brian.
    The curriculum: a comparative perspective.
Includes index.
1. Curriculum planning—Cross-cultural studies.
2. Education—Curricula—Cross-cultural studies.
I. McLean, Martin.   II. Title.
LB2806.15.H65   1989   375'.001   88–33752
ISBN 0–04–375002–8 (alk. paper)
ISBN 0–04–375003–6 (pbk.: alk. paper)

Typeset in 10 on 11 point Garamond by Nene Phototypesetters Ltd,
and printed in Great Britain by Billing and Sons Ltd, London and Worcester.

Contents

Preface

This book is for readers who want to know what should be taught in schools. Since the creators of the United Nations declared education to be an inalienable human right most governments have attempted to provide universal primary education, secondary schools for all and higher education for large numbers of students. Since 1945 compulsory education has been introduced in many countries and its length increased. The number of school-age children has risen and costs have escalated. Nevertheless it is unlikely that in answer to the question 'Who shall be educated?' governments will in future abandon their policy of providing an 'education for all'.

Indeed, for many years, they were able to persuade taxpayers that 'free' education was an investment which would raise standards of living, ensure peace and promote democracy. These unreasonable expectations were voiced in London in 1945 by the founders of Unesco. They asked teachers to eliminate illiteracy as the source of poverty, war and totalitarianism. A succession of international and national literacy campaigns in developing countries have failed. Investment in education has not narrowed the gap between the wealthy northern countries and the poor southern countries. Local wars proliferate. It is doubtful whether peace studies in schools will prevent them. The failure of teachers to achieve unrealistic educational objectives has provoked a great deal of criticism of education as a societal panacea.

The explosion of scientific knowledge and its applications which have transformed industry, commerce, communications and transport systems, have made the teacher's task more difficult. These changes have prompted the movement of a great many people from rural to urban areas and from one country to another. To retain credibility teachers can no longer simply pass on the accumulated wisdom of their own small community or society by teaching what they themselves had learned at school and in a university. Unless they are familiar with the world of work,

international problems and the tensions which arise in multi-
cultural conurbations they cannot prepare young people for their
life as adults.

Under these circumstances the question 'What knowledge is of
most worth?' is crucial if teachers are to face the future with any
chance of success. There is, however, no universally accepted
curriculum panacea to the problems created by post-1945
socioeconomic and political changes and the reluctance of
teachers to accept novel or foreign curriculum theories and
practices. Common educational problems find unique expression
in national systems. Curriculum responses to them depend upon
an ethos informed by ethnocentric theories of man, society
and knowledge. The case studies in this book are based on
the assumption that four major curriculum theories have their
origins in Europe. An early curriculum model, based on Platonic
Aristotelian assumptions and supported by the Catholic Church,
was challenged by Comenius. His views, mediated by the French,
came to dominate curricula throughout Europe except England.
Some comments by Marx gave rise to a third European curriculum
model. In the late nineteenth century John Dewey formulated a
curriculum theory to meet the changing needs of American society.

Some European and American curriculum practices were freely
incorporated into emerging systems in other parts of the world. On
the other hand, imperialists transferred European curricula to their
colonies where they were modified to accommodate indigenous
beliefs about worthwhile knowledge. The assumption on which
the analysis in this book is based is that the deeply held beliefs of
teachers about individual abilities, the characteristics of the just and
good society and the nature of knowledge make curriculum
change slow and difficult. In the first part of the book these
difficulties are exemplified in four countries where European
models have indigenous roots. In the second part the difficulties
associated with the transfer of curriculum models are examined in
national and regional case studies. These case studies will help
students, teachers and administrators better to understand the
need for curriculum reform and the difficulties of bringing it about.

Since the first draft was prepared a major new Education Bill has
been passed in England and Wales (1988) and a major critical
report on the condition of education in Japan has been published
(1988). The consequences of these attempts to improve education
are not yet known. Both reform proposals have been mentioned
but no attempt has been made fully to anticipate the curriculum

changes which may subsequently occur. In both countries even radical teachers will find it difficult to abandon deeply held beliefs and behaviour patterns.

Both authors are comparative educationists. In the preparation of this volume they have worked closely together but inevitably see events from somewhat different perspectives. Professor Holmes trained as a physicist. Dr McLean is an historian. Rather than attempting to prepare consensus chapters each author has finalized individual chapters within a structure designed to illuminate the questions 'Who shall be educated?' and 'What knowledge is of most worth?'. In each case the politics of educational change since 1945 have been analysed.

Dr McLean is largely responsible for the chapters on educational transfer (6), England and Wales (2), France (3), India (7) and Latin America (8). Professor Holmes wrote the chapters on curriculum models (1), the USA (4), USSR (5) and China (10) and finalized the chapter on Japan (9) when a Japan Society for the Promotion of Science Visiting Fellow at Waseda University. The structure of each chapter is sufficiently similar to facilitate easy comparison but is by no means identical. The presentation of each case study has been influenced by the way each system has evolved since 1945.

Brian Holmes
Martin McLean

London, August 1988

Chapter One

Curriculum theory

'What knowledge is of most worth?' In comparative and historical perspective curriculum theory has been based on answers to this question. In practice, whether overtly stated or covertly accepted, the answers given by priests and teachers to this question have also determined the content of school education. In performing their public service they have selected for transmission from one generation to the next only that knowledge which they considered worthwhile. Definitions of knowledge, of course, themselves restrict what parts of the information accumulated by mankind can be regarded as 'knowledge'. In either case teachers, whether religious or secular, have been able to decide what should be taught. In so far as they possessed much more school knowledge than other adult members of society and their pupils, teachers have been able to say how it should be taught. The power of teachers to decide what knowledge is of most worth and how it should be taught has not yet been seriously challenged.

Until fairly recently if they performed the task of transmitting knowledge to the satisfaction of the public they served, teachers had the power to decide who should be educated. In Europe, and wherever European-type universities have been established, the power of teachers to decide what is taught, how it is taught and to whom it is taught, is best exemplified in the freedom and autonomy enjoyed by university academics. Responsibility has been associated with these privileges and the professional authority of teachers in general has depended on their willingness to perform a service approved by the public in accordance with a self-imposed code of ethics and on the basis of their special skills and knowledge acquired after a long period of training.

The professional authority of teachers was justified by psychological theories about the innate nature of men and women and by elitist theories about the nature of society. Only when these kinds of theory were challenged politically was the central role played by teachers in the organization and control of school education seriously questioned. The most significant change which affected the position of teachers after 1945 was the widespread articulation and acceptance of the view that education should be provided for all as a human right. In 1944, for example, politicians in Britain formulated and adopted the 1944 Education Act which accepted that education should be provided for all children and young adults in accordance with their 'age, aptitude, and ability'. International support was given to these heightened aspirations when the United Nations, having been established in 1945, adopted at its General Assembly in 1948 the Universal Declaration of Human Rights. Article 26 of the declaration set forth 'the right to education' as one of the rights to which all human beings are entitled. In fact, the declaration went little further than statements made at the end of the eighteenth century by French and American reformers who held that primary schooling should be freely provided for all and that secondary and higher education should be available to all those capable of benefiting from these levels of education. Theories of man and society have changed since then and the declaration stimulated demands for universal provision at all levels of education. The power of teachers to decide 'Who shall be educated?' was in effect taken from them by politicians.

The second explosion – of scientific knowledge and its applications – made the task of selecting what was worthwhile from the accumulated wisdom and knowledge of mankind much more difficult. It slowly became apparent that, on any definition of knowledge, it was impossible within existing systems to pass all of it on to all human beings. Teachers were faced with major choices. They had to choose between traditional forms of knowledge on which, for carefully selected pupils and students, a satisfactory general education had been based and 'new' knowledge created by the scientific revolution. Moreover, choices had to be faced in the light of new definitions of knowledge. Already, traditionally sharp distinctions between abstract, theoretical and practical knowledge were being eroded. Emerging curriculum theory persuaded many educators that historical distinctions between 'forms of knowledge' were erroneous. To be sure not all teachers were persuaded of this.

2

A third major post-1945 change affected the position of teachers, namely the emergence of world-wide acceptance of faith in education as a societal panacea. This faith was most strongly favoured by the Americans in marked contrast to Soviet educators. American views found expression in discussions which took place in London in 1945–6 among the founders of Unesco. These educators and scientists expressed the view that teachers should and could do more than pass on knowledge. Most of them argued that, particularly through the promotion of literacy, education was capable of raising standards of living, promoting democracy and safeguarding world peace. To be sure the notion of 'fundamental education' discussed at these early meetings blurred the historically sharp distinction between education and training. In so doing it suggested that the public service teachers should perform is many-faceted.

In the event it has become less clear. As before, teachers have to satisfy university academics that their secondary school products are capable of studying at a university. In addition they are required to prepare students for a wide range of occupations in complex economies in order to promote national economic growth. They are charged with the task of inculcating moral, social and sometimes political values in urban and multi-cultural societies in which traditional patterns of authority are breaking down. They are held responsible for promoting social mobility and for preventing drug and other abuses and familial disharmony. Radically different answers have to be given to the question 'What knowledge is of most worth?' if these diverse tasks are to be undertaken by teachers.

In many parts of the world, particularly in the USA and England and Wales, teacher-training programmes, and the rhetoric of those who prepare and teach on them, suggest that many teachers have been prepared to accept many of these tasks as legitimately part of the public service they should perform. The prominent place accorded to psychology and sociology in English and US teacher-training courses suggests that teachers should know more about children than their parents and as much about society as industrialists and politicians. Since manifestly not every teacher is capable of possessing esoteric knowledge in these areas which goes far beyond the knowledge possessed by many members of the adult population, their authority to select and pass on social scientific knowledge has been questioned. In so far as teachers have attempted to do more than pass on knowledge and have

3

claimed that they can and should improve society their traditional status has been eroded and their freedom and autonomy undermined.

The conditions under which teachers have accepted these new roles were transformed shortly after the Second World War by increases in birth-rates and decreases in infant mortality figures. Primary schools first experienced post-1945 baby booms in the early 1950s. Towards the end of the decade secondary schools were expected rapidly to expand to accommodate all young adolescents. In the 1960s institutions of higher learning, including universities, were expected to find places not only for larger cohorts of secondary school leavers but to satisfy the heightened demand for post-secondary education from young men and women whose parents had not been to university. Governments responded to the population explosion as it worked its way through the system by increasing the number of schools and universities. Few educationists were prepared to accept that in responding to population growth pupil-teacher ratios should be allowed to rise. Indeed great efforts were made in many countries to reduce the size of classes in the belief that such reductions would improve the quality of education. The soundness of this kind of assertion is very questionable. Nevertheless systems of teacher training were expanded as quickly as possible to keep pace with the demand for teachers.

In response to heightened demands for education to be provided as a human right many governments paid more attention to the reorganization of secondary school systems than to the content of education. Movements to reorganize secondary schools along comprehensive lines were initiated by or received the support of left-wing politicians in most countries in Europe. The Japanese government was persuaded to increase the period of compulsory attendance and reorganize the school system under pressure from the Americans. To be sure, many teachers supported these moves, convinced that through increasing equality of opportunity at all stages of schooling the right of all human beings to an education would be achieved in practice. Evidence indicates that they were over-optimistic in accepting that structure was more important than content in equalizing provision.

Interest in curriculum reform was doubtless delayed by the preoccupation of teachers, social scientists and politicians with the expansion and reorganization of secondary education. At the

4

same time, for a variety of reasons, many teachers have resisted changes in the content of school education since by training, temperament and traditional mores they see themselves as the guardians of traditional knowledge. The resistance to change of such teachers is based principally on long-established concepts of what knowledge is of most worth. Some knowledge of historically important answers to the question is important if problems of curriculum change are to be identified and analysed in terms of the resistance of teachers. Some religious and secular answers which continue to inform present-day debates will now be briefly considered.

Teachers as the guardians of traditional knowledge

Many answers have been given to the question 'What knowledge is of most worth?' Not all of them are relevant to present-day curriculum debate. Those which informed the major civilizations of the ancient world are. They account for many of the cultural differences we are aware of today. They help to explain the sources of teacher resistance to major curriculum change and make it possible to anticipate some of the difficulties likely to arise when attempts are made to transfer a curriculum model from one national system of education to another.

From this perspective the most significant long-established answers have several common features. They have all been permanently recorded in some way or another so that the transmission of knowledge is not by word of mouth only and does not necessarily depend on the presence of a teacher. In the major cultures of the world a book, or books, contains what is regarded as worthwhile knowledge. Finally in most cases the answer, and the records in which it is found, have become the foundations on which groups of people have built politically powerful institutions.

In ancient China, for example, the classics of Confucius, which stressed the importance of human relationships, became the texts used by tutors preparing carefully selected students for a series of demanding examinations on the results of which successful candidates entered, as scholar-officials, the service of the emperor. These tests determined the content and methods of teaching in China for centuries. Although the imperial examination system was formally abolished in 1905 its persisting influence

5

is apparent in the People's Republic of China, Taiwan, Hong Kong and indeed wherever Chinese people run schools. Apart from the intrinsic value of the knowledge tested by examinations, possession of it had practical value in that it conferred status and power. In China the Confucian classics acquired the status of religious texts; elsewhere, particularly in Europe, the Chinese examination system influenced the development of competitive examinations as the most democratic method of selecting senior government officials.

In India, Brahmins protected Hindu traditions. They attracted young scholars to their households and introduced them to the sacred Hindu texts – originally collected in the voluminous three (and later four) Vedic hymns. Privileged Hindus, however, studied medicine, physiology, psychology, astrology and the principal systems of philosophy as well as the sacred texts. Thus the content of education in ancient India was designed to provide future leaders with an all-round education. As priest-teachers the Brahmins enjoyed the highest status among Hindus, although members of the Kshatriya caste possessed *de facto* political power. While modern India is a secular state, communal differences based on religious beliefs continue to sustain political conflict.

In Islamic countries, and between them, sectarian differences mobilize national sentiments and justify conflict. In these countries power was, and in some cases even today is, shared by religious teachers. Initially the Koran was the source of all knowledge. After Muhammad's death, practices spelled out in the *Tradition* were accepted as supplementing the holy text or filling gaps that existed in it. Even today, among Shi'ite Muslims, the view that an infallible *imam* has the master key to the inner meaning of the Koran and the *Tradition* is accepted. In spite of the intellectual differences which exist among Muslims worthwhile knowledge for all of them is a blend of practical prescriptions to guide behaviour and that supremely important understanding of God which is the right of every Muslim. Theology and jurisprudence, and their handmaiden Arabic, constitute the central core of traditonal studies. Today some distinguished Islamic scholars are attempting to reconcile the knowledge contained in the Koran with modern Western science and technology. At the same time wherever Muslims are found in large numbers there is pressure to ensure that the ethos of the schools attended by their children retains its religious character.

For many centuries in Europe the priest-teacher not only decided what should be taught, and to whom, but was the adviser of kings and princes. The religious content of education in Western Europe for Christians was taken from the Bible and for Jews from the Talmud. For Christians the Bible became the source of moral principles and the basis of canon law. As a predominantly legal document, the Talmud helped to shape the daily lives of the group of people for whom it was originally intended. Sectarian differences among Christians gave rise to political conflicts and to attitudes towards the ethos of schooling, if not to the secular content of education, which are still not resolved. Even today, in some Jewish schools, the content of education is constrained in a very definite way by the holy texts.

A major difference between curricula in European schools and those established by Hindus, Muslims and Buddhists was that from an early date the former incorporated secular knowledge and the non-religious justification for it from the literature of classical Greece. The origins of the three most influential European curriculum theories and the epistemological, psychological and political/sociological theories associated with them can be found in this literature. The fourth major theory – polytechnicalism – is designed in Soviet debates less to answer the question what knowledge is worthwhile than to suggest how all knowledge should be presented in schools.

The choice of four European models as the framework of analysis is not simply ethnocentric. European answers to the questions 'What knowledge is of most worth?' and 'Who shall be educated?' are debated wherever European traders, missionaries and soldiers set up schools in countries other than their own; where educators setting up their own school system deliberately 'borrowed' from European prototypes; and in international forums such as those provided by Unesco, the International Bureau of Education in Geneva, OECD and regional agencies in Latin America, Asia and Africa.

Faced with heightened aspirations for education at all levels, phenomenal increases in scientific knowledge and its applications, and their willingness to accept new societal tasks, educators have done little more than adapt curriculum models, two of which, essentialism and encyclopaedism, go back to before the seventeenth century and two, pragmatism and polytechnicalism, in their modern form are products of the late nineteenth and twentieth centuries. In many situations, traditional curriculum solutions have been offered in response to new 'problems', particularly those created by post-1945 demographic changes. Few national efforts have been made voluntarily to consider radically different curriculum theories other than the one familiar to most teachers. Where attempts have been made to transfer curriculum models the political and psychological difficulties faced by teachers willing to introduce transferred models have been very considerable. In subsequent chapters in this book some of these difficulties are analysed.

Major curriculum theories

In Europe, and indeed throughout the world, changes in political theory have been more readily and widely accepted than the theories of knowledge on which curriculum theories depend. In so far as political and to a lesser extent psychological theory changes have influenced some aspects of national educational systems the retention of traditional epistemologies creates normative inconsistencies and curriculum lag in systems of education undergoing change. It is within the paradigm of political, psychological and epistemological theories advanced in the works of Plato and Aristotle that 'problem'-creating changes can best be analysed. It is at the same time the case that within the corpus of Greek literature the theories of some of Plato's precursors and contemporaries have present-day supporters. The ideas of Democritus about the natural world are remarkably similar to those held by some modern physical scientists. The political theory of Pericles that all men possessed civic virtue was central to justifications given by eighteenth-century French and American revolutionaries for the action they took against their own and foreign masters respectively and for the proposals they made to set up political democracies. It is therefore against the paradigm exemplified in Plato's *Republic*, in which the origins of essentialism as a curriculum theory are found, that subsequent developments will be identified.

(1) ESSENTIALISM

In Plato's *Republic* the public service that teachers were expected to perform was basically political. In this model the aim of education is to sustain a just society the main feature of which is its stability. Political leadership should be exercised by

8

philosopher-kings, or guardians. Auxiliaries should support them and workers should be content to remain in a specific occupation. Social and political change are antithetical to good government and great harm is done if unsuitable workers are promoted to positions of leadership.

The justness of this elitist political model is sustained by a theory of individual differences which while politically unacceptable today continues to dominate much educational thinking. At the heart of Plato's theory of individual differences is the view that men and women are intellectually different and that among men inequality is simply a biological fact. Men inherit qualities which fit them for assigned roles in society. With few exceptions clever parents beget clever children; less clever parents have less clever children. Educational provision should take account of these facts by educating potential guardians to be guardians and the sons of workers should be trained as workers. Arrangements should be made to ensure that the few exceptions to this general rule should be promoted out of their class. Plato's myth of innate individual differences justified elitist authoritarian political systems, class-structured societies and selective systems of education. By 1940 Plato's concept of the politically just society had been abandoned in most industrialized countries. Rigid social class structures were also under attack. There persisted among many European educators belief in the decisive influence of innate intellectual ability on the educability of individual children.

Plato's sole interest was in the education of future political leaders. His psychology of learning is in keeping with his theory of individual differences. He divides the soul into three parts: reason, energy and animal instincts possessed respectively by guardians, auxiliaries and workers. Education should cultivate reason; training should develop the animal instincts appropriate to workers. Today few such crudely stated views are openly admitted even by the most conservative teachers. The importance in education of cultivating qualities of reason, wisdom, the vision of truth and love of beauty in present-day educational debates cannot be dismissed. These two Platonic theories continue to receive support long after his political and sociological theories have been rejected.

Central to the achievement of his educational aims is Plato's somewhat general theory of knowledge. It was Aristotle who, within the same tradition, spelled out how knowledge could be acquired either inductively or by logical deduction. For all

9

Greeks, however, what was knowable among ceaselessly changing experiences was that which is permanent. Materialists hold
that atoms are permanent; idealists that ideas which transcend or
are immanent in individual objects are permanent and therefore
knowable. For Plato, beauty in the abstract is knowable but
material things are not beautiful because pure ideas are imper-
fectly realized in practice and as they change become less perfect.
Things which can be touched, smelled, seen, or heard are the
objects of opinion not knowledge. This view of knowledge has
had an important bearing on debates between the relative merits
of the natural sciences and the humanities in the education of the
future leaders of society. It excludes from the sphere of education
the vocational training of future workers.

Plato's suggested curriculum for guardians dominated European practice for centuries. Generously interpreted, music and
gymnastics should constitute the content of education. The former should be taken to mean virtually everything connected with
high culture. The study of arithmetic, geometry, astronomy and
harmony should develop reason and prepare the mind for a
vision of eternal things. This non-utilitarian purpose of mathematics has been a feature of the education of political leaders in
Europe with the exception of Britain. It may also have persuaded
teachers that only those subjects whose content can be arranged
to satisfy the logical criteria of mathematics should be taught at
school. The essentialist curriculum therefore consists of a few
carefully selected subjects whose internal logic and coherence are
self-evident. Such subjects, presented in logical sequences, provide learners with the intellectual skills, and presumably the
moral fibre, expected of a societal leader.

In line with this theory, the Seven Liberal Arts curriculum
dominated the content of education in the Middle Ages. The
quadrivium – music, astronomy, geometry and arithmetic – made
for a sound general education. The subjects of the trivium –
grammar, rhetoric and philosophy or logic – provided methods
by which essential knowledge should be studied. The status of the
Seven Liberal Arts curriculum owed much to the support it
received from leading figures – particularly Aquinas – in the
Roman Catholic Church. It might be said that the power of the
Christian Church made it possible to incorporate secular knowledge into European curricula and to justify this inclusion by
reference to Platonic and Aristotelian theories.

Indeed, it was only when the power of the established church was seriously challenged that an alternative to the essentialist curriculum was proposed. The persecution of Galileo and other natural scientists during the seventeenth century was a response to the liberating expansion of scientific knowledge. The political climate, however, changed sufficiently for Protestant educators to formulate new answers to questions about worthwhile knowledge. To Comenius, a renowned and widely travelled Czech educator, can be given credit for a curriculum theory – identified here as encyclopaedism – which is the antithesis of essentialism and which profoundly affected European curricula except those in England.

(2) ENCYCLOPAEDISM

Encyclopaedism is based on the premiss that the content of education should include all human knowledge. Comenius pioneered the theory by first criticizing systems of education which did not follow nature. His own scheme of universal learning was based on the observation of nature and an examination of its laws. Since learning takes place first through the senses Comenius's curriculum was designed to develop these first. This assertion justifies the view that instead of first learning from books pupils should learn from the 'book of nature'. In an encyclopaedic curriculum a knowledge of things and words should go together.

Comenius proposed that in vernacular schools children should learn to read and write grammatically in their mother tongue in order to learn about things. They should learn how to add, weigh, measure and how to sing and say sacred passages by heart. Moral values, economics, politics and the history of the world, the position and make-up of the earth, the motion of the planets and stars, physics, geography and a general knowledge of the arts and handicrafts should be included in a comprehensive curriculum.

These radically different curriculum proposals found expression in proposals made by French revolutionary governments towards the end of the eighteenth century. They were part of a comprehensive pattern of policies designed to transform the French political and social systems. Among the most significant of these was the reiteration of some of the ideas expressed by Pericles. Fundamental to the new curriculum paradigm was the theory, shared, for example, by Condorcet (1743–94), that all men are capable of reason and the acquisition of moral ideas, from which it follows that men should not be sharply divided into rulers and the ruled. Reason, or the civic virtue possessed by all

11

men according to Pericles, made it possible for citizens in a democratic society, if not to formulate policies, to pass judgement on those of their leaders. The political tasks ascribed to the schools by Condorcet were to appraise all citizens of their rights and make them aware of their civic duties and responsibilities. Secondly a national school system should select out and educate an aristocracy of talent to provide national leadership.

The curriculum proposed included mathematics, the classical languages, modern languages, the physical and biological sciences, geography, history, the fine arts and mechanical drawing. Throughout the nineteenth century, following the creation under Napoleon of a national system of education, a curriculum including more than ten compulsory subjects typified the content of education in secondary schools whose task was to prepare young people for national leadership. It was a model disseminated throughout the whole of Europe with the exception of Britain where, in spite of its well-established democratic political system, specialized curricula were retained in the secondary schools which were established to satisfy the demand for commercial and political leaders and administrators.

While the encyclopaedic model survives in all continental European national systems of education, national specific theories about the nature of knowledge and how it can be acquired make it possible to compare and contrast the way universal knowledge is presented in the schools of France, Spain, Italy, Germany, Poland, the Scandinavian countries and the Soviet Union where, until recently, all the academically respectable subjects were included in school curricula. Distinctions should be made, however, between the influence on French curricula of the epistemological assumptions of Descartes whose effect is clearly visible, and philosophers like Hegel whose theories inform the way knowledge is treated in some other European countries. The kernel of Descartes' theory lies in his well-known statement that 'I think. Therefore I am' which justifies an intellectual, rational approach to the acquisition of knowledge which is reflected in the way French teachers spend a great deal of time critically analysing written texts.

(3) POLYTECHNICALISM

The most obvious alternative to the French approach to knowledge is expressed by Soviet educators who accept Lenin's assertion that the whole socioeconomic and historical experience of mankind should be included in school curricula. In this they differ little from their Western European counterparts. What sets polytechnicalism apart as a curriculum theory is found in the comments made by Karl Marx on the factory school run by Robert Owen in Lanarkshire, Scotland, in the early nineteenth century. The fundamental premiss on which it is based is that the content of education should be deliberately interpreted in terms of the productive life of society. The political theories of Marx have been readily accepted and there is little doubt that the few remarks he made about the treatment of knowledge have given credence in socialist countries to the argument that school education should be brought nearer to productive life in societies in which the capitalist class system has been eliminated. It is not a theory which can be put into practice while a class sytem similar to that advocated by Plato continues to determine the attitudes and consciousness of individuals. The political task of a polytechnical curriculum is to eliminate, once workers have been freed from exploitation by the private owners of the means of production, the false consciousness they have inherited from a capitalist society.

The polytechnical curriculum is designed to prepare good communists who as the most resolute members of society offer leadership in the inevitable progress of society from capitalism through socialism to communism. Teaching must take account of the fact that the behaviour of individuals is conditioned by biologically inherited factors and external stimuli and a consciousness based on the accumulated experience of mankind seen principally as a series of conflicts between the classes. Among Marxists, psychological theory is materialistic and has its basis in physiology. There are no intrinsic reasons, therefore, why all children, other than those with brain damage, should not follow and complete the same encyclopaedic curriculum.

There is no doubt that this alternative approach to a broadly based subject curriculum has been accepted in theory by educationists in countries in which communist governments are responsible for educational policy. At the same time it must be said that the principles of polytechnicalism are extremely difficult to internalize by teachers. To relate theory to practice and education to the productive life of society requires a fundamentally different approach to the concepts of worthwhile knowledge proposed by Plato and re-enforced by generations of teachers. Even teachers committed in theory to the polytechnical treatment of knowledge find it difficult systematically to illustrate general principles, in whatever subject they occur, by reference to their social implications and economic applications.

Nevertheless, Soviet curriculum theory and the physiologically based theories of learning associated with it offer a more realistic approach to the provision of education as a human right under conditions characterized by advances in scientific knowledge on which industrialization depends whatever the ideological commitment of governments, than theories inherited from Plato who rejected change as a process of degeneration, and knowledge of other than permanent ideas as impossible. It is hardly surprising that in the USA, which changed more rapidly than most countries in response to the application of science and technology to industrial processes, a viable alternative to polytechnicalism was developed towards the end of the nineteenth century.

(4) PRAGMATISM

The American pragmatists shared many of Marx's concerns. They were aware of the impact of industrialization, commercialism and urbanization on American life. Collectively they set out to develop an alternative rationale for American democracy in which the institutions established at the time of the war of independence had been created by Jefferson and his colleagues to serve an agrarian slave-owning democracy. The civil war and the emancipation of women had transformed the political bases of American society. The application of science was transforming its economic base. The pragmatists recognized that theoretical changes in law, psychology, mathematics, medicine and education were needed if American institutions were to respond adequately to societal change.

As part of the discussions which took place among the early pragmatists John Dewey gave credence to a radically new curriculum theory. It was similar to that advanced by Herbert Spencer in his book *Education* in which he asked the question 'What knowledge is of most worth?' His answer was: that knowledge which enables young people to tackle problems and prepares them to solve the problems they are likely to meet as adults in a democratic society. In the light of this theory curriculum debate turns on the identification and analysis of 'worthwhile problems'. Spencer stated that the problems associated with healthy living, earning a living, family life, civil participation, the enjoyment of leisure and the making of moral decisions were the most important. Dewey and other pragmatists accepted this classification of problems as the basis of a sound curriculum not based on sharp distinctions between general education and vocational training.

Dewey located the problems which should be used to select the content of school education in the urban environment. His most influential early essays on education were prepared when he was at the University of Chicago in a city which had grown at an unprecedented rate. Like Marx, he was aware that industrialization had created problems for which radical solutions were needed. Unlike Marx, he did not see them as arising exclusively from the struggle between workers and capitalists. On the contrary, while not satisfied that a constitution drawn up more than a hundred years earlier was a satisfactory basis on which to run a rapidly changing society, he wished to retain the American frontier values which he had learned during his childhood in Vermont. Dewey recognized that in urban Chicago it was impossible to re-create the kind of small educative community he so admired. He therefore proposed that primary schools should become, vicariously, small communities with curricula which would provide children with the problem-solving learning activities they would have experienced in a small frontier town. The school was to become the community.

For Dewey, as for Marx, productive work was the most educative activity. Both, therefore, assigned to teachers the task of inculcating moral values through vocational activities. The former located these desirable activities in the occupations with which he had become familiar in Burlington and accepted the values associated with nineteenth-century agrarian democracy. Marx analysed modes of production in capitalist factories, took as his educative activities those which would be developed in the productive life of a socialist society and stressed the values associated with such a society. From these politically different perspectives both philosophers proposed that vocational activities should form the core of a sound general education. Aspects of productive life should be central features of the school curriculum. The dichotomy drawn by Plato between education and training was for Marx and Dewey as false as that between intellectual endeavour and productive activities. Failure to recognize that for both of them vocational activities should constitute the core of a sound curriculum perpetuates the dichotomies which lie at the centre of traditional European curriculum theory.

While Dewey's theory was designed for primary schools, his followers later adopted it when they established the main principles of secondary school curriculum development. Pragmatic curriculum theory therefore offers a radical alternative to earlier European models. It has been implicitly accepted by many, if not most, English primary school teachers and in so far as it is a process rather than a fixed content model, has had an influence on the higher levels of education in Britain. Two trends, however, should be identified in pragmatic 'progressive' curriculum theory. One stresses child-centred aims which make the needs of the developing child the criteria for selecting curriculum content. Society-centred progressive educators, who also take Dewey as their intellectual leader, consider that the main purpose of the schools should be to reconstruct society. The two views can be reconciled only if the needs of individual children are analysed in the context of present-day societal problems. As stated earlier, Dewey's curriculum solution was to make the urban primary school an educative community. The extent to which rural, small town values can successfully be perpetuated in urban schools is problematical. Nevertheless the pragmatic paradigm and the curriculum theory developed by Dewey were designed to accommodate the kind of societal change which has taken place since 1945 in many countries.

Indeed of the four curriculum models briefly described in this chapter only pragmatism and polytechnicalism offer in theory viable curriculum solutions to the problems created after 1945 in countries where European-type selective second-level academic schools and distinctions between education and training and different forms of knowledge have survived. However, the emergence of the USA and USSR as superpowers espousing antithetical political ideologies polarized the commitment of teachers throughout the world and re-enforced the parochialism of their curriculum debates and their responses to change.

The politics of curriculum non-reform

Nevertheless, from time to time anxiety about the content of education has been articulated since 1945. In 1945–6 the founders of Unesco proposed that the elimination of illiteracy could best be achieved through curricula designed in accordance with Dewey's pragmatic principles. Over the years under different names the

16

notion incorporated in 'Fundamental Education' has informed the initiatives taken by Unesco to tackle world illiteracy. The principle behind all of them is that children learn best through participating in activities which are relevant to life in their community. Few of these internationally inspired non-formal approaches have been significantly more successful than attempts to introduce systems of universal primary education based on early European prototype curricula.

In some cases international pressure was more direct. In Japan members of the American Mission proposed changes in school curricula immediately after the Second World War. They considered that morals education (*Shushin*) in prewar schools had promoted ultra-nationalism. American advisers recommended that courses in morals education should be removed from the curriculum and replaced by social studies. They also recommended that a Deweyian process curriculum model should replace a subject-centred approach.

The establishment of a communist government in China after a long armed struggle initiated curriculm debate. The leaders of the People's Republic found in the ideology of Marx, Lenin and Stalin policies which they hoped would bring the knowledge of the west to their people. Such knowledge, it was maintained, was necessary if a modern industrial state under the leadership of the Communist Party was to be created. The uneasy relationship between the USSR and the government of the People's Republic of China shows how difficult it is freely to transfer curriculum practices from one nation to another and how difficult it is for teachers of any political persuasion to put the principles of polytechnicalism into practice.

The failure of international illiteracy programmes and the effective resistance of teachers and officials in Japan to proposals supported by politically motivated leaders of the Teachers' Union to promote curriculum change illustrate the difficulties associated with the reform of curricula through international action. The parochialism of educational debate in general and about the content of education in particular is well illustrated in the omission of education from the terms of reference of the Treaty of Rome, on which the European Community was founded. Over the years community agencies have collected and disseminated information about education. In 1976 a resolution of 9 February provided a specific basis for community-level action in education by making it possible for ministers of education, voluntarily, to discuss educational matters of mutual concern. In the event the community has restricted itself to discussing problems and policies which in the European context do not have long histories to which national solutions have been offered. It is unlikely that a common European curriculum will be proposed although if qualifications are to be harmonized and the free movement of labour facilitated such a curriculum is badly needed. Parochial national views are bound to prevent agreement if any such proposal was made.

Unesco's International Bureau of Education in Geneva provides a forum for the discussion of curricula. It has no power to influence national policies although at its international conferences agreement among delegates is frequently reached on some very general statements of intent. OECD reviews of national systems of education have had little direct influence on curriculum reform in those countries on which reports have been made. In short the provision by these and other international organizations like the Organization of American States (OAS) in Washington and the Association of South East Asian Nations (ASEAN) agencies in Bangkok of forums in which curriculum issues can be debated has had little effect on national curriculum debates. It is unlikely that the long-term influence of international debates will in practice be profound – the most they may achieve is to organize and mobilize opinion in highly charged political atmospheres which do little to encourage consideration of alternative curriculum theories on their merits.

Concern about the content of education has been articulated in several major countries. It is not surprising that expressions of concern occurred first in the USA and the USSR where selective second-level schools had been replaced under different circumstances before 1945. During the 1950s American high schools came under severe criticism from scholars and laymen who compared school curricula unfavourably with those in the schools of Europe. Criticism of progressive – pragmatic – curriculum theory came to a head when Soviet engineers launched the first earth satellite in 1957. The protagonists in this acrimonious battle were on the one side teachers and professors of education and on the other university academics in subjects other than education, industrialists and politicians. In spite of the formidable political pressure brought to bear on teachers the appearance in 1983 of *A Nation at Risk* and other critical reports in which the appalling weaknesses of American high school curricula were exposed by

American scholars suggests that, in spite of internal concern, school curricula in the USA did not change significantly between 1958 and 1983.

The Khrushchev reforms of 1958 designed to bring education nearer to life through the polytechnicalization of the curricula failed in spite of the fact that they were approved by members of the Communist Party and had the support of leading members of the Academy of Pedagogical Sciences. It is apparent from the internal debates which took place at that time that historically significant differences of interpretation of the term 'polytechnicalization' gave rise to conflict within the educational establishment. It is also apparent that deeply held European educational traditions made it difficult for teachers, many of whom had little or no knowledge of modern technology, to internalize principles which would have made it possible for them to relate the principles of their subject to the productive life of Soviet society. If the internal debate was less publicized than the debate in the USA there can be little doubt that teachers were able successfully to prevent the introduction in practice of a curriculum theory which had been accepted from the early 1920s.

As in the USA and the USSR, in France, Britain and other Western European countries curriculum change has been slow and undertaken almost exclusively within traditional curriculum theories – essentialism and encyclopaedism. Regardless of the power of the central administration to formulate and adopt curriculum policies the real protagonists have been teacher–guardians of worthwhile knowledge and radical educationists who have advocated pragmatic or polytechnical curriculum theories. In some cases the motivation of the radicals has been based on a political ideology. In few cases has a direct appeal been made by the reformers to foreign curriculum models and theories. In most cases admission requirements established and controlled by university academics have effectively prevented change in the curriculum of second-stage schools in spite of the difficulties associated with the retention of university preparation courses in comprehensive or unified schools.

To be sure, American progressive theory has made some headway particularly in English schools. It has enjoyed less success in other European systems. In France, for example, advocates of *les classes nouvelles* attempted after 1945 to introduce the kind of content and methods of teaching favoured by American and British progressive educationists. *Les classes nouv-*

elles had a short-lived vogue among some teachers but failed to gain universal acceptance among the profession. Staunch opponents of change were members of the Société des Agregés who as teachers in the *lycées* opposed bureaucrats in the ministry who favoured reform. The curriculum remains *encyclopaedic*. By the same token curricula in English secondary schools remain highly specialized in spite of attempts made to broaden the content of sixth form studies. The protagonists in this debate have been university academics and educational administrators particularly at the national level whose influence on the formulation, adoption and implementation of curriculum policies has been notoriously weak. Attempts by the Thatcher government in the late 1980s to introduce a more broadly based national curriculum may be fiercely opposed by teachers' organizations and Labour Party politicians on the ground that teacher control over the curriculum in individuals schools is in the best interests of the system.

The demise of colonialism has made curriculum reform in recently independent nations no less difficult. In these countries government leaders and educationists have wished to revive indigenous values by replacing European colonial curricula with those more consistent with national aspirations. Among these aspirations the replacement of an imperial language (French, English, Spanish) as the medium of instruction by a local language (or languages) has given rise to political problems created by internal linguistic diversity. In addition the introduction of a local language frequently is not in accordance with the wishes of parents who want their children to benefit from the acquisition of a world language. Within this framework of competing interests curriculum reform becomes highly charged politically and less restricted to protagonists within the educational establishment than in most countries with long histories of independence.

In summary, international influences on curriculum theory and practice are inhibited by the sovereignty of national governments and the conservatism of many teachers. International statements are usually pious expressions of intent which have little practical effect. Bilateral pressures are not much more effective. The examples of Japan and Germany illustrate the fact that the attempts of educators from one country to shape curricula in another have little lasting effect unless maintained for many years as they were in former European colonies because of the power of teachers, as the guardians of worthwhile knowledge, to resist change. The victorious allies divided Germany into American,

British, French and Soviet spheres of influence. Each tried to reform the German system in its own image. Over more than forty years German traditions have reasserted themselves and continue to inform the content of education and maintain distinctions between academic education and vocational training.

Proposed curriculum changes legitimized by theories generated by educationists in their own country are effectively disseminated very slowly. Not until novel theories have been fully internalized by a majority of teachers is it possible to guarantee that curriculum innovations will be put into practice effectively. Even in the USA, where pragmatic philosophies have been in vogue for nearly a century, prescribed textbooks differ little in content from European school textbooks. Indeed in view of the conservatism that can be observed in American education the number of vehement attacks that have been made from time to time on progressive curriculum proposals to meet the needs of 'all American youth' seem misplaced.

Comparative evidence, therefore, demonstrates how difficult it is to formulate adequate curriculum responses to societal change. Changes brought about in Europe after 1945 when party politicians initiated structural changes increased the need for radical curriculum change. It has not been forthcoming in Western Europe. Curriculum reform has been limited to (1) reordering subject priorities for specific groups of pupils, e.g. downgrading Latin and Greek in schools preparing students for admission to a university, (2) reducing the syllabuses of individual subjects by selecting from the historical development of each of them only that knowledge regarded as most worthwhile, e.g. selecting from the history of physics those principles which inform a whole range of phenomena, and (3) increasing the choices open to students by creating optional subjects from the whole range of acceptable subjects.

This failure is serious and probably accounts for the disenchantment expressed by previously firm supporters of comprehensive schools, like Torsten Husen, with an educational experiment which it was hoped would equalize the provision of education as a human right. Whether in the Western European context the American pragmatic response would be adequate and accepted by European educationists is a moot point. Equally problematical is the prospect that governments in non-socialist countries might accept and develop a Soviet polytechnical curriculum. If they were to do so how many teachers in any school

21

system would be able so to internalize the theory that it could be put successfully into practice in their schools?

The dilemma is equally serious in school systems influenced by European models and where teachers cling to traditional concepts of what knowledge is of most worth. Educationists face the task of developing curriculum theories which can be successfully adapted to their attempts to create modern industrialized societies without destroying traditional values – the problem Dewey faced. This analysis is designed to show that no real alternatives to the four curriculum models described in this chapter have yet been formulated. At best minor modifications have been proposed.

Even these modest attempts to introduce new curriculum theories have been resisted. Yet it is unlikely that a return, as is often advocated, to traditional theories will make it possible adequately to solve present-day educational problems. In the absence in the literature of a curriculum model which is fundamentally different from essentialism, encyclopaedism, polytechnicalism and pragmatism it is instructive to examine how each of them have been debated and modified in its country of origin and how attempts have been made to transfer pragmatic and polytechnical theories from one system to another.

Further reading

Adamson, John E., *The Theory of Education in Plato's 'Republic'* (London: Swan & Sonnenschein, 1903).

Adamson, J. W., *The Educational Writings of John Locke* (New York: Longmans Green, 1912).

Archer, R. L., *Rousseau on Education* (London: Edward Arnold, 1912).

Ashby, Eric, *Universities: British, Indian, African* (Cambridge, Mass.: Harvard University Press, 1966).

Bereday, George Z. F., and Lauwerys, Joseph A. (eds), 'Education and philosophy', in *The Yearbook of Education 1957* (London: Evans, 1957); see Arabinda Basu, 'Hinduism and Buddhism', pp. 93–112, Djemal Saliba and George J. Tomeh, 'Islam', pp. 65–79 and A. L. Tibawi, 'The philosophy of Muslim education', pp. 80–92.

Bowen, James, *A History of Western Education*, Vol. 1, *The Ancient World* (London: Methuen, 1972).

Brubacher, John S., *A History of the Problems of Education* (New York: McGraw-Hill, 1947).

Bury, J. B., *A History of Greece* (New York: Random, Modern Library, n.d.).

Butts, R. Freeman, *A Cultural History of Western Education* (New York: McGraw-Hill, 1955).

Compayre, Gabriel, trans. W. H. Payne, *The History of Pedagogy* (London: Swan & Sonnenschein, 1904).

Condorcet, Antoine-Nicolas de, trans. June Barraclough, sketch for a historical picture of *The Progress of the Mind* (London: Weidenfeld & Nicolson, 1955).

Dewey, John, *The Child and the Curriculum* (Chicago: University of Chicago Press, 1902).

Eaton, Ralph M., *Descartes Selections* (New York: Scribner, 1927).

Flexner, Abraham, *Universities: American, English, German* (New York and Oxford: Oxford Univerity Press, 1930).

HMSO, *Treaty* [establishing] *The European Economic Community*, Rome, 25 March 1957 (London: HMSO, 1972).

Holmes, Brian, *Comparative Education: Some Considerations of Method* (London: Allen & Unwin, 1981).

IBE, *Recommendations, 1934–60*, Publication No. 222 (Geneva: International Bureau of Education, n.d.).

Keatinge, M. A., *Comenius* (New York: McGraw-Hill, 1931).

The Koran, Interpreted, trans. J. Arberry (Oxford: Oxford University Press, 1983).

La Fontainerie, F., *French Liberalism and Education in the Eighteenth Century* (New York: McGraw-Hill, 1932).

Lieberman, Myron, *Education as a Profession* (Englewood Cliffs, NJ: Prentice-Hall, 1956).

Locke, John, *Some Thoughts Concerning Education* (Cambridge: Cambridge University Press, 1889).

Locke, John, *An Essay Concerning Human Understanding* (London: Dent, 1947).

Marx, K., and Engels, F., ed. Samuel H. Beer, *The Communist Manifesto* (New York: Appleton-Century-Crofts, 1955).

Marx, K., and Engels, F., *The German Ideology, Part One* (London: Lawrence & Wishart, 1974).

National Society for the Study of Education, ed. Nelson B. Henry, *Modern Philosophies and Education* (Chicago: University of Chicago Press, 1955).

Plato, trans. J. L. Davies and D. J. Vaughan, *The Republic of Plato* (London: Macmillan, 1935).

Quick, R. H., *Educational Reformers* (London: Longmans Green, 1984).

Russell, Bertrand, *A History of Western Philosophy* (London: Allen & Unwin, 1946).

Russell, Bertrand, *Human Knowledge* (London: Allen & Unwin, 1948).

Scheffler, Israel, *Four Pragmatists* (London: Routledge & Kegan Paul, 1974).

Spencer, Herbert, *Education, Intellectual, Moral & Physical* (London: Dent, 1860).

Unesco, *Learning to Be: The World of Education Today and Tomorrow* (Paris: Unesco, 1972).

Unesco, *In the Minds of Men 1946–1971* (Paris: Unesco, 1972).

Unesco/IBE, *International Guide to Education Systems*, prepared by Brian Holmes (Paris: Unesco, 1979) (see also *International Yearbook of Education* from 1980 onwards, a Unesco/IBE annual).

Chapter Two

Individualism and the English curriculum

The 1944 Education Act for England and Wales asserted that secondary education should be provided for all in accordance with age, aptitude and ability. The Act did not specify how secondary education should be organized in the locally administered system of national education and, apart from making religious education compulsory, it did not state what should be taught in schools. The sources of dominant curriculum aims and typical curriculum practices for most of the period since 1944 must be sought elsewhere.

Traditional curriculum practice in England can be understood in terms of the essentialist view, derived from Plato and Aristotle. This philosophy, which came to predominate in the nineteenth century, held that a truly liberal education could best be provided through certain selected subjects.

It has been difficult to reconcile the democratization of the secondary school curriculum with a residual view that high-status knowledge could be acquired only by future 'philosopher–kings', namely the political, social and intellectual elite. Nor has it been easy to introduce into the curriculum knowledge which is related to the occupational and social futures of the majority of students when traditional concepts of high-status knowledge have been so restricted.

The question of producing a relevant curriculum for a democratized school system after 1944 was left mainly to educationists and was answered largely by school-level innovations. Since 1976 central government has attempted to create a national curriculum. The 1988 Education Act specified the content of the school curriculum in ways that challenged some of the principles of the essentialist view while leaving others untouched. The traditional monopoly of power of educationists in determining the content of schooling was more certainly threatened. The outcome of these changes is, as yet, unclear.

What knowledge?

During the twentieth century, the curriculum of liberal education, for both the elite and the majority, has been restricted to a few, mainly 'academic' subjects. Choice between subjects has been encouraged and has been determined by student interest and ability. Fundamental to the English notion of what constitutes worthwhile knowledge is a belief in the value of distinct subjects which meet clearly defined criteria.*

In England, a third principle has had importance besides specialization and individual choice. The idea of morality was expressed in Plato's *Republic*. In the English essentialist tradition it has been translated into a belief that the education of the elite should develop qualities such as fairness, integrity and constancy – in short, wisdom rather than cleverness.

The moral imperatives of Plato were taken up by John Locke in the eighteenth century. His ideas on the moral education of good leaders became the working principles of English education in the mid-nineteenth century when the elite secondary ('public') schools and the old universities of Oxford and Cambridge were reformed. Thomas Arnold's Rugby School and Benjamin Jowett's Balliol College (at Oxford University) typified elite institutions which took responsibility for the moral training of future members of the political-administrative class which was to participate in the expansion of the empire abroad and the government bureaucracy at home. It was a morality intended to guide the leaders of a hierarchically structured society in their relations with those they governed.

---

* A version of the encyclopaedist tradition was deeply entrenched in education in Scotland, where the content of secondary and university education differed markedly from the curriculum of England in the eighteenth and nineteenth centuries. A broadly based curriculum embracing many subjects contrasted with the narrow and specialized content of education in England. However, Scottish educational practice increasingly has become harmonized with that of England in the later twentieth century.

These moral purposes made humanistic studies central in the curriculum. In the nineteenth and early twentieth centuries, the classics – particularly Greek and Latin literature, philosophy and history which were the main subjects of the prestigious Literae Humaniores degree course at Oxford – were regarded as the most important subjects. Through such studies the finest moral lessons and precepts could be adduced by those sufficiently sensitive to discover them.

Modern history and English literature later replaced the classics as the sources of moral enhancement. Sciences and linguistic studies struggled to compete. The defenders of subjects such as mathematics and sciences often tried to justify their study by the moral or aesthetic value that they could contain. The study of foreign languages in upper secondary schooling focused on fine literature in foreign languages rather than linguistic structures or everyday language use.

Platonic moralism had acquired another interpretation in the sixteenth century when Erasmus emphasized the cultivation of aesthetic appreciation, good taste and elegance. There was a stress on external appearance and etiquette rather than on inner morality. This view was never pre-eminent, especially in the earnest and Christian nineteenth century when the foundations of twentieth-century education were laid. But it allowed aesthetic subjects (most particularly literature but also art, music and even mathematics) to gain some status.

The moral purpose of elite education designed to develop future leaders excluded practical, useful, or vocational knowledge which was relegated to the inferior category of 'training'. This included particularly those manual activities, associated with craft occupations, which had a distinctly lower status in the Platonic social structure.

The principles of individualism and specialism complemented moralism. Plato argued that wisdom was learned intuitively. The acquisition of knowledge was not logical, sequential and standardized as rationalists claimed but was the outcome of the interaction between the innate qualities of the learner and potential sources of reinforcing morality in the texts. Since each individual might find different material appropriate to his or her moral development the content of education should be selected in the light of individual differences.

If the purpose of education is to develop moral values, the need for comprehensive coverage of many knowledge branches is weakened. In the essentialist tradition, a greater case can be made for the depth study of a few appropriate subjects than for a superficial coverage of a wider range of knowledge. Specialization, individualism and a moral purpose of education each gave weight to the English view that only through the study in depth of a few subjects could a sound education be provided.

There were other bases for the emphasis on specialization. The scientific method of Aristotle suggested that, while some subjects – such as mathematics – met criteria of logical coherence, others acquired the status of a body of knowledge through the discovery and careful collection and classification of data. Natural sciences were justified by these canons of scientific method. Induction as a method of science through the works of Francis Bacon in the seventeenth century and John Stuart Mill in the nineteenth century has dominated English concepts of knowledge creation.

This view of scholarship encouraged further a high degree of specialization in university courses. Single subject 'honours' degrees were established and gradually became the norm throughout higher education in the twentieth century. Students spent their entire courses on the study of one subject such as mathematics, or English literature, or geography. The power of university academics to determine how secondary school students should be prepared for higher education has also resulted in highly specialized upper secondary school courses.

The essentialist view of knowledge, which dominated the curriculum of elite secondary schools and universities from the nineteenth century, was not intended to apply to mass education. Indeed, vocational studies, so lowly regarded by followers of Plato, and mass primary education, where child-centred philosophies had an impact, were far less influenced by the essentialist view. As educational access began to be democratized at post-elementary level in the twentieth century so the essentialist approach began to be applied to a wider range of the population.

Secondary education for all

The major debates about curriculum in England have centred on secondary education as it changed from the socially exclusive preserve of a future professional and managerial elite to a universal system in which all children and young people had the right and obligation to participate.

The essentialist tradition was brought into question also by external economic, social and political pressures on schools. Changes in the occupational structure of Britain as well as hopes or plans for economic growth led to demands for an education with greater vocational relevance. The growth of youth unemployment by the mid-1970s led to calls for a secondary school curriculum which would be appropriate to the future working lives of students who would fill skilled and semi-skilled manual jobs.

Social changes after 1945 included the emergence of a society with greater racial, religious and linguistic diversity created largely by immigration especially from the Caribbean and the Indian subcontinent in the 1960s. Patterns of family life also changed with greater occupational and professional aspirations among women, increasing divorce rates and numbers of one-parent families and powerful influences on values from the mass media and a mass consumption economy. Debates about the curriculum consequently focused on social and moral issues as well as demands from the economy. But the impact of these social and economic changes was felt mainly through the new clientele of students introduced into educational institutions by changes in policy over educational access.

How did secondary education change after 1945 and what was the impact of this change on debates about the curriculum? Secondary education had been provided in grammar schools since the Middle Ages. By the mid-nineteenth century, a few of these emerged as 'public' schools providing an education, often boarding, for the upper and upper middle classes. They continued to be the apex, in status, of the independent, fee-paying school system which still had about 8 per cent of all secondary level enrolments in the 1980s. The graduates of the independent schools throughout the twentieth century contributed a disproportionately high number of students to the elite universities of Oxford and Cambridge and of members of high-status occupations. The curriculum of these independent schools continued to influence the state school sector through their commitment to long-standing traditions which had been undisturbed by democratization of access.

Most grammar schools were brought into the state education system from the late nineteenth century. After 1945 they drew all their students from state primary schools on the basis of the 11+ examination. They provided an academic education for pupils aged 11 to 16 or 18 who left to enter mainly professional occupations or higher education.

Before the Second World War, most of the population had received only elementary education up to the end of compulsory schooling at 14. The 1944 Education Act led to the provision of universal secondary education in a 'tripartite' system. Between 20 and 25 per cent of primary school pupils were selected for grammar or technical schools. The others were educated in newly established 'secondary modern' schools until the end of compulsory schooling at 15. In practice the 'tripartite' system was 'bipartite' since few technical schools were set up and they never recruited more than 2 per cent of the age group.

The 'tripartite' system began to be replaced by 'comprehensive' neighbourhood secondary schools, mainly after a central government circular of 1965. While the first comprehensive schools had been established as early as 1944, it was not until after 1970 that most secondary age students were in comprehensive schools.

Comprehensive schools were provided for the age range 11–18 but the majority of pupils left at the end of compulsory schooling (16 from 1974). Even in 1985, only 46 per cent of 16 year-olds were continuing in full-time education. This imbalance between enrolments of lower and upper secondary levels was one factor that led some local education authorities to vary the 11–18 pattern by introducing separate lower and upper secondary institutions. A few maintained some selective grammar schools.

Despite the almost universal adoption of common secondary schools, the secondary level curriculum continued to reflect the older tripartite system. Grammar and public schools since the later nineteenth century had prepared students for a School Certificate examination at the age of 16 in academic subjects. Credits in five subjects including English language, mathematics and a modern language qualified students for university entrance. Later a more specialized Higher School Certificate examination developed.

Following the recommendations of the 1943 Norwood Report, the School Certificate was replaced by the General Certificate of Education (GCE) Ordinary ('O') Level. Though 'O' level passes were no longer sufficient for university entrance, they became the passport for many intermediate-level occupations in large business organizations and government service. Candidates were permitted to take any number of subjects and were credited separately for passes in each subject. The intention was to allow pupils to concentrate on their strong subjects and not to be penalized for their weaknesses.

In practice it was not uncommon for some pupils to drop all studies in science or modern languages or history at the age of 14 when 'O' level specialisms were selected. The first response to the anticipated expansion of access to secondary education was to permit student selection between subjects in the lower secondary school.

Specialization was and remains more intense in the two-year upper secondary course, GCE Advanced ('A') level. Normally students pursue courses in only three (usually cognate) subjects such as English literature, history and French, or mathematics, physics and chemistry. This excessive specialization is encouraged by university entrance requirements which demand only two or three 'A' level passes (in addition to three in different subjects at 'O' level or its equivalent) but which put greatest emphasis on the grades achieved in 'A' levels. Though the pass grade is 'E' it has been rare for universities to accept less than 'C's and popular university departments have demanded 'A's.

The secondary modern schools never had the 'parity of esteem' that was claimed for them. But they imitated the curriculum of the grammar schools, especially since the more ambitious head-teachers aimed to enter their best students for GCE 'O' level examinations. Many secondary modern schools consequently offered a watered-down version of the essentialist curriculum even for the vast majority of students who took no external examinations.

The introduction of comprehensive schools had little immediate impact on the curriculum. The schools were usually streamed by ability or attainment. Even where mixed ability classes were introduced in the first two or three grades, around 25 to 30 per cent were allocated to the top stream preparing for the GCE 'O' level by the beginning of the fourth grade.

The middle streams prepared for the Certificate of Secondary Education (CSE) which had been introduced after 1964. CSE syllabuses were similar in type to those of 'O' level – focusing on academic areas – but with lower expectations of student achievement. While there was more continuous assessment than the 'O' level examination (which usually consisted largely of time-limit essay-type answers to unseen questions) and more class teacher participation in examining, the same kind of content prevailed. The lowest ability band prepared for a few CSE examination subjects or for no external examinations but again was offered a curriculum content of a similar type (but at a lower level) than the other streams.

The development of comprehensive schooling in some ways strengthened the place of essentialist curriculum in secondary schools. Deep divisions between streams and examinations persisted in the secondary school. GCE 'O' level courses were offered to a minority. Other courses gave little if any opportunity for higher education or entry to intermediate level occupations. This clear defeat for the comprehensive school ideal embarrassed teachers and other curriculum planners who sought to preserve the appearance if not the reality of a common curriculum based on a content that traditionally had been offered to the elite.

Abolition of the GCE/CSE divide had been proposed in the mid-1970s but very slow progress was made until the General Certificate of Secondary Education was introduced in 1986. Even this new examination, which combined GCE and CSE, is available in a range of subjects for only 60 per cent of students. The academic bias and subject specialisms continue despite a greater emphasis on continuous assessment and the specification of objectives in behavioural as well as in academic terms.

Restricted higher and further education

The continued domination of essentialist views in the secondary school curricula has been aided by the survival of a narrow and elitist system of higher education and by forms of technical/vocational education which remain specialized and separate from mainstream education.

The medieval English universities of Oxford and Cambridge (together with four old universities in Scotland) had been supplemented by universities in London and the other major cities or large towns in the nineteenth and early twentieth centuries. There was an expansion of university places and a creation of new universities following the 1963 Robbins Report. 'Public sector' institutions (polytechnics and colleges of higher education) began to emerge after 1966 and by the 1980s they provided about half the places in higher education. But despite this expansion, the age participation rate in higher education remained very low at around 14 per cent in the mid-1980s.

First degree courses usually last three years in England and

Wales (but four years in Scotland). In England and Wales, these courses very largely concentrate on one academic subject. While 'public sector' institutions have been expected to focus on subjects which are relevant to new technical vocations, there has been a tendency towards 'academic drift' in public sector institutions just as the new universities created after 1963 imitated many features of Oxford and Cambridge. The persistence of highly specialized and academic degree courses is used by university academics to justify resistance to any broadening of the secondary school curriculum.

Technical and vocational education in Britain has been sharply differentiated from the mainstream system. The 'education' v. 'training' dichotomy survives strongly not only because of the essentialist view of knowledge but because of the self-imposed isolation of technical education. There has been a historical tradition of 'on-the-job' training rather than formal vocational education. This applied at all levels of occupation. Most lawyers, accountants and professional engineers until the 1960s and after, for instance, acquired professional qualifications during and after an 'apprenticeship' in well-established businesses rather than in universities. Craft level training for skilled manual workers still occurs largely 'on the job'.

Vocational/technical education since the nineteenth century was provided in technical colleges but very largely on a part-time basis for full-time workers. Courses led to very specific vocational qualifications such as City and Guild Certificates for craft workers, though these craft workers 'qualified' by completing an apprenticeship rather than by passing an examination. Most City and Guilds courses contain very little general education.

At technician level, the Ordinary and Higher National (later the Business and Technician Education Council National and Higher National) Certificates and Diplomas often contain more theoretical mathematical and science elements but are still predominantly vocational. Like City and Guilds they are controlled by institutions dominated by employers. The education/training divide is entrenched not only because of essentialist views predominating in educational establishments. It is reinforced by the narrow vocationalism of employer-dominated courses.

Technical colleges or colleges of technology which had provided 'advanced further education' often became polytechnics (or in some cases technological universities) from the 1960s. Lower-level further education colleges offered second-chance academic courses in GCE 'O' and 'A' levels as well as part-time City and Guilds courses for craft apprentices and, increasingly from the 1970s, work-orientation courses, including, for instance, basic study skills for 16–19 year-old unemployed youth. These various courses were not usually integrated in a coherent or sequential framework nor were there clear links with the school system.

Primary education

In contrast, the main challenge to the supremacy of the essentialist curriculum in secondary schools has come from the influence of a child-centred curriculum which increasingly has predominated in primary schools in the later twentieth century.

Curriculum change in primary schools in the twentieth century has been associated with the removal of certain external pressures and the adoption by many primary school teachers of a child-centred rather than knowledge-centred approach to education. Elementary schooling for children aged 5 to 11 or older has been universal and compulsory since the 1880s. However, the nineteenth-century elementary school had centrally defined timetables and syllabuses which were enforced by a formula which related financial support to pupil achievement in these curriculum areas. Strict government control over curriculum was maintained in a rapidly expanding system of first-generation pupils and teachers whose education and training was very limited.

As the mass elementary education system matured so greater school-level determination of the curriculum was permitted. Broad curriculum aims and outlines were provided by central government. Teachers at school level were allowed informally to decide how these broad aims were to be put into practice. A guidebook on the teaching of each subject in the curriculum was published and regularly revised until 1935. But this guide was advisory rather than mandatory.

The relative freedom of primary school teachers to determine the details of the curriculum was constrained by pressures arising from the development of the primary schools as agents for the selection of pupils for admission to the secondary grammar schools at the age of 11. The 11+ examination, with its emphasis on cognitive learning especially in English language and arithmetic, influenced the primary school curriculum, the streaming of pupils and the frequency of pupil assessment. It was only with the abolition of the 11+ examination in the early 1960s that the primary school curriculum was freed from external constraints.

A substantial proportion of English primary school teachers, especially under the influence of the teacher education institutions, have wholeheartedly accepted an individualist and child-centred philosophy of education as proposed by a variety of progressive educationists of the nineteenth and early twentieth centuries including Pestalozzi, Froebel, Montessori, John Dewey and Susan Isaacs. Child-centred views allowed for selection of curriculum content according to the needs and interests of children with little reference to the essentialist idea that some kinds of knowledge were intrinsically more valuable than others.

The 'integrated day' curriculum approved by the Plowden Report of 1967 involved the organization of knowledge content around themes drawn from pupils' experience (for instance, water, autumn, or the shopping centre) to which subject matter from a wide range of 'disciplines' (language, mathematics, history, art, geography, science, literature) could be introduced. In this kind of curriculum, knowledge is not presented in a structured way but is brought in if and when necessary to illuminate the topic.

An approach similar to that favoured in many primary schools has had some influence on the reform of curriculum for lower grades of some secondary schools. Not only has some teaching allowed for child-centred discovery learning processes but there has been also a move to combine traditional subjects into broader groups such as integrated science, environmental studies, humanities. The battle between the subject-centred and child-centred philosophies is often fought in the teaching of classes in the lower age range of secondary schools. Essentialism, however, occupies the higher ground (of the universities and upper secondary education) and still maintains a predominant advantage.

Curriculum debates

Debates about the curriculum before the late 1970s took place mainly between professional educationists. The question which engaged them was how far and in what ways the traditional elite curriculum could be made available to a much wider school population. From the mid-1970s politicians have tried to force new questions on to the curriculum agenda. They have been concerned mainly with standards of achievement and with the economic relevance of the content of schooling.

AN ESSENTIALIST CURRICULUM FOR ALL?

The promulgation of universal secondary schooling in the 1944 Education Act was preceded by the 1943 Norwood Report which notoriously rejected a common curriculum for secondary schools based on the postulation of three kinds of intellectual capacity and interests among children – 'academic', 'technical' and 'practical'. There was some support for this position from educationists such as G. H. Bantock (1968) who argued that a curriculum based on 'folk' culture was more appropriate for the majority of pupils than one derived from elite 'high' culture. By the 1970s, proposals to differentiate the curriculum according to different abilities or backgrounds of students had been largely rejected.

It was hoped that a common curriculum for all students at secondary level based on that formerly prevailing in the grammar schools would genuinely offer equality of opportunity of access to high culture and the social rewards that possession of such knowledge conferred. The central claim was that the same kind of knowledge, organized in broadly the same ways, could be shared by all pupils through the same kind of curriculum content.

The main elements of the traditional curriculum of the elite schools were adopted for the new comprehensive schools. Proposed modifications focused not on the epistemological principles of essentialism but on the pedagogical techniques by which it could be made accessible to a wider school clientele.

This approach was upheld in the major curriculum projects of the 1960s. The Schools Council Humanities Project contained materials on topics such as poverty, war and society, and family and marriage, and was aimed at the low-achieving 14–16 year-olds. While the pedagogical principles emphasized open (but structured) discussion among pupils, the content stressed the acquisition of moral values through the study of literary and historical texts and illustrations. The project was directed by Lawrence Stenhouse whose extensive writing on the curriculum stressed the intrinsic value of 'fine texts', which could be appreciated intuitively by the whole range of students (Stenhouse, 1970).

The Nuffield Science and Schools Mathematics Projects were

also intended initially to cater for a comprehensive school population. They focused on individual and active discovery of physical phenomena and relationships as the prelude to learning general principles. The concreteness of the stimuli for discovery was intended to cater for children of a wider ability range. However, in practice, the projects began to be associated with elite pupils especially because these projects had been developed mainly by teachers in high-status independent schools.

Another kind of 'democratization' of essentialist knowledge began in universities rather than in schools. The intention was to change the content of study so that it reflected the culture of ordinary people rather than that of the rich and powerful. But these changes did not disturb the logical structures or intellectual principles underlying traditional university studies.

Two examples may be given. The study of great literature had been one of the highest peaks of the essentialist knowledge topography. In the nineteenth and early twentieth centuries, this literature had been mainly Greek and Latin. English literature courses initially had concentrated on linguistic history. But the focus began to shift to great works which contained moral lessons (or which sharpened the moral and aesthetic sensibilities of students). Under the influence of F. R. Leavis at Cambridge, emphasis was given to literary works of, for instance, Charles Dickens, Joseph Conrad and D. H. Lawrence which also dealt with the experiences of 'ordinary' people. This democratization of content, allied to the moral and individualistic definition of purpose, then was reflected on curriculum and methods courses in teacher education dealing with the teaching of English in schools.

History had emerged as a major area of university study from the late nineteenth century, especially at Oxford. The content initially focused at constitutional development and the work of great political leaders (whether monarchs or prime ministers). Radical academics such as R. H. Tawney and G. D. H. Cole shifted the emphasis to the lives of the poor and oppressed through social history but without challenging the moral enhancement purpose of the study. School history curriculum projects moved towards the use and evaluation of sources of evidence for the history of ordinary people though perhaps the emphasis shifted from moral lessons of great lives to the morality of respect for evidence (especially of different groups of people) in making judgements.

37

There was a conflict inherent in the democratization of the content of essentialist areas of study. The purpose originally had been to make a future governing elite more aware of the lives and aspirations of ordinary people. It was not intended primarily to underlie the educational experience of the mass of the population. Even democratized essentialism had elitist purposes. It did not accommodate easily the demands these people might make themselves for a relevant humanistic educational experience.

The major weakness in the movement to democratize the essentialist curriculum in comprehensive schools was that a collection of a few traditional academic subjects, taught in a diluted form, did not meet the needs or aspirations of the majority of students. This patent insufficiency allowed politicians to enter the debate about the curriculum and to make very different kinds of proposals.

A NATIONAL CURRICULUM?

After 1976 central government agencies attempted to define a national curriculum and, in the process, to regain control of the school curriculum from teachers. The rationale was that a school curriculum in which only one subject, religious education, was compulsory by law could lead to the neglect of central areas of study. This was the thrust behind the 1977 Green Paper and subsequent government statements (DES, 1977a, 1980, 1981) culminating in the 1988 Education Reform Act.

The 1988 Act identified 'core' subjects – mathematics, English and science – and other 'foundation' subjects (history, geography, technology, music, art, physical education and, for secondary pupils, a modern foreign language). Schools and teachers were required to follow programmes of study and attainment targets established by the DES for these core and foundation areas. Furthermore, uniform national testing of pupils at the ages of 7, 11, 14 and 16 would also bring greater central government influence over what was taught in schools.

The main justification for the national curriculum in the 1988 Act was that it would allow consumers to know their rights and to have uniform criteria by which they could judge the education provided by schools. Secretary of State Kenneth Baker suggested that 'parents will be far better placed to know what their children are being taught and what they are learning' (DES, 1987b).

Other concerns also impelled these demands for national uniformity. Research reports (Bennett, 1976; Rutter, 1979) added support to the belief that teacher control of the curriculum at school or classroom level intensified differences in opportunities between students at one school compared to another.

Questions also arose about the difficulties experienced by students moving between one school and another in the country when curriculum content was specific to individual schools (DES, 1977a). This last issue was of importance to governments concerned with labour shortages in the expanding south of the country and high unemployment among populations in the declining northern areas. British participation in the European Community may have given even wider significance to the issue of mobility of labour.

While the mandatory content prescriptions which the secretary of state is entitled to make under the terms of the 1988 Education Reform Act are not yet known, earlier statements suggest that they are likely to be relatively traditional (DES, 1980, 1981, 1987a). There have been no indications from government that the content of the 'core' and 'foundation' subjects will differ significantly from what has traditionally prevailed.

The national curriculum applied only to compulsory schooling. The highly specialized 'A' level system for upper secondary education was not seriously undermined. There had been proposals in the early 1970s for an upper secondary course of five subjects spread across the 'arts' and 'science' divide. A more modest version of this scheme was introduced in 1987 when students could follow 'Advanced Supplementary' studies, at the same intellectual standard but with only half the content of 'A' level. But even this modest scheme was not widely accepted.

However, in other sections of the 1988 Act, government reserves the right to influence the content of higher education studies. This power may eventually force changes in the content of upper secondary education.

The relative conservatism of curriculum proposals in the debate about a national curriculum after 1976 can be related to the overlap with the somewhat different issue of 'standards' or 'quality' in school teaching and pupil achievement. The concern for standards was one element in the demand for a national curriculum. But rather different solutions were also proposed for this perceived problem, including more frequent and systematic assessment of the achievements of both students and teachers and a suggestion that there should be greater parental opportunity to choose schools for their children. It was hoped that the latter would force schools to raise standards by the application of 'market forces'. The Conservative governments after 1979 were unclear about whether standards could be raised most effectively by the 'nationalization' of the school curriculum or the 'privatization' of school admissions procedures.

This dual approach has been pursued by governments since 1977 before it was enshrined in the 1988 Education Act. Following the 1977 Green Paper, the Assessment of Performance Unit (APU) was set up in the DES to evaluate achievement in the school curriculum throughout the country. Other measures taken since the late 1970s included the publication of examination results of each school and of the reports of the national inspectors into the quality of teaching in individual schools. The intention was that such information would lead parents and other interested people to put pressure on schools to improve teaching.

These measures challenged the power of teachers rather than the content of the curriculum. Often the debates over standards tended to reinforce older and more traditional views of the 'worthwhile' content of the school curriculum. Indeed, the national curriculum as proposed in the 1988 Act threatens rather more the child-centred approaches adopted in primary education and the lower grades of secondary schools. The sanctity of separate 'subjects' has been reaffirmed. The essentialist view has been challenged only in that specialization involving choice between subjects has been removed from the compulsory period of schooling.

A NEW VOCATIONALISM?

The major attempt to challenge established notions of worthwhile knowledge has been the government-led demand for a stronger technical and vocational element in the curriculum of mainstream schooling.

The pressure for more technical and vocational education which grew in the 1970s and 1980s reflected wider economic and social changes. First, there was a more intense concern about the decline of manufacturing industry and about the lack of the social and work attitudes which might support industrial growth (Weiner, 1981; Dore, 1985). There was concern that not enough skilled workers at every level were being prepared in the education system and also that schools created anti-industrial attitudes among students who then avoided careers in manufacturing industry (DES, 1980).

The second development was the dramatic increase in youth unemployment from the mid-1970s in Britain as in other countries. Work-experience courses such as the Youth Training Scheme (YTS) were developed. These programmes often had a formal educational element in further education colleges, especially for low-attaining 16–19 year-old school leavers. The tension between manifest vocational preparation and latent work substitution functions of these courses was not resolved. But, regardless of the conflict in purposes, there was an emphasis on the development of positive work attitudes and 'generic' work skills.

These courses had been developed by the Manpower Services Commission (MSC) (later, the Training Agency) which had responsibility for employment creation and training at every level. It was quite separate from governmental education agencies and had its own substantial budget. The major initiative to introduce vocational studies in mainstream education was directly funded by the MSC. The Technical and Vocational Education Initiative (TVEI) was established in 1983 and had the support of the Secretary of State for Education but it was controlled and funded by the MSC. This was a pilot scheme introduced into most local authorities but for students aged 14–18 in a minority of schools though it was planned in 1986 that TVEI would be universally available within ten years. It was accepted by teachers and LEAs because it meant an external injection of funds from the MSC at a time when general educational spending was being cut.

Evaluation of TVEI did not produce unanimous findings. It was clear that the 'education' and 'training' divide still operated in that TVEI courses, despite the objectives, were patronized largely by students with low attainments in academic subjects. The extra resources were accepted and TVEI courses were developed enthusiastically. A post-16 Certificate of Pre-Vocational Education was introduced, in practice for 'less academic' sixth form students. But rarely did pupils of above average academic ability depart from the traditional humanistic curriculum to follow new technical and vocational studies.

The vocationalism represented by the introduction of TVEI courses was rejected by many teachers and other educationists. It was seen to represent a return to the differentiation of the curriculum according to student abilities proposed by the Norwood report.

It is unclear whether teachers will be able to sabotage the vocational purposes of MSC projects by their ability to control the

41

details of curriculum content or whether government pressures will succeed. The struggles over a common curriculum, a national curriculum and the 'education' v. 'training' divide have continued for twenty years or more and are far from being resolved. The outcomes are likely to depend on the strengths of the various parties engaged in the politics of curriculum control.

OTHER UNRESOLVED ISSUES

Debates about the curriculum in primary and secondary schools since the 1960s, at least at national level, gave little attention to the socializing function of schools. This was surprising since English schools had had a pre-eminently moral function expressed not only in the place of moralism in the essentialist curriculum but also in widely held views of the moral and pastoral role of teachers and the residually strong place for (Christian) religious education in the curriculum.

Issues such as moral education, sex education and political education were not strongly pursued in debates about the national curriculum. Even the issue of the rights to cultural autonomy of ethnic minorities (especially in language and religion) were largely ignored in central government curriculum statements.

Partly this neglect of socializing functions of schooling may be linked to a perception, in government reports, of the problems of education in socially decaying big cities as those of equality of access to education rather than of socialization. Later, there was concern with the chronic underachievement of certain ethnic minority children (particularly Afro-Caribbean) which had been stimulated at least in part by inner city riots of the early 1980s.

The neglect of the way that the curriculum might contribute to encouraging cultural and social identities particularly in large cities tended to strengthen the essentialist tradition that morality was inculcated through the values of a school community and of a humanistic curriculum. Yet the social crisis of large cities especially was marked by the increasing divorce between secondary schools and the values of local communities or of sub-cultures, particularly of youth. Schools had been seen as citadels of civilization in nineteenth-century urban jungles. They were as much fortified outposts of an alien culture in the later twentieth century.

Curriculum issues in England since the 1960s particularly have as much involved competing groups of protagonists as competing ideas. Generally until the mid-1970s, curriculum debates took place between different groups of teachers. Since that time, governments have tried to exert a greater influence. The outcomes of these struggles are likely to be of major significance in the development of the curriculum in England. The nature of the forces and groups engaged in the battles should be examined further.

Curriculum control and management

It was suggested earlier that teachers and other professional educationists are the arch-defenders of established curriculum traditions. Yet arguments that the school curriculum in England and Wales is dominated by teachers have been challenged by assertions that central government has exerted an increasingly powerful influence since the 1970s.

These arguments may be evaluated by considering the influence of various groups or agencies separately. But first the legal or 'official' structure of curriculum decision-making should be described. It is within the framework of this official structure that the various groups compete for influence.

THE LEGAL AND OFFICIAL STRUCTURE OF CURRICULUM CONTROL

The one hundred or so local education authorities since 1902 have had the legal and actual power to raise and allocate financial resources, to decide the location and organization of schools, to appoint teachers and to control all matters of internal school organization including the curriculum. The policy of LEAs is formulated by locally elected councils. Educational policy is implemented through LEA permanent officials. LEA inspectors and advisers maintain close relationships with individual schools and teachers.

Educational matters are controlled at central level by the Department of Education and Science (DES) in England (and in practice Wales) the political head of which has been a cabinet minister. Scottish and Northern Irish education is the responsibility of the Scottish and Northern Irish Offices. The influence of the DES, however, does extend over the whole of Britain in university policy.

The uncertainty of the relationship between central and local government revolves particularly around financial and, to a lesser extent, legislative power. Central government has provided about half the financial resources employed by LEAs (but as part of a block grant covering also services outside education). Central government also possesses the power to enforce educational change through legislation. The 1988 Education Reform Act has broken with recent traditions by permitting the DES to prescribe curriculum content for schools. Furthermore, this Act permits individual schools, after a ballot of parents, to 'opt out' of LEA control and to enter a direct relationship with the DES.

All aspects of curriculum control and policy to determine timetables, syllabuses, texts and equipment, teaching methods and forms of assessment up till 1988 have lain officially with LEAs. In practice, this control has not been effectively exercised by local authorities. LEAs have not enforced consistent curriculum policies. Curriculum power has passed to teachers in schools or to a variety of agencies at national level because of the local authority unwillingness to intervene.

National advisory bodies have had considerable influence. The DES and its predecessors have established numerous committees of inquiries often on education at particular levels such as the Plowden Report on primary education (DES, 1967) or on broad curriculum areas (Bullock, 1975) which have been taken often as guidelines by teachers. Many reports on curriculum matters, often on the teaching of specific subjects, have been issued by HM inspectors since the late nineteenth century. The recent prescriptive statements of central government on curriculum matters have developed from a longer tradition of informal central government advice on curriculum matters.

A number of quasi-official bodies have also had influence. The Schools Council (1965–83) sponsored many advisory reports on curriculum matters. Though set up by government, the Schools Council contained a majority of teaching members. Its projects and reports were largely permissive rather than prescriptive reflecting a view that curriculum innovation should be based on individual schools and led by teachers. With the abolition of the Schools Council, teachers have been relatively under-represented in official curriculum bodies at national level.

The Schools Examination Council which was established after the demise of the Schools Council has had the function of liaising with examination boards. These have been independent of government at either national or local level. The eight GCE (later six GCSE) boards mainly are based on universities. There are

questions of which groups control these boards whose requirements have a major impact on the secondary school curriculum.
University academics certainly have a major influence on the
maintenance of a curriculum of specialist academic subjects
through the examination boards.

The 1988 Education Act has shifted the balance of power in that
lists of compulsory subjects, programmes of study, attainment
targets and assessment procedures are to be controlled ultimately
by the DES. Details will be decided by committees and working
groups of educationists and others under the aegis of the National
Curriculum and Schools Examinations and Assessment Councils.
The major change is that the secretary of state will have stronger
powers of veto over the adoption of the recommendations of
these organizations. Whether there will be a major reduction in
the power of professional educationists outside central government to determine the details of curriculum content remains to
be seen.

The claims that teachers have controlled the curriculum in
English schools and that central government has begun to exert a
greater influence since the 1970s both have validity but neither
is easily justified if reference is made only to official curriculum
control structures. The power of teachers and the growing
influence of central government need to be investigated in
relation to informal power configurations that are highly significant in determining the curriculum of schools in Britain.

THE POLITICS OF CURRICULUM CONTROL

The main question in examining the actual processes of curriculum control is how the essentialist tradition has been entrenched
so strongly despite pressures for democratization of access and
demands for vocational relevance. What groups have been able to
preserve the pre-eminence of the specialist humanities-based
curriculum? How far has this influence been disturbed in recent
years by other groups which have different views of the curriculum?

The power of teachers may be examined first. In the period
1945–75 the politicians and officials of central and local government have insisted neither on what subjects should be taught nor
on what the content of each subject should be. In effect teachers
were left to decide what to teach and in what combinations.

It has been argued that teacher control over the curriculum
emerged from an informal arrangement in the twenty years after

1945 between leading officials of the then Ministry of Education, LEAs and the teacher unions (or, more particularly, the largest, the National Union of Teachers – NUT). These officials, it was claimed, met frequently to determine local and national education policy behind the backs of their respective political masters. By this arrangement, the Ministry of Education controlled finance and resources, the LEAs determined school organization and local provision, while the teachers gained control over the curriculum (Manzer, 1970).

The capacity of central government to control the curriculum has been weakened primarily by the determination of teachers at school level to continue to teach the content that they feel is appropriate to individual children and to maintain the right of individual teachers to make these choices.

Teachers do not form a unified group. There are different interests among different groups of teachers. It is not always clear which groups of teachers have the greatest power over curriculum matters – classroom teachers, heads of subject departments (especially in secondary schools), or headteachers. These last two grades of teacher often have a very considerable influence. In many cases, teacher control over the curriculum may mean power for these elite grades rather than the majority of teachers (Richardson, 1973). Elsewhere control is more diffused.

Teachers are subjected to external pressures, especially from the higher education system which they may be unable to resist but which they may also willingly accept. University influence on secondary school teachers is formally maintained through the GCE (or GCSE) examination boards. University academics exercise ultimate control over the running of these organizations even though teachers and central and local government are represented. University control over the examination boards is most significant in the use of these examinations primarily for selecting students for higher education.

The question then is why teachers who resist government intervention in the curriculum appear to accept the influence of university academics over examination syllabuses. The answer would seem to be that teachers in secondary schools notoriously have been dominated by their subject discipline affiliations which are created and maintained in the universities and other institutions of higher education in which the teachers received their own higher education.

Subject specialization identities have been very strong among

46

teachers. Subject associations have been influential among teachers. The school curriculum and school organization are built around a number of academic subject-based hierarchies which divide teacher from teacher and destroy curriculum unity for students (Bernstein, 1977). Even noted 'progressive' schools which, successfully in the short term, abolished formal classes and timetables and replaced them by pupil-teacher individual contact, failed to persuade 'progressive' teachers to abandon their subject identities in ways needed for completely interdisciplinary teaching (Bernbaum, 1973).

Departments of educational studies in universities may have had some countervailing influence. There has been a tradition of support for child-centred views of education in these institutions upon which the Plowden Committee, for instance, drew and also of support for critical perspectives on the educational process which may have influenced teachers. But education courses are far less highly regarded by future teachers than the academic studies that preceded or accompanied them. The identities of most teachers in secondary schools are based mainly on the subjects they teach rather than on a commitment to 'progressive' styles of pedagogy.

What is striking about the politics of curriculum control in Britain is not only the power of teachers but also the powerlessness of the inspectorate. The functions of both levels of inspector – the (national) Her Majesty's inspectors (HMIs), and the LEA advisers – have been limited largely to advice rather than direction of teachers. The HMIs may have higher status but their reports both on general developments and on individual schools have no mandatory force. Despite the enhanced position they have gained since the mid-1970s following greater central government attention to curriculum matters, the HMIs at most contribute only to forming opinion. Their powerlessness, together with suspicions that HMIs are overly sympathetic to the views of teachers, has led to attempts by central government politicians to bypass them in the process of creating a national and vocationally relevant curriculum (Lawton and Gordon, 1987).

Despite the higher national political profile given to curriculum affairs since the 1970s, groups outside the education system have had a very limited impact on curriculum decision-making. Employers have had little influence on the curriculum of mainstream education. While employer organizations (especially the Confederation of British Industries) have complained about the lack of motivation and achievement of their new recruits which they blame on the schools (a perennial complaint), they rarely have made positive curriculum proposals. Indeed, employers have relied heavily on conventional school and higher education certificates in the selection of new recruits. At intermediate and higher level initial recruitment they have preferred students with traditional high-status education.

Employers have preferred to provide their own 'on the job' vocational education. Their involvement in curriculum matters has been mainly in vocational qualification courses in further education. The attempts by the Manpower Services Commission to gain control over lower-level vocational education and qualifications have indicated that employer influence at these levels may have been weak.

Parents traditionally have had practically no influence on the curriculum decisions in Britain. The establishment of universal and compulsory education in a highly urbanized society in the nineteenth century created a tradition of antipathy between teachers and parents especially in urban areas. The social elite since the late eighteenth century tended to abandon their children totally to boarding-schools with little concern for what the schools provided for them. Teachers have been loath to consult parents on curriculum matters and parents have rarely interfered.

Despite calls for greater consumer control of education by governments since the mid–1970s, little has been done to strengthen parent consultation on curriculum matters. The 1980 Education Act made it obligatory for school governing bodies to include elected parent representatives while the 1981 Education Act allowed parent appeals against the allocation of their children to particular schools. But neither Act implemented the recommendation of the 1977 Taylor Committee (DES, 1977c) that headteachers should be required to win the approval of governing bodies for general curriculum aims. Consumer power has meant choice between pre-set alternatives rather than the right to demand that a particular offering should be made available.

Any attempt to weaken the dominance of the essentialist tradition in the curriculum of English schools must either lessen the informal influence of schoolteachers and of university academics on curriculum practice or persuade these groups to change their positions. Government actions since 1976 have not indicated any ways in which curriculum practice can be changed without the co-operation of these two groups.

Not all teachers and academics are totally averse to change, especially when child-centred views of the curriculum are widely held by many teachers and when rigid university entry requirements may eventually lead to a decline of university places to the detriment of academic careers. But the essentialist tradition of worthwhile knowledge is still deeply ingrained among both groups and, without a change in these deeply held values, proposals for major changes in the curriculum will encounter significant resistance.

Conclusion

The essentialist tradition in the curriculum of educational institutions in Britain has been challenged in two main ways. First, primary schools and to some extent the lower grades of secondary schools have been able to adopt curricula based on child-centred philosophies. This movement has been in progress since the mid-nineteenth century and has had a high degree of success. However, the 1988 Education Reform Act appears to bring it to a halt.

Secondly, there has been a sustained effort since the mid-1970s to introduce a greater vocational element to the curriculum especially for lower-achieving pupils aged 14 and above. The outcome of these demands is difficult to judge at this stage.

Yet the essentialist tradition has not been seriously challenged in planning curricula for the majority of pupils aged 14 and above in the mainstream system. The attitudes not only of teachers but also of university academics and, rather strangely, of employers in their recruitment practices suggest that the essentialist view is still very fully entrenched.

Further Reading

Axtell, James J. (ed.), *The Educational Writings of John Locke* (Cambridge: Cambridge University Press, 1968).

Bamford, T. W., *The Rise of the Public Schools* (London: Nelson, 1967)

Bantock, G. H., *Culture, Industrialisation and Education* (London: Routledge, 1968).

Bennett, Neville, *Teaching Styles and Pupil Progress* (London: Open Books, 1976).

Bernbaum, Gerald, 'Countesthorpe College', in OECD/CERI, *Case Studies in Educational Innovation*, Vol. 3 (Paris: OECD, 1973) pp. 7–88.

Bernstein, Basil, 'On the classification and framing of educational knowledge', in Basil Bernstein (ed.), *Class Codes and Control*, Vol. 3 (London: Routledge, 1977) pp. 85–115..

Board of Education, *The Montessori Method* (London: HMSO, 1905).

Board of Education, *The Education of the Adolescent* (Hadow Report) (London: HMSO, 1926).

Board of Education, *Primary Education* (Hadow Report) (London: HMSO, 1931).

Board of Education, *Handbook of Suggestions for Teachers* (London: HMSO, 1935).

Board of Education, *Grammar and Technical High Schools* (Spens Report) (London: HMSO, 1938).

Board of Education, *Curriculum and Examinations in Secondary Schools* (Norwood Report) (London: HMSO, 1943).

Bullock Report, *A Language for Life* (London: HMSO, 1975).

Centre for Contemporary Cultural Studies, *Unpopular Education* (London: Hutchinson, 1981).

Department of Education and Science (hereafter DES), *Children and their Primary Schools* (Plowden Report) (London: HMSO, 1967).

DES, *Public Schools Commission Report* (Newsom Report) (London: HMSO, 1968).

DES, *Education in Schools: A Consultative Document* (London: HMSO, 1977a).

DES, *Modern Languages and Comprehensive Schools* (London: HMSO, 1977b).

DES, *A New Partnership for our Schools* (London: HMSO, 1977c).

DES, *Local Authority Arrangements for the School Curriculum* (London: HMSO, 1979).

DES, *A Framework for the School Curriculum* (London: HMSO, 1980).

DES, *The School Curriculum* (London: HMSO, 1981).

DES, *Teaching Quality* (London: HMSO, 1983).

DES, *Better Schools* (London: HMSO, 1985).

DES, *The National Curriculum 5–16* (London: HMSO, 1987a).

DES, 'Education Reform Bill' (press release, mimeo) (1987b).

Dore, Ronald, 'Technical change and cultural adaptation', *Compare*, vol. 15, no. 2, pp. 109–20 (1985).

Flemming, Wilfred, 'The Schools Mathematics Project', in Lawrence Stenhouse (ed.), *Curriculum Research and Development in Action* (London: Heinemann, 1980) pp. 25–41.

Goodson, Ivor, F. (ed.), *Social Histories of the Secondary Curriculum* (Brighton: Falmer, 1985).

Gordon, Peter, and Lawton, Denis, *Curriculum Change in the Nineteenth and Twentieth Centuries* (London: Hodder & Stoughton, 1978).

Hall, Stuart, and Jefferson, Tony (eds), *Resistance Through Rituals* (London: Hutchinson, 1975).

Hirst, Paul H., *Knowledge and the Curriculum* (London: Routledge, 1974).

Inner London Education Authority (ILEA), *Race, Sex and Class* (London: ILEA, 1983).

Jackson, Brian, *Streaming: An Education System in Miniature* (London: Routledge, 1964).

Kogan, Maurice, *Educational Policy Making* (London: Routledge, 1975).

Kogan, Maurice, *The Politics of Educational Change* (London: Fontana/Collins, 1978).

Lawton, Denis, *Social Change, Educational Theory and Curriculum Planning* (London: University of London Press, 1973).

Lawton, Denis, and Gordon, Peter, *HMI* (London: Routledge, 1987).

Manzer, R. A., *Teachers and Politics* (Manchester: Manchester University Press, 1970).

Ministry of Education, *15 to 18* (Crowther Report) (London: HMSO, 1959).

Ministry of Education, *Half Our Future* (Newsom Report) (London: HMSO, 1963).

Plaskow, Maurice (ed.), *Life and Death of the Schools Council* (Brighton: Falmer, 1986).

Plato, *The Republic* (Harmondsworth: Penguin, 1955).

Richardson, Elisabeth, *The Teacher, the School and the Task of Management* (London: Heinemann, 1973).

Robbins Report, *Higher Education* (London: HMSO, 1963).

Rubinstein, David, and Simon, Brian, *The Evolution of the Comprehensive School 1926–1966* (London: Routledge, 1969).

Rutter, Michael, *et al.*, *Fifteen Thousand Hours* (London: Open Books, 1979).

Salter, Brian, and Tapper, Ted, *Education Politics and the State* (London: Gran-McIntyre, 1981).

Stenhouse, Lawrence, 'The Humanities Curriculum Project', *Journal of Curriculum Studies*, vol. 1, no. 1, (1969) p. 26–33.

Stenhouse, Lawrence, 'Some limitations on the use of objectives in curriculum research and planning', *Paedagogica Europaea*, vol. 6, (1970) pp. 73–83.

Stewart, W. A. C., and McGinn, W. P., *The Educational Innovators*, 2 vols (London: Macmillan, 1967, 1968).

Taylor, William, *The Secondary Modern School* (London: Faber, 1963).

Walker, Rob, 'Nuffield Secondary Science', in Lawrence Stenhouse (ed.), *Curriculum Research and Development in Action* (London: Heinemann, 1980) pp. 79–93.

Weiner, M. J., *English Culture and the Decline of the Industrial Spirit 1850–1980* (Cambridge: Cambridge University Press, 1981).

White, John P., *Towards a Compulsory Curriculum* (London: Routledge, 1973).

Whitty, Geoff, and Young, Michael F. D. (eds), *Explorations in the Politics of School Knowledge* (Driffield: Nafferton, 1976).

Young, Michael, F. D. (ed.), *Knowledge and Control* (London: Macmillan, 1971).

Chapter Three

Universal knowledge and the French curriculum

The end of the Second World War in France gave impetus to educational reform. There was a need to reconstruct a country which had suffered defeat and occupation. There was a desire to rid the country of the Nazi-influenced education system of the puppet Vichy government. The 1947 Langevin–Wallon Commission proposed that education should be made available for all children and young people until the age of 18 and there should be equality of opportunity of access to all kinds of education.

It was only after Charles de Gaulle became President of the Fifth Republic in 1958 that secondary education was made available for all and the democratization of access to each level of the education system was begun. By this time, France was experiencing an economic revolution which turned it, broadly, from a nation of peasants containing islands of industrialization into a high-technology economy and an urban society. The democratization of educational access had economic as well as political imperatives.

These changes in France have been confronted by a curriculum tradition of encyclopaedism which had been institutionalized since the 1789 revolution. Despite its origins, the bastions of the encyclopaedic view in the nineteenth and early twentieth centuries were the socially and intellectually elitist secondary schools – the *lycées* – and the institutions of higher education which the *lycées* fed. Democratization of educational access brought the appropriateness of the encyclopaedic tradition into question. Debates about curriculum in the second half of the twentieth century in France have been largely about the ways in which this dominant tradition can be modified to suit mass secondary education.

What knowledge

The philosophy and pedagogy of the encyclopaedic tradition were expressed by seventeenth-century writers, especially Comenius. But its central position in French educational thought owed much to the rational philosophy of Descartes and to the Enlightenment view of social reform of the eighteenth-century encyclopaedists such as Montesquieu. This latter position influenced the revolutionary governments after the 1789 revolution. Indeed, one of the fullest expositions of an encyclopaedist view of knowledge in relation to educational (and curriculum) policy can be found in Condorcet's plan for educational reform presented to the National Assembly in 1792 (see Barnard, 1970).

The encyclopaedist view has three main elements. First has been the principle of rationality. Those subjects which have the most coherent rational structures and which are perceived to encourage the development of rational faculties in students are regarded as most important. In the nineteenth century these were seen to be classical languages and philosophy. In the twentieth century, mathematics and physical sciences have had the highest status. Subjects such as expressive arts or physical education have struggled for recognition. The traditional French secondary school curriculum has been almost completely intellectual.

The second principle has been universality. This has two applications. First, all students should acquire as much 'valued' knowledge as possible of all kinds and branches. There should be no early specialization, since this would entail exclusion of valid subjects. Secondly, all students should acquire broadly the same knowledge at the same time and in the same order. There has been a common curriculum in which all or most students in all institutions throughout France acquired the same knowledge by the same stages.

The third principle has been utility. This was important for the eighteenth-century encyclopaedists and for the revolutionaries of 1789 who believed that social progress should be achieved by reforming and efficient central governments. Rational knowledge could and should be used to improve society. Social, economic, political and technological organization could be enhanced by the application of rational thought and rational knowledge.

The utilitarian principle was relatively neglected during the conservative regimes (both monarchist and republican) of the nineteenth century. It has become important again in later twentieth-century educational policies. Technical and vocational education is justified because it may lead to the economic improvement of society. But technological and vocational education is also valid in terms of curriculum traditions because it is seen to be based upon and drawn from rational knowledge (often the 'pure' physical sciences).

There have been debates about which encyclopaedic principles are most important, which subjects should receive particular attention. In the socially conservative periods of the nineteenth century 'the essential goal of education was to be to train the pupils to appreciate the masterpieces of Greek and Rome and to imitate them intelligently' (Durkheim, 1977) . This view was challenged in the second half of the twentieth century. Symbolically its defeat can be associated with the relegation of Latin from a central to a marginal place in the lower secondary school curriculum and the replacement of letters by mathematics and physical sciences as the most prestigious specialization in upper secondary education by the late 1960s.

Some educational aims adopted in France have entailed attention to kinds of knowledge which could not be justified easily by encyclopaedist principles. Democratization of education has involved acceptance of the idea that students are different and may have individually different knowledge needs. Changes in the social role of families have given schools a socialization function which involves the transmission of certain kinds of moral or expressive knowledge which are not easily justified by encyclopaedist views. In both cases there has been conflict between the residual dominance of encyclopaedism and these new curriculum imperatives.

Support for child-centred philosophies of, for instance, Freinet has been marginal. While these views have had some impact on the primary school curriculum, they have hardly touched the teaching of central subjects such as French and mathematics. At lower secondary school level, pupil-centred views have been applied to the teaching of less able pupils and not the mainstream curriculum (Nieser, 1979).

Curriculum debates in France have rarely challenged the basic assumptions of encyclopaedism. Few suggest that other curriculum theories should be adopted. But the encyclopaedic curriculum which applied in the elite *lycées* in the nineteenth and early twentieth centuries cannot remain unchanged if an effective education is to be provided for a democratized education system in a highly industrialized society in the later twentieth century.

For which students?

The expansion of educational opportunities after 1958 followed upon the growth of a high-technology economy. There was also an acceleration of urbanization and of immigration from abroad (particularly North Africa and Portugal). There were changed family and social relationships and new perceptions of human rights. These wider social changes triggered demands for more education and brought the existing content of education into question.

In 1945, elementary schooling in the years 6–14 had comprised the complete formal educational experience of most French men and women. Secondary and higher education had been reserved for stringently selected future elites. By 1980 90 per cent of 3 year-olds and practically 100 per cent of 4 year-old children were in kindergartens. Elementary education had become a separate stage before universal secondary schooling rather than a complete formal education in itself. Universal lower secondary education was provided in neighbourhood comprehensive schools. Nearly 80 per cent of the relevant age group entered upper secondary institutions, whether of the general or professional kind. And 30 per cent of the age group was admitted to higher education.

The encyclopaedist curricula had operated in an education system in which the rigorously intellectual secondary school knowledge diet had been confined to less than 20 per cent of the age group who mainly were preparing for traditional professions, often via higher education. Education had concentrated on exclusively academic concerns. The changes of the 1960s and 1970s gave schooling a wider social and economic function and extended the range of pupils to whom this education was offered.

ELEMENTARY EDUCATION

The content of pre-school and primary education was perhaps least affected by socioeconomic changes. There has been a tradition that pre-secondary schooling should be linked to some degree to the familial and local environment, reflecting the introduction of universal state primary education into a diverse rural society in the nineteenth century.

Nineteenth-century elementary schools had had the functions of creating a national political solidarity and of selecting a few children for *petit fonctionnaire* positions. There had been a national curriculum and standardized examinations at the end of the course. But there was a tradition also of linking the elementary school to the local life of village children. Standardized French, mathematics, history and geography syllabuses existed in a system in which the children of peasants were not pressed too hard when the majority would also become peasants.

The primary school curriculum after the introduction of universal secondary education from 1959 was also fairly relaxed. Standardized, intellectually based syllabuses in French and mathematics were balanced by more flexible 'curiosity awakening' subjects (*activités d'éveil*).

In one respect, however, French primary schools were expected to follow encyclopaedist principles. The idea that all children should reach a pre-ordained standard at the end of each grade of primary education has survived – and this is consistent with the encyclopaedist view that there is a standard body of knowledge that all should acquire. So children in primary schools are still forced to repeat grades – including between 10 to 15 per cent of both the first and last grades of primary education in 1982–3. In effect, children are not promoted from the first grade of primary school until they can read fluently.

SECONDARY EDUCATION

The major debate about which students should receive what knowledge has centred on secondary and post-secondary education. In the first part of the twentieth century, a minority of state elementary school pupils was selected for the *lycées* on a meritocratic basis by examination. Fully comprehensive neighbourhood secondary schools began to be set up following the Fouchet decrees of 1963 (in the 1980s termed *collèges uniques* or simply *collèges*). They catered for students aged 11–15 or 16. There was pressure for all their students to follow the same curriculum to achieve full equality of opportunity.

This did not happen in practice. Three bands or *filières* emerged in the comprehensive *collèges*. The first was a fast stream whose students took extra subjects such as a classical or second foreign language after the second year. The second stream concentrated on the central subjects of the core curriculum. The third (some 25 per cent of pupils) followed a far more restricted curriculum (concentrating on French, mathematics and craft subjects) which did not meet the ·encyclopaedist criterion of universality. Various attempts were made after the Haby reform of 1975 to abolish the *filières* and to replace them by a more flexible system of setting. But the Haby reform and later attempts such as that of the Legrand Commission of 1982 to introduce mixed ability teaching at least in the first year were resisted by teachers at school. In practice the slow and restricted streams have survived, though sometimes in a disguised form.

The *filières* had been justified in the 1960s by the application of the principles of *observation* and *orientation*. In the first two grades, students were to be observed continuously to ensure that they were placed in the right stream. But initial placements were rarely changed in practice. *Orientation*, which was applied in the final two grades of the college, was to ensure that students were prepared for those educational or occupational futures for which they were best suited. But this process could be in conflict with the provision of full educational opportunities for all as was recognized by government reports in the 1980s.

The development of streaming indicates a conflict between encyclopaedist rigour and the range of abilities and motivations of children in the democratized schools. It is also symptomatic of organizational constraints such as the grading of teachers by intellectual criteria which links their qualifications to the academic level of teaching they do and the persistence of grade repeating in primary schools which means that around 20 to 25 per cent of children reach secondary schools at ages which preclude them from completing the full four-grade lower secondary school course in the normal time.

Despite the incapacity of French secondary schools, operating by encyclopaedist principles, to provide a coherent and valuable education for the lowest 25 per cent of the ability range, the encyclopaedist tradition has meant that the rest do follow a reasonable common curriculum without greater variations in basic standards at least up to the end of compulsory schooling at 16. Almost 80 per cent of pupils stayed on for some form of post-compulsory education in 1980.

There is, however, quite sharp curriculum differentiation after the end of compulsory schooling at 16. Academic education continues in three-grade general *lycées* leading to the *bacca-laureát* at around the age of 19 and thence to higher education. The core curriculum is combined with depth study of a few subjects. About 35 per cent of the age group follows this track. The others take one out of a variety of technical vocational qualifications, full-time or part-time, in *lycées professionels*. At the lowest level, they give work orientation to future semi-skilled workers – in effect a continuation of the lowest streams of the secondary school. At the highest level, there are courses for future technicians or junior managers and in the middle (though for the largest number) highly specialized vocational part-time courses for apprentice skilled workers. The curriculum at every level of the *lycée professionel* track is orientated towards the skills required in work.

The separation of a specialized vocational track of upper secondary education is reconciled partly with encyclopaedist views in that the vocational courses do include a general education element and the vocational content often follows on from introductory courses in subjects such as mathematics and the physical or biological sciences. The utility principle of encyclo-paedism is employed to justify a curriculum which is strongly vocational but which starts from the study of rationally structured academic subjects.

HIGHER EDUCATION

The relationship between rationality and utility is also found at higher education level. The most prestigious kind of higher education is provided in the *grandes écoles* which select students by high-level entrance examinations and which are linked to particular vocations, such as engineering and public administration. But the actual curriculum of these professional institutions is strong on the rational academic disciplines.

Even the universities retain some of their older function of preparing for traditional professions such as medicine and law. Reforms after 1971 reorganized the universities into *unités d'en-seignement et recherche* which were linked to particular future careers for students which were seen to be relevant to the new industrial and urban France. But the sub-elements of such courses focused on traditional academic knowledge. So conventionally a law degree in a French university contains substantial elements of philosophy, politics and economics.

Short-cycle higher education has been developed. University

institutes of technology (IUTs) began in 1966 to provide technically orientated shorter courses. From 1971 the older university degree (*licence* or *maîtrise*) was punctuated by a mid-stage diploma (DEUG) after which it was hoped that many students would enter work. But few students were prepared to complete their studies with the DEUG, which was also treated with suspicion by many employers.

The principles of encyclopaedism have continued to inform the curriculum choices of educational institutions in France after they have widened their intake to include much broader social and ability ranges and after the reorientation of the educational system to meet the technological need and social outcomes of industrialization in France.

Curriculum debates

Curriculum decision-makers in France have had to take into account both new general aims of education and older curriculum traditions. Conflicts have arisen between supporters of aims, on the one hand, that education should be provided as a human right to all, that it should contribute to economic development and that it should encourage social adjustment and, on the other hand, the adherents of a traditional curriculum view that rational knowledge is most worthwhile and that as much as possible of the total stock of rational knowledge should be imparted to all students. Curriculum debates have centred on this conflict. Curriculum decisions have been attempts to resolve it.

A COMMON CURRICULUM FOR STUDENTS WITH DIFFERENT OCCUPATIONAL FUTURES?

Both the encyclopaedist view of the curriculum and the administrative structure of French education traditionally have supported a common curriculum for all pupils in the same kinds of institutions. On the one hand, the universalism of encyclopaedism has been consistent with all students at the same stage acquiring broadly the same kind of knowledge. On the other hand, the centralized system of educational administration in France has meant that curriculum content is prescribed in considerable detail at national level for uniform application in every school.

The demand, expressed strongly since the 1947 Langevin–Wallon Report, that education should be provided as a human right and that there should be equal opportunities for educational success, has supported the maintenance of a common curriculum. Equality of opportunity is perceived by most groups concerned with education, including teacher unions, parents and the main political parties, to require a common curriculum. When comprehensive lower secondary *collèges* were established from 1964, the policy was to offer, as far as possible, a common curriculum to all pupils. This meant that the old academic curriculum of the selective *lycée* would be made available to as many pupils of the new *collèges* as could follow it.

There are three major obstacles to the implementation of a completely common curriculum. First, the encyclopaedist ideal of universality is seen to mean that all pupils shall reach minimum standards of attainment in the acquisition of a standardized body of knowledge. When a substantial group of students entering democratized secondary schools has failed to reach these standards, the reaction was to offer a modified curriculum to around 25 per cent of the pupils in the lower secondary school. These classes contain many pupils who are socially disadvantaged and those who have fallen behind in the primary school.

This differentiation has not been accepted passively by policymakers. A variety of measures has been introduced to prevent rigid divisions within lower secondary schools. The attempt by Minister Haby in 1975 to replace streaming by setting and to introduce reinforcement (*soutien*) and enrichment (*approfondissement*) lessons in the core subjects of mathematics, French and modern languages was an attack on the three tracks (*filières*) which emerged after 1968. The effort by the Legrand Commission (supported by Minister Savary) to create totally mixed ability classes in the first year of the lower secondary school (and to abolish the pre-vocational classes) in 1982 was an attempt to recover from the failure of the Haby proposals.

But teachers in schools, especially principals, have been unwilling to implement mixed ability teaching, despite the commitment of their unions at national level to a common curriculum. These teachers have been following the encyclopaedist view that a common curriculum means similar attainment standards of pupils and that if some pupils clearly cannot cope then they should be offered something different.

This obstructionism of some teachers has in part been a response to popular criticism expressed particularly in the press that attainment standards in the *collège* are low and falling. The unwillingness of the curriculum designers in Paris to lighten the factual load and intellectual demands of many syllabuses has also made teachers feel that mixed ability classes are unfeasible.

The second obstacle to the implementation of mixed ability teaching has been the professional interests of teachers. The various separate grades of teacher in lower secondary schools not only have different pay scales and conditions of work but, because their gradings are linked to initial academic attainment levels, tend to teach different ability levels of pupils. The elite *professeurs agrégés* and the university graduate *professeurs certifiés* traditionally have taught more able pupils. They feel that if they lose this right, their other privileges are likely to come under attack. Only over time, when those former primary school teachers (*instituteurs*), who were upgraded to teach middle and lower ability classes in *collèges*, are replaced entirely by university graduate teachers, will the stratification of the teaching force cease to be an obstacle to the removal of streams within the *collège*.

The third constraint on the achievement of a common curriculum has been the sharp division at upper secondary level between the academic courses of the general *lycées* and the vocational courses followed by most students in the professional *lycées*. At the highest level of the professional *lycées*, the technician *baccalauréat* does not differ substantially in the status or opportunities it offers from the more academic *baccalauréats*. The next level course, the *Brevet d'Enseignement Professionelle* (BEP), contains broad theoretical as well as vocational studies and has some status in preparing future technicians and supervisors.

It is the course leading to the *Certificat d'Aptitude Professionelle* (CAP) for apprentice skilled workers that most diverges from the general encyclopaedic ideal of a common curriculum based on rational knowledge. The CAP is taken by the majority of students in the professional *lycées* yet is very specialized and highly vocational. There are some 260 specialisms and a failure rate of around 60 per cent (compared to less than 30 per cent for the *baccalauréat*). The orientation towards vocational futures at the end of lower secondary education has produced a sharp bifurcation between the continuance of general education for around 35 per cent and limited vocational studies for others.

This division cannot be attributed simply to educationists. National economic plans have assumed distinctions between workers of different levels of skill in the future economy. Upper secondary education has been planned partly on the basis of these assumptions. Furthermore, the historical provision of craft training in state educational institutions since the 1919 Astier law has brought vocational education, which in some other countries would be carried out within industry, into the educational system. At best, this may have injected a greater theoretical and general element into craft training than is found elsewhere but it has also widened the division between the content of the curriculum of general and vocational upper secondary education.

The encyclopaedist tradition has allowed for a high status to be attached to studies leading to scientific and technological vocations. Engineering and technology are prestigious subjects in universities and the *grandes écoles*. But the same students reject such studies at the lower level of the *lycées professionels* when they are associated with less prestigious occupations and with limited vocational education.

In the academic branch of upper secondary education, differentiation between students on the basis of educational specialisms is accepted and practised. But each course leads to the *baccalauréat* which gives entry to higher education. There is much communality across these specializations. A core curriculum is maintained in that all students whatever their specialisms take subjects such as French (until the penultimate grade), mathematics, social studies, a foreign language, sciences and (in the final grade) philosophy. But specialization means that non-specialist subjects may be studied rather superficially and examined only by short oral tests.

Also, though specialisms are notionally equal, the mathematics and physical sciences option has much higher status than those in, for instance, letters, social and economic sciences, biological sciences, or technology. There is in effect competition to enter the mathematics and physical sciences option. Students may repeat the last year of the *collège* course in order to enter the mathematics and physical sciences option rather than one of the less prestigious alternatives.

This informal prestige ranking does have an important impact on entry to higher education and is closely related to the socioeconomic background of students. Mathematics and physical sciences specialists are more likely to have come from higher social class groups and are much more likely to enter the *grandes écoles* or the prestigious faculties of universities such as medicine than their fellows who follow other specialisms (Neave, 1985).

Quite apart from the implications of creating an elite primarily of mathematicians, for which French ministers of education have shown concern, subject specialisms in the general (academic) *lycées* have an impact on the achievement of equality of opportunity in upper secondary education.

A high degree of communality does exist in the French school curriculum. In every *collège* 75 per cent of pupils do follow broadly the same courses with more or less the same content. Reasonable standards of attainment are demanded of the majority of pupils. But there are exceptions. The lowest 25 per cent of attainers are abandoned at a fairly early age. Only about 35 per cent are permitted to follow the higher-status general upper secondary course. In the first case, it is the high intellectual demands of an encyclopaedist curriculum together with the large range of subjects which militate against attempts to bring the lowest 25 per cent of attainers into the common curriculum. In the second case it is the impact of an external socioeconomic structure and of governmental economic planning which insists that the 40 per cent of mainstream lower secondary pupils are diverted into vocational courses at the age of 16.

INDIVIDUALISM AND LOCAL INTERESTS

Encyclopaedism has been associated with collectivist governments such as the revolutionary and Napoleonic regimes of 1789–1815. It has been of value in guiding education systems which have had the aim of creating a new highly ordered society based on the application of rational knowledge. Encyclopaedism has never accommodated individualist and localist demands very comfortably.

Yet there has been always a libertarian, individualist and even anarchistic strain in French culture and politics which has been in direct conflict with the encyclopaedist and collectivist ethos of government and education. This individualism has had an educational impact. Most recently it has been expressed in the libertarianism following the 1968 student revolt which developed in the 1970s into regionalism, sub-culturalism and demands for local participation in government and education. Urbanism and industrialism have also brought self-orientated, consumerist aspirations in the 1970s and 1980s which have had an impact on schools. Quite apart from these developments, the democratization of access to education has produced socially and culturally more heterogeneous secondary school populations than prevailed at earlier times. The standardization of the encyclopaedic curriculum has been challenged.

Localism, sub-culturalism and individualism traditionally have not been accommodated in the curriculum. The largest 'opposition' movement in education has been the Catholic Church, especially as government educational policy was a vehicle for anti-clericalism from the 1880s. Yet the curriculum of the private church schools – catering for between 15 and 20 per cent of all pupils – has closely mirrored that of the state education system except for the additional element of religious education. The church school curriculum has been as encyclopaedist as its state counterpart.

Some demands for local cultural autonomy have been partly met in the curriculum without sacrificing encyclopaedist principles. Regional languages (Breton, Occitan, Basque and Corsican) have been permitted as additional (non-examined) subjects in the secondary school curriculum since 1951 and (with the major immigrant group languages such as Arabic and Portuguese) have been added to the list of foreign languages which may be taught in the main (examined) curriculum since the early 1970s. This partial breach of the universalist principle of encyclopaedism has been seen to be consistent with rationalism since any language with a logically structured grammar could be admitted to the inner circle of rational bodies of knowledge.

Similarly, the content of history courses has been expanded to include non-European civilizations. But this new subject content has been organized in the same lines as the more conventional history of France and Europe. Some concessions were made to the everyday use of language by pupils in French syllabuses recommended since the late 1960s, but the emphasis on grammatical structures and on the study of great works of literature has survived.

What has not been permitted has been total decentralization of curriculum decision-making either to local authorities or to teachers in the schools. Local curriculum decision-making was encouraged marginally by the 1972 decrees which prescribed that the content of 10 per cent of curriculum time could be decided at school level. But the rest of the curriculum continued to be determined centrally. The response by teachers and often by pupils and parents was to reject any local decison-making and to devote the 10 per cent of time to additional classes in the mainstream curriculum. The universalist, standardized and uniform curriculum was supported both by teachers and by pupils who felt that its abandonment even marginally would threaten teachers' security or damage pupils' chances of success in conventional assessment procedures.

There has been sympathy from some groups at national level for a concept of individualism which stresses the physical, aesthetic, emotional and social elements of the human personality. Non-intellectual elements have been given more prominence in the curriculum as prescribed by national government. But these elements of the curriculum have not been treated seriously by teachers and pupils at school level. Physical education has been given a substantial slice of the timetable of secondary schools since the 1960s but in practice this teaching has been undertaken by auxiliary or part-time teachers and its status in the eyes of students and other teachers has been low. Similar developments have been experienced in subjects such as art and music. Whatever the pronouncements of the Ministry of Education in Paris, encyclopaedist views predominate at school level and these can subvert ministry intentions.

While individualist approaches to the curriculum have had relatively little success in French schools, there have been greater pressures to emphasize the socialization role of the school. Traditionally, the function of schooling has been intellectual and academic. Social and moral education has been left to the family – an arrangement that could work when most French primary schools were situated in rural areas and most secondary schools in small towns. Moral/social education was confined to the subject *morale* in primary schools (largely precepts on day-to-day behaviour) and civics in secondary schooling. The pastoral role of teachers in secondary schools was practically non-existent. Discipline in school was in the hands of the deputy principal aided by part-time auxiliaries (often university students).

The Legrand Commission of 1982 did propose that all teachers should have a contractual three hours a week for pastoral duties (compared to a proposed 15 hours a week of teaching). But teachers in higher grades opposed the whole package because it assumed equal hours of teaching for all lower secondary school teachers. Even this modest proposal assumed that pastoral functions could be separated clearly from the main teaching activity of the school.

Such neglect of a social adjustment role for schools has created strains in common secondary schools in an urban industrial society. Teachers have been encouraged to take greater interest in matters of personal and social relationships. But the intellectual traditions of the curriculum have obstructed the development of an effective socialization function.

ENCYCLOPAEDISM AND THE KNOWLEDGE EXPLOSION

One of the major problems faced in the adoption of curricula based on universalist criteria of encyclopaedism has been to accommodate the growth of knowledge. There is no principle of exclusion except for rationality. So there is a tendency for the amount of facts that pupils have to learn to expand without a corresponding growth in the amount of time in which these facts can be learned. A common criticism made by parents and others is that pupils spend much time accumulating a mass of information.

This expansion of knowledge is marked both by the emergence of new subjects which are seen to be relevant such as technology or computer science and by the expansion of the boundaries of relevant knowledge in the conventional subjects. Yet any proposals to abandon existing elements of the curriculum are fiercely resisted by interested parties. Proposals to include new areas of knowledge are more likely to be accepted than suggestions that any existing fields should be dropped. The consequence is not only pressures on students to acquire larger and larger amounts of information but, in practice, a tendency towards superficiality in many areas of the curriculum.

Some specialization is permitted in the upper secondary school so that students may concentrate on their special subjects. In practice they do not take other areas of the curriculum very seriously. It has been suggested that French students are failing to acquire a broad *culture générale* especially when mathematics and physical sciences are given the highest status and the greatest attention. It is felt by some that the broad encyclopaedist view of knowledge is now being undermined and the broader education of the most able students is being neglected.

However, in most areas of the curriculum, the encyclopaedist tradition remains strong despite pressures to modify or abandon it. The question then is what forces sustain this approach and how do they operate. These forces may be examined in analysis of curriculum control and management.

Curriculum control and management

Which groups and individuals have the power to change the curriculum or to obstruct proposals for curriculum change? In France, curriculum decision-making occurs within a highly centralized system of government. Yet in France, as in other countries, curriculum management and control can be investigated also by exploring the influence of various groups such as politicians, officials, academics, teachers, parents, students, employers and the interaction of these groups both within and outside the formal decison-making structures.

THE OFFICIAL STRUCTURE OF CURRICULUM DECISION-MAKING IN FRANCE

Most issues concerning the overall structure and organization of public education and the allocation of resources are decided in Paris. Relatively few decisions, especially in curriculum matters, are left to regional, local, or school authorities. Curriculum aims, content, methods and evaluation are prescribed predominantly at national level.

There is consistency between a highly centralized system of educational control and the predominance of the encyclopaedic view of the curriculum which emphasizes the externality of knowledge, the uniformity and standardization of the curriculum and the subordination of individual interests to those of a wider national society.

Viewed from the position of teachers and students in schools, the Ministry of Education in Paris appears to be a central monolith. Timetables for each grade and kind of schooling and the syllabuses of each subject arrive from the Ministry of Education in Paris. Advisory recommendations on textbooks are also made. Examinations at the end of secondary education are controlled by the Ministry of Education. Inspectors supervise teachers and can ensure conformity to the national curriculum as well as influencing teaching methods.

But, viewed from Paris, the central monolith appears rather as a forum of competing influences. There is a variety of groups operating in several arenas. The outcomes of power struggles between these groups can differ from one issue to another.

Education laws are proposed by the Minister of Education and are placed before the National Assembly. There is a considerable scope for consultation and influence for many different groups in this process. Some of these influences are formalized as, for instance, in the interministerial committees which allow for governmental agencies outside education to exert some impact or the Conseil Supérieur de l'Education Nationale which is a forum for teachers, employers and other groups to express opinions on educational matters.

Curriculum decision-making is a more specialist, closed and professional matter. The decrees and circulars issued by the Ministry of Education on curriculum matters are discussed by various *ad hoc* and standing committees within the Ministry of Education. These committees are dominated by inspectors, teacher representatives and academics. Curriculum-planning is controlled largely by professionals with little lay intervention but the professionals are not exclusively officials based on the Ministry of Education. Schoolteachers do have a major formal influence in curriculum management but through their unions at national level rather than in individual schools.

Since the 1960s, a number of curriculum commissions have been established to advise on specific reforms. While they included the national *inspecteurs généraux*, a majority of members of these commissions have come from outside the Ministry of Education particularly university academics. Examples have included the Rouchette (1965) and Emmanuel (1972) Commissions on the teaching of French and the Lichnerowicz (1966) Commission on mathematics as well as the Lagarrighe Commission on physics, chemistry and technology of 1971.

These commissions have often challenged traditional curriculum practice. The Rouchette committee suggested that French teaching should start from the colloquial language of pupils while the Lagarrighe committee recommended a greater place for technology and technical subjects within the lower secondary school curriculum. The Commission of Sages of 1972, which was concerned with more general educational reform, urged that the role of national inspectors should be less one of curriculum prescription and more one of mediation between innovative schools and the central administration.

The general direction of change has been for politicians in government to involve more groups in curriculum-planning especially through committees and commissions based on the Ministry of Education. The monopoly of control of the inspectorate over the curriculum, if it ever existed, has passed.

But curriculum formulation and adoption still occur at national level and are as much as ever in the hands of professionals (teachers, inspectors and academics). School-level decisions are confined in practice to choice of textbooks and other supplementary material and of teaching methods though even in these areas there are central recommendations.

However, the official structure does not indicate which groups exert the greatest actual power. The important questions then are which professional groups exert the greatest influence and to what external pressures they are subject.

THE POLITICS OF CURRICULUM CHANGE

If a number of groups compete to influence curriculum decision-making at national level, which exert the greatest power, what demands do they make and what are the consequences of these interventions? A distinction may be made between those groups that are formally involved in curriculum policy formulation and adoption – especially Ministry of Education officials, national teacher union representatives and university academics – and those which exert informal influences such as employers, government agencies outside education, teachers at school level, the media, political parties, parents, and students. These latter groups may be able to persuade the official curriculum designers to introduce new policies or they may obstruct decisions which are adopted at national level.

The curriculum decisions traditionally have been taken by the national inspectorate. These individuals in the past have been conservative in their conceptions of worthwhile knowledge and a valid curriculum. This view was held by various ministers of education in the late 1960s and 1970s who attempted to introduce other groups, especially university academics, into the decision-making process. There were certainly grounds for this view. The 129 national inspectors in the past have been mainly concerned with teaching in selective secondary schools (inspectors for primary schools have been based at regional level). They are mainly subject specialists who tend to defend the position of their subjects in schools (Corbett, 1977). There are pressures within the inspectorate to resist the exclusion of any traditional branch or body of knowledge from the curriculum. The overloading of the curriculum and its persisting intellectualism may be associated in part with the continuing power of the national inspectorate.

Yet there are also national inspectors concerned with levels of education or non-subject specialisms rather than with curriculum subjects. Some of these have advocated rather freer and more individualistic approaches to the curriculum (as in the Rouchette Commission on the teaching of French). They may be in the minority but these inspectors have been a force for curriculum reform of a kind which recognizes the diversity of pupil origins and interests.

The influence of the inspectorate at national level may be in decline. Changes in the administration of French education have reduced its traditional dominance. Since the late 1960s, attempts have been made to streamline the centralized administration of the Ministry of Education and other government agencies to improve efficiency, coherence and speed of administration and to counter traditional charges against centralized administration that it is slow, cumbersome and internally divided.

Two specific changes have affected the power of the national inspectorate. First, there has been some devolution of central power to regions to enhance efficiency (quite apart from political arguments about decentralization). This has given more weight to the regional inspectorate. Secondly, there has been a development of corporate management techniques in the ministry in Paris to improve efficiency. These give greater influence to new professional administrators rather than the older educationist/ administrator (Broadfoot, 1985). These new administrators have not been concerned mainly with curriculum matters. But their increased power may have weakened the influence (including curriculum influences) of the traditional inspectorate.

Representatives of schoolteachers have been established members of curriculum design committees for some time. It is quite wrong to argue that teachers have no impact on curriculum policy-making. They are fully and formally involved through their national union representatives. But teachers have not been generally strong advocates of curriculum reform. Their attitude has been traditional and conservative because teachers tend to defend their subject specialisms and to defend the privileges of their grades. In a stratified profession, self-protective restrictive practices tend to weaken curriculum reform proposals.

The major teacher unions (apart from the elitist Société des Agrégés) have strongly supported a common curriculum in which different kinds of pupils receive equality of treatment consistent with equality of opportunity. Yet teachers also tend to support curriculum uniformity throughout France partly because they feel this protects their professional positions.

University academics have been brought into school curriculum decision-making especially since the 1960s. The impact of this group on curriculum reform is not clear. Specialists in new areas of knowledge can lend their authority to the expansion of these areas in the curriculum. So newer university departments of Celtic studies can support proposals for a stronger position for regional languages in the school curriculum. Professors of education such as Henri Legrand in 1982 have been associated with pupil-centred curriculum proposals.

However, most university academics have been committed to maintenance of traditional knowledge categories upon which their social status is in part based (Bourdieu, 1984). Their overall position has been to encourage greater specialization of pupils in upper secondary education in order that they should be better prepared for university studies. The general influence of academics has been to strengthen the role of the traditional academic subjects and the encyclopaedist view of knowledge (though perhaps encouraging a greater degree of specialization than older views of encyclopaedism would permit).

Within each of the main groups officially involved in curriculum policy-making, there are radicals and reformers. But the dominant influences within each group are conservative and traditionalist. The main pressures for curriculum reform come from outside the official agencies though the success of these pressures depends on the responsiveness of members of the groups with formal power in curriculum matters.

Of the external pressures for reform which can be seen since the late 1950s, the greatest has been for the expansion of technical and vocational education. There have been employer pressures. But these pressures have been most evident in the impact of governmental economic departments on educational policy-making. The growth of industry which occurred in France after the late 1950s was encouraged by state planning and intervention. The apex of the state economic planning exercise is the four year national economic plan. These plans have specified educational targets for the training of future workers which have been adopted by government, though some recent plans have included more socially orientated educational objectives.

The process by which the economic plans affect curriculum policy-making is that interministerial committees specify targets for each ministry which will meet the objectives of the plan. The Ministry of Education is given guidelines from above on technical and vocational education (as well as objectives which affect the balance between science and other subjects in the general curriculum). Resources within the Ministry of Education's budget are earmarked by the interministerial committee for certain kinds of education that will fulfil economic objectives.

The power of economic interests should not be exaggerated. First, though employers are represented on major educational consultative committees, they may have relatively little influence on the curriculum details of vocational and technical education in specific areas. Since the 1919 Astier law, technical education for young workers in precursors of the *lycées professionels* has been provided by government but financed largely by a training levy on employers. So employers have not directly controlled the content of vocational education.

Second, governments may provide resources for science and technical education (which leads to the training of teachers and the provision of facilities and equipment) but curriculum committees in the Ministry of Education and particularly teachers at classroom level may give the curriculum a less vocational orientation than was intended. Third, the fact that more scientific and technical/vocational education is made available does not mean that students will choose to take these options. The nature and importance of student choices will be considered below but there have been examples of scientific and vocational educational resources being unused because of lack of student demand.

There are few other effective and organized groups influencing curriculum decision-making at national level. Some pressure groups do exist and there have been isolated examples of their influence affecting the curriculum. The media and television were used skilfully by one group to gain acceptance of the idea of sex education in schools (Beattie, 1976). Regionally based groups have used national political means to gain a greater place for regional languages. But generally the non-official pressure groups operating at national level, particularly political parties, teacher unions and parent organizations have focused on access to education rather than on the curriculum.

Though official curriculum decision-making is concentrated at national level, groups operating at school level can exert some informal influence. There is some evidence that parental concern for a more individualistic and less exclusively bookish education at primary level (especially since the late 1960s) has in practice led to a rather freer approach by teachers. In secondary and primary schools, individual teachers have experimented with different kinds of methods and especially media. There are also various officially sponsored experimental pilot projects existing in a variety of schools. Minister of Education Savary in 1982 suggested that the ministry would consider favourably proposals for curriculum change put forward for individual schools.

More usually the reaction of teachers has been negative. The exhortations following the 1975 Haby reform for teachers to relate the curriculum to the background and interests of pupils were ignored by most teachers. Ultimately, despite the impact that the inspectorate has on teachers' requests for transfer (crucial in a system where teachers are allocated to schools), teachers have a considerable autonomy in what they teach and especially how they teach it. Well-established classroom teachers, even in the most efficient and highly centralized education systems, have much freedom in practice to do what they will behind closed classroom doors. This power is all the greater when they choose to follow traditional practices and to ignore national exhortations for curriculum change.

Another crucial influence is that of student choice (and that of the parents who guide it). This applies particularly at the end of lower secondary education when choices between broad areas or types of study are permitted. These choices may affect informal priorities throughout the lower secondary school course. There has been a marked move towards mathematics and physical sciences options in upper secondary education which reflects student and parent valuation of this kind of knowledge (though presumably in reaction to wider economic and labour market conditions). The consumers of the curriculum ultimately have a decisive impact on the implementation of change.

The encyclopaedic tradition has entrenched support among certain groups with major power in determining the official curriculum. Most particularly the inspectorate and the teachers and, to some degree, university academics are committed, for various professional as well as more ideological reasons, to maintaining a school curriculum based on encyclopaedic criteria of rationality and universality. Economic interests, especially in government, have been able to influence the curriculum to give it a greater scientific and technical orientation within encyclopaedist principles.

Even within these professional groups, there are anti-encyclopaedist factions which may gain sufficient outside support, especially at a political level, to effect curriculum change. Indeed, the view that an elite curriculum should be based on classical languages was entrenched among important professional groups until the late 1960s yet they still lost the battle to maintain a humanistic curriculum – symbolized by the central position of Latin in the fast stream of lower secondary schools – in 1968. The configurations of future curriculum power struggles are not predictable simply on the basis of past battles.

Conclusion

This analysis has tended to view the encyclopaedic view of the curriculum in France as traditional, conservative and unsuited to the needs of students in a democratized school system in an urban industrialized society. Encyclopaedic principles have been invoked by those involved in curriculum decision-making who do not wish to accept some necessary curriculum reforms.

This view is partial and not entirely fair. Encylopaedism is still a revolutionary and reformist view of the function of knowledge in transforming society in the interests of the majority of its members. It may be argued that an encyclopaedist curriculum in France has allowed for a degree of equality of treatment of students which has not been achieved in some other countries, especially those such as England which have more elitist curriculum traditions. It may be claimed also that an encyclopaedic curriculum was suited to the economic transformation of France since the 1960s. Certainly the French education system has produced the high-quality engineers and technologists that other countries have envied. The intellectual and professional qualities of the French administrative elite are widely admired. Both characteristics may be associated with an encyclopaedist approach to the curriculum.

The challenge for French curriculum planners is to maintain the undoubted value that the encyclopaedist approach has brought while somehow adjusting teaching in ways that will accommodate the individualist and social aspirations that have been strengthened by wider social and political changes.

The outcome of solutions to this problem in France is of wider international interest. Many non-industrialized countries (and industrial countries such as the Soviet Union) have adopted elements of the encyclopaedist approach to the curriculum. They face some of the same problems as France but also their own specific concerns. How these issues have been faced in other 'encyclopaedist' countries will be considered in later chapters.

Further reading

Ardagh, John, *France in the 1980s* (Harmondsworth: Penguin, 1983).

Barnard, H. C., *The French Tradition in Education* (Cambridge: Cambridge University Press, 1970).

Beattie, Nicholas, 'Sex education in France: a case study in curriculum change', *Comparative Education*, vol. 12, no. 2, (1976) pp. 115–28.

Bourdieu, Pierre, *Homo Academicus* (Paris: Editions de Minuit, 1984).

Bourdieu, Pierre, and Passeron, J. C., *The Inheritors* (Chicago: University of Chicago Press, 1969).

Broadfoot, Patricia, 'Towards conformity: educational control and the growth of corporate management in England and France', in Jon Lauglo and Martin McLean (eds), *The Control of Education* (London: Heinemann, 1985), pp. 105–18.

Corbett, Anne, 'Programme Control', *Times Educational Supplement* (4 February, 1977).

Durkheim, Emile, *The Evolution of Educational Thought* (London: Routledge, 1977).

Halls, W. D., *Education, Culture and Politics in Modern France* (Oxford: Pergamon, 1976).

Hignette, Marcel F., 'The primacy of the rational in French secondary education', in G. Z. F. Bereday and J. A. Lauwerys (eds), *Yearbook of Education 1958* (London: Evans, 1958), pp. 223–41.

Horner, Wolfgang, 'The evolution of culture in French pedagogical discussion', *Western European Education*, vol. 12, no. 2. (1980), pp. 62–79.

Lewis, H. D., *The French Education System* (London: Croom Helm, 1985).

Neave, Guy, 'France' in Burton R. Clark (ed.), *The School and the University: An International Perspective* (Berkeley, Calif.: University of California Press, 1985), pp. 10–44.

Nieser, Bruno, 'Innovations in primary and secondary school education in France', *Western European Education*, vol. 10, no. 3 (1979), pp. 28–50.

Organization for Economic Co-operation and Development, *Youth Employment in France: Recent Strategies* (Paris: Organization for Economic Co-operation and Development, 1984).

Poujol, Jacques, 'The lower secondary school in France: a note on the Haby reforms', *Compare*, vol. 10, no. 2 (1980), pp. 187–91.

Prost, Antoine, *L'Enseignement en France 1800–1967* (Paris: Armand Colin, 1968).

Rothera, Harold, 'The "New Baccalauréat" in its context', *Comparative Education*, vol. 4, no. 3 (1968), pp. 183–97.

Singer, Barnett, *Village Notables in 19th Century France: Priests, Mayors, Schoolmasters* (Albany, NY: State University of New York Press, 1983).

Touraine, Alain, *The Post-Industrial Society* (London: Wildwood, 1974).

Zeldin, Theodore, *France 1848–1945*, 2 vols (Oxford: Clarendon Press, 1977).

Zeldin, Theodore, *The French* (London: Fontana, 1985).

Appendix: Programmes

UPPER SECONDARY

Baccalauréat options

(2nd and 3rd years)
A. Letters (language and literature)
B. Economics and social sciences
C. Mathematics and physical sciences
D. Mathematics and biological sciences
E. Mathematics and technology

Brevet d'enseignement professionelle (24 branches)

(Baccalauréat de technicien)
F. Industrial studies (various)
G. Secretarial and accountancy studies
H. Information science

Certificat d'aptitude professionelle (260 branches)

1st year *Baccalauréat* common programme

Compulsory core subjects

French (5 hrs)
History/geography (4 hrs)
Modern language (3 hrs)
Mathematics (4 hrs)
Physical science (3.5 hrs)
Biological science (2 hrs)
Physical education (2 hrs)

Obligatory options (one of):

1. Industrial technology
2. Laboratory science and technology
3. Medical and social science
4. Craft
5. Economics and social science with one of: Greek, Latin, 2nd modern language, office management, technology, art, music, sport

Non-obligatory options
3rd modern language, art or music, family and society, typing, technical education

LOWER SECONDARY EDUCATION

Core subjects	1st and 2nd Grades	3rd and 4th Grades
French	5 hours (+ 1 hr)	5 hours
Mathematics	3 hours (+ 1 hr)	4 hours
Modern language	3 hours (+ 1 hr)	3 hours
History/geography, etc.	3 hours	3 hours
Experimental science	3 hours	3 hours
Artistic education	2 hours	2 hours
Technical and handicraft education	2 hours	1.5 hours

Obligatory options (one of):
Latin or Greek or 2nd modern language
or extra 1st modern language or technology   3 hours

(+ 1 hour = reinforcement or enrichment classes)

ELEMENTARY EDUCATION

Subject	1st–5th Grade
French	9 hours
Mathematics	6 hours
Physical education	5 hours
Activités d'éveil (history, geography, art and craft, science, moral education, music)	7 hours

Chapter Four

Curriculum pluralism in a mass system of education – the USA

After the Second World War the majority of Americans were optimistic and had great faith in education and their own know-how. In contrast to their Western and Soviet allies and their wartime opponents they had been neither invaded nor bombed. Their children had suffered neither the traumas of an occupation nor evacuation from vulnerable cities. Moreover, they already had a system of education which was intended to meet the needs of 'all American youth'.

The optimism and the faith in popular education which goes back to 1642, when the 'Old Deluder Satan Act' laid down the principle of compulsory education in Massachusetts, explain the role US leaders played in the creation of Unesco and the United Nations. Many American ideas were incorporated into Unesco's charter and into the United Nations Universal Declaration of Human Rights. The Americans proposed for the world what they had achieved in their own country during the nineteenth and first half of the twentieth centuries, namely a universal system of education based on the principle that 'all men are created equal'.

Who shall be educated?

American faith in education gained momentum after the War of Independence when in Massachusetts and elsewhere a system of common, eight-year elementary schools was set up; after the Civil

War when in 1874 the Michigan Supreme Court ruled in the Kalamazoo decision that high schools could receive public funds; and after 1896 when the Federal Supreme Court ruled that facilities could be provided separately for blacks and whites only if these facilities were equal. The ruling was taken to apply to education. Consequently by 1945 the demand for first- and second-level schooling had virtually been satisfied (though not equally) in a system of six-year first or elementary schools, three-year junior high and three-year senior high schools. To the pattern of four-year liberal arts colleges granting first degrees and universities awarding postgraduate degrees had been added two-year junior colleges which enrolled senior high school graduates and provided them with terminal vocational courses or programmes which counted towards a four-year first degree.

In this system, pupils passed from elementary schools to junior high schools and from these middle schools to senior high schools without having to enter for and pass, as in Europe, selection tests. Each type of school enrolled pupils across the whole spectrum of abilities. Consequently, long before European educators faced the task of devising curricula for intellectually heterogeneous groups of adolescents the Americans had tackled the problem and devised a curriculum theory based on pragmatism.

One consequence of these profound changes from an elitist system of education which had its origins in European theories is that many foreign observers, and indeed some American critics, argue that university admission standards in the USA are much lower than in Europe and that the first two years of an American college or university course do no more than complete the secondary education of students leaving senior high schools. Nevertheless, in 1945 the American system had completed a stage of development on which European school systems were about to embark. For this reason the problems faced and the solutions offered in the USA in developing education as a human right are instructive.

For example, cultural diversity there gave rise to inequalities of provision. The First Amendment to the constitution has consistently been interpreted by the Supreme Court to deny the provision of equalizing public financial support for religious, particularly Catholic, schools. Blacks have had to struggle to be regarded as equal even when they were emancipated after the Civil War. Both groups have been disadvantaged relative to the

'White Anglo-Saxon Protestants'. Since 1945 attempts have been made to equalize provision. A 1964 Supreme Court decision overturned the 1896 'Separate but Equal' ruling by stating that segregated schools were inherently unequal. In the 1965 Elementary and Secondary Schools Act and in equal opportunities legislation about the same time, federal attempts were made to equalize provision and, through compensatory education, outcomes in schooling throughout the nation. On the other hand the Supreme Court consistently refuses to allow public funds to be made available to religious organizations for the promotion of schools. These rulings place the Roman Catholic authorities at a great disadvantage. The reasons are political rather than educational.

On the other hand the human rights argument is used to persuade local authorities to ensure that all public schools have a mix of black and white children. Parents with children suffering from mental or physical disabilities and in need of special care successfully promoted legislation guaranteeing that their children are admitted to regular rather than special schools. Mother tongue teaching is designed to provide equal opportunities for the children of linguistic minorities. It is still the case that great difference in per capita expenditures on education mean that considerable inequalities of outcomes exist.

Failure to equalize educational provision cannot, however, disguise the success of campaigns since 1945 to educate everybody throughout their whole lives in a flexible, consumer-centred system of education. For Americans the immediate postwar challenge was to extend third-level education in colleges and universities to virtually everybody who wanted it. Some 2 million demobbed servicemen and women took advantage of the GI Bill to enter institutions of higher learning. Some 3.5 million veterans enrolled in institutions at a lower level and another 3 million took trade, craft and industrial courses.

The expansion of higher education in response to demands for it from applicants with widely different educational backgrounds and whose interests varied greatly makes it difficult in the USA for a small group of university academics to determine the content of education in senior high schools. The absence of selection tests at the points of transfer from elementary, junior and senior high schools allows teachers at each level of education considerable freedom to decide what should be included in the content of education. Harvard President Eliot's nineteenth-century dictum that any subject was worth teaching in his university places few restrictions on concepts of 'What knowledge is of most worth?' and 'Who shall be educated?'

What knowledge is of most worth?

The Declaration of Independence, the constitution and amendments to it (in the Bill of Rights) provide a framework for political debate in the USA. Appeal is made to them by protagonists in any educational discussion about education as a human right. There is no disagreement on this basic issue. How it should be provided is a matter of lively debate and focuses on curricula, university admission requirements and standards of achievement in traditional high-status subjects. The conflict reflects differences between the protagonists about social change, the needs of individuals and the permanence of knowledge.

The key to John Dewey's almost total rejection of Plato's theories of knowledge, society and the individual lies in the latter's view that change is a process of degeneration. Dewey also rejected Plato's theory that real knowledge of changeless, permanent 'ideas' was accessible only to a few potential 'philosopher-kings'. Hence Dewey did not draw a distinction between worthwhile abstract knowledge of the kind found in school and university textbooks and 'practical knowledge'. He rejected the proposition that knowledge of ideas would fit individuals for societal leadership and vocational skills would prepare other individuals to be carpenters, shoemakers and the like.

Dewey considered that these traditional dualisms and dichotomies downgraded applied science compared with pure science and justified the sharp contrasts drawn between manual work and intellectual activity, and between liberal education and vocational training. All the pragmatists accepted that knowledge is not permanent but conjectural; it is not universal but contingent; and it can be acquired without ignoring changes in the worlds of experience. These new theories of knowledge had a profound influence on American curriculum theories after 1900. They were accepted by most professors of education but rejected by a number of philosophers such as W. C. Bagley (Teachers College, Columbia University), Robert M. Hutchins, a somewhat eccentric chancellor of Chicago University, and Philip Phenix (Teachers College, Columbia). In spite of widespread American acceptance of pragmatism frequent criticisms have been made of high school curricula constructed in accordance with the principles of pragmatism.

The conflict turns on the relative merits of child-, society- and knowledge-centred curricula. Pragmatists advocate child- and society-centred theories and downgrade subject-centred curriculum theories. Knowledge was defined in a new way by the pragmatists and was given a new role to play in a changing democratic society. Dewey maintained that education should prevent pupils from becoming pawns in the new corporate society. Knowledge should help them control, rather than simply accept, political events. The pragmatic curriculum is not, therefore, based on pre-digested knowledge. Selected problems are used to determine what information and experiences should be included in a pragmatic curriculum. In 1918 the Commission for the Reorganization of Secondary Education, in considering the principles of secondary education, proposed that the problems associated with healthy living, worthy home-membership, occupational success, citizenship, the worthwhile use of leisure, ethical character and a command of fundamental processes should form the core of a sound general education. Problem-solving, as a fundamentally important educational process, should not be based on established knowledge but on the ability of individuals to think reflectively. For Dewey 'reflective thinking' is synonymous with 'scientific thinking' and hence the methods of science should inform methods of teaching in American schools.

For pragmatists, the components of scientific thinking are different from those advocated by Aristotle, Francis Bacon and nineteenth-century philosophers like A. Comte and J. S. Mill who argued that the careful collection and classification of 'facts' should precede inductive generalizations. On the contrary, Dewey maintained, children use the true methods of science when by playing they solve their own problems by trial and error. This belief gave support to the 'play way' of teaching, to 'learning by doing' and to 'learning from experience' as the slogans of his followers. Scientific method implies the application of intelligence to the solution of problems; an activity in which all individuals can participate collectively. This curriculum theory and the view of intelligence it incorporates justify the extension of education to everybody on the grounds that all individuals can benefit from it and hence society will benefit.

Dewey's theories were, as stated, warmly accepted by many

professors of education, not least by the powerful group at Teachers College, Columbia University during the 1930s. They influenced professors of education everywhere and gained support from classroom teachers who joined the Progressive Education Association. The association was closed down in 1955 in the presence of its chairman, secretary, two members and a foreign visitor. But it had achieved its purpose by making it impossible for its opponents to regain complete control of American curricula. The spokesmen of the opposition to pragmatic curriculum theory were, and are, American academics and their allies from industry and commerce. In most countries, university academics are the guardians of 'worthwhile knowledge'. Their autonomy and freedom allow them to decide what should be taught in universities. Their power to restrict entry to their own university, by selection tests designed to determine what the applicants know, extends their influence over the whole system of education. American university academics decide what is taught in third-level institutions and influence what is taught in second-level schools but their power has been reduced by the expansion of education and the inclusion of technological institutions within the university system. The Land Grant Colleges, now among the most prestigious universities in the country, were set up under the 1862 Morill Act to promote subjects which would serve agriculture and an emerging industrial economy. Other new universities set up after 1870, like Johns Hopkins and Chicago, were influenced by imported German professors who emphasized research rather than undergraduate teaching.

Consequently, high-level research in traditional fields of learning still informs much of what is done in high-status private universities like Chicago and in outstanding state universities like Michigan at Ann Arbor and California at Berkeley. Other state, municipal and private universities respond to the more practical needs of the huge number of Americans who prepare for, and receive every year, degrees in a wide range of subjects. In most states the number and size of third-level institutions and the variety of courses on offer make it possible for the vast majority of applicants to find a place and to study in a field of their choice. One result is that university entrance requirements do not dominate the content of education at the second level of education. It also allows serious debate to continue between 'progressives' and conservatives at each level of education.

Primary school and junior high school curricula

For many years the most ardent advocates of pragmatic curriculum theory have been primary school teachers who promote child-centred education and the professors of education who train them. Dewey's early books on education, *The School and Society* (1900) and *The Child and the Curriculum* (1902), were about first schools. They laid down principles in the light of which Dewey analysed the role of the school and how children should learn. In his experimental laboratory school attached to the University of Chicago his colleagues attempted to put his principles into practice.

Practical expression was given to Dewey's approach in the Project Method and the Dalton Plan. The word 'project' invaded the pedagogical vocabulary about 1900 in the field of manual training and involved making things for the home and farm as a pedagogical exercise. Projects were legitimized philosophically by W. H. Kilpatrick of Teachers College, New York and found their way into American first-level schools, junior high and even senior high schools. Projects are designed to inculcate knowledge and basic skills but their main aim is to provide pupils with opportunities to solve problems.

Essentially the Dalton Plan devised by Helen Parkhurst (1887–1958) was a scheme in which each pupil entered into a contract to complete a carefully planned project over a stated period of time, usually one month. Pupils were allowed to work at their own rate and were free to plan it. When it became clear that pupils were accepting the freedom it gave without behaving responsibly the plan fell out of favour. Nevertheless, many features of it continue to inform progressive curriculum theory in the primary schools.

In the mid-1970s several schemes were designed to improve the teaching of mathematics and science along similar lines by emphasizing process rather than content. The University of Minnesota Mathematics and Science Teaching Project (MINNE-MAST) was launched. At Berkeley there was a Science Curriculum Improvement Study (SCIS) and the Elementary School Science Project (ESSP) was undertaken at the University of Illinois. The Commission on Science Education of the American Association for the Advancement of Science and the School Mathematics Study Group (SMSG) also undertook work along these lines.

Support for the process model is provided by Jerome S. Bruner in *The Process of Education* in which he emphasizes the importance of introducing pupils to the principles of a subject. The selection of worthwhile knowledge on this criterion makes it possible for pupils to generalize. It stimulates intellectual excitement and facilitates memory. Movements reflecting Bruner's process approach to the curriculum are best exemplified in proposals to improve the content of established subjects or to create new 'broad fields' of study. In English, for example, attempts are made by those who plan new syllabuses to introduce inner or core structures round which sequential programmes are built. The Gateway programme, developed at Hunter College for pupils aged 11 to 15, succeeded in being open-ended and pupil-centred.

In response to federal pressure social studies for the primary and early junior high school grades were developed to introduce pupils to core concepts in the various social science disciplines and involved bringing life situations into the classroom to provide an interdisciplinary course. *Man: a Course of Study* prepared by the Curriculum Development Associates is organized round three core questions, namely:

(1)   What is human about human beings?
(2)   How did they get that way?
(3)   How can they be made more so?

The interdisciplinary approach bridges the natural sciences, the social sciences and the arts. The unifying principles are, as in the case of integrated natural science courses, abstract principles rather than the day-to-day problems of young people.

At the same time as movements to adopt discovery methods of teaching gained support, the psychological theory of 'readiness' profoundly influenced the curriculum in elementary schools. In the absence of selection tests in the American system, child development theories about sequential learning abilities found fertile ground. They alerted teachers to the fact that certain levels of maturity are necessary before certain subjects can be taught and learned effectively. Notions of 'readiness' justified individualized curricula. Thus children should be taught to read only when they are 'ready'. Premature training often results in loss of skill, frustration and a loss of enthusiasm for learning.

These pyschological theories fit in admirably with pragmatic proposals that curricula should be not subject-centred but process-orientated. Carried to extremes these child-centred, problem-solving curriculum models mean that in many schools in the 1950s, in spite of the regular testing of reading ability, young children who had not learned to read at the age of 8, 9, or 10 were excused on the ground that they were not yet 'ready' to read or write. Failure was a natural consequence of the process of cognitive maturation. Since children mature at different rates some of them must be expected to learn how to read, write and solve arithmetical problems sooner, or later, than other children. This assumption and the belief that reading is a natural activity explain the failure of teachers to diagnose reading difficulties. It is fallacious to assume that reading and writing do not have to be taught. In societies where communication is by word of mouth reading is not necessary. In industrial societies it is. Dewey's attachment to the educative value of the small rural community cannot be entirely acquitted if blame is to be allocated for the failure of many adolescent Americans to read fluently. Indeed the consequences of allowing 'readiness' theories and a process curriculum model to dominate American primary school curricula gave rise to alarm in the USA when it was discovered that many adolescents were unable to read or write when seeking to enter a university. Indeed in the mid-1950s at one well-known state university hundreds of freshmen were required to attend remedial English courses.

In spite of the criticism made by Harry S. Broudy of the research associated with the behavioural objectives approach to curriculum development the work of Benjamin S. Bloom and Robert M. Gagne and the tradition in American primary schools of regular testing helped to save American schools from the excesses of child-centred process curriculum models. In *Taxonomy of Educational Objectives* Bloom provides a classificatory system which includes cognitive, affective and motor objectives. The value of the objectives approach lies in the way it can be used to select curriculum material and the encouragement it gives to the statement of objectives, the achievement of which can be measured using suitably designed tests. In her extremely influential book, *Curriculum Development: Theory and Practice*, Hilda Taba states that objectives should describe both the kind of behaviour expected and the content to which the behaviour applies. They should be formulated in ways which make it possible to say what learning experiences are needed if the objectives are to be achieved.

The testing movement associated with the behavioural objectives approach perhaps did no more than encourage the reorganization of subject matter into broad fields and the integration of previously separately organized but related disciplines, e.g. physics, chemistry and biology. It offered an alternative to the pragmatic, problem-solving model accepted by 'progressive' educators by suggesting that the problem-centred approach should not be abandoned but made more methodical.

Thus, in the construction of primary and junior high school curricula several influential theories compete. Some 'progressive' educationists support a child-centred process model. Other 'progressive' educationists advocate a social problem-centred model. The 'broad fields' and 'behavioural objectives' models give more structure to curricula designed to develop the all-round abilities of individual children.

The influence of the behavioural objectives model and the testing movement on practice at the first and second levels of education has been profound. This influence has, in fact, been to re-enforce the traditional domination of textbooks and subjects. In *An Educational History of the American People*, Adolphe E. Meyer asserts that the curriculum which started with reading and religion has long since vanished and music, drawing, history, geography, literature, health, hygiene, safety, citizenship, arts and crafts and manual instruction have been added to the primary school curriculum. Nevertheless, in the 1970s Arthur W. Foshay could write that instruction in elementary schools still relied heavily on the authority of a textbook and that the schools are products not on sociological and psychological theories but of the school itself. They still are. Knowledge-centred curricula prevail. Traditional teaching practices persist. School subjects are separate entities the content of which is treated in logical sequence with mathematics as the model.

In short, in spite of radical and competing curriculum theories which have received wide acceptance among professors of education and some teachers, and the enormous amount of research which informs curriculum discussion, the explosion of scientific knowledge has been accommodated in primary and junior high schools for all Americans in separate parcels although somewhat differently wrapped. Much goes on as usual in American first schools.

High school curricula

The same is true of high school curricula. Debates about them are far more vicious and, from time to time, highly politicized. In the 1920s and 1930s after John Dewey, John Childs and George Counts among others visited the Soviet Union and commented favourably on what they had seen, Counts suggested that American schools should set out to create a new social order. Even in the 1930s critics opposed this view. When the Cold War between the USA and the USSR dominated international relations after 1948, Joseph McCarthy's Senate committee quickly associated progressive educationists with the subversives it had been set up to uncover. Fuel was added to the fire when in 1957 Soviet engineers successfully launched Sputnik. Nicholas de Witt's evidence on the number and training of Soviet technological personnel persuaded Congressmen that Soviet education had made it possible for the USSR to steal a march on Americans in a field (technical know-how) they regarded as peculiarly their own. In 1958 Congress made vast sums of money available under the National Defense and Education Act (NDEA) to improve the content of mathematics, the natural sciences and modern language syllabuses in elementary and secondary schools. In 1964 the Act was amended to include history, civics, geography, English (including the elementary school subject – language arts) and reading. These Acts, and the 1965 Elementary and Secondary Education Act, represent changes in the interpretation of the preamble to the Constitution of the United States. Previous interpretations of the 'common defense and welfare' clause had restricted federal aid to education to subjects, like the mechanic arts, directly linked with the nation's economic activities.

USA–USSR rivalry should not obscure the real issue in the USA which is control of the high school curriculum. The battle is between essentialists and pragmatists. The protagonists are professors of education and academic subject professors. The crux of the argument is whether the high school curriculum should be 'subject-centred' as the professors of history, mathematics, physics, chemistry, biology and foreign languages want, or based on the kind of problems adolescents are likely to face as adults.

The attack on curricula favoured by progressive educationists has a long history. Relatively few professors of education have supported essentialism. Bagley and Phenix of Teachers College, Columbia are exceptions as philosophers who support the

Platonic-Aristotelian tradition by maintaining that teaching and learning the basic disciplines is the principal task of education. The majority of critics of pragmatic curriculum theory are university academics. Over many years the most articulate of them has been Hutchins. In *The Higher Learning in America* (1936) he argued that neither engineering subjects nor modern languages were fit subjects for inclusion in a university course. By 1956, in *Some Observations on American Education*, Hutchins had modified his position somewhat but was still arguing that universities ought to be elitist institutions, that vocational training in schools and universities was futile and that there was chaos, mediocrity and curriculum vagaries in colleges and universities. Although Hutchins's critique applied principally to university education it has implications for high school curricula.

Certainly the attack on pragmatic curriculum theory was pressed home by university academics like A. E. Bestor, businessmen like Albert Lynd and servicemen like Admiral Hyman Rickover who claimed that curricula in American high schools were a hodge-podge of unrelated, frequently trivial, subjects. Major criticisms were made of life-adjustment programmes justified by child- and society-centred curriculum theories. The replacement of traditional subjects by driver education and similarly less demanding courses was regarded as a heinous crime. None of these critics argued that in order to reintroduce an essentialist curriculum the American system should become more selective.

Less polemical critics like James B. Conant were more persuasive. Their major complaint was that too many young people were receiving a high school education which lacked coherence in the absence of a unifying core of worthwhile knowledge. This was as much due to the proliferation of 'electives' in large urban schools in line with Eliot's principle as to the progressive educationists' pragmatic curriculum theory. Moreover, there had crept into the enormous number of 'electives', or optional subjects, many so-called life-adjustment courses. This loss of cohesion persuaded members of the Harvard Committee in its report *General Education in a Free Society* (1944) to stress that high schools should serve the needs of all American youth by ensuring that they could think effectively, communicate clearly, make relevant judgements and discriminate among values. To these ends the Harvard Report, under Conant's leadership, recommended that a core of studies in the humanities, the social sciences and the physical and natural sciences should constitute the curriculum in all public high schools.

In a later book, *The American High School Today* (1959), Conant maintained that high schools should offer non-college-bound students some vocational courses and provide the academically gifted students with advanced courses in mathematics, science and modern languages. Both the Harvard Report and Conant's book became best-sellers. Arguably they influenced public opinion more than any other commentary on high school education partly because of Conant's reputation and partly because they did less violence to American academic traditions than the proposals made by the Progressive Education Association which had conducted an eight-year study between 1930 and 1938 to show that curricula to meet the needs of all American youth constructed along progressive lines would not place students seeking to enter a university at risk. The high school graduates from thirty experimental schools were admitted to co-operating universities without having to satisfy normal entrance requirements. Their college achievements were compared with the results obtained by an equal number of students from regular high schools. They did neither much better nor much worse. Neither the 'progressives' nor the conservatives won a decisive victory. At least the experiment showed that for well-motivated college-bound students what they were taught in high schools did not make much difference to their future success.

Today high school curricula usually follow Conant's model and trend-setting universities like Harvard require applicants for admission to have credits in the humanities (including English), the social sciences and the natural sciences. Moreover, students applying to well-known universities, whether state or private, are expected to take a standard aptitude test (SAT) on the results of which they are admitted to the university of their choice. The required minimum SAT scores vary greatly from one institution to another and competition to gain admission to high-status institutions is severe.

Pragmatic curriculum theory permits the individual needs of pupils and students to be accommodated within this broad framework. Doubtless for this reason the human rights lobby fought and won the battle to ensure that children with special educational needs should be admitted to regular schools and classrooms. The pedagogical consequences of 'mainstreaming' have still to be revealed (1988) but some parents at least consider

91

that their children might be better served educationally in special schools in which teachers have special training in the teaching of children with a specific handicap. By the same token a pragmatic curriculum made it possible to accommodate compensatory programmes for those children whose family background placed them at a disadvantage in terms of academic achievement *vis-à-vis* children from affluent 'white' homes because no school board is required to provide an established sequence of programmes laid down in legislation by the state as may happen in some European countries.

There can be little doubt that progressive educationists are right when they maintain that the process – problem-solving – curriculum model facilitates the education of all young people regardless of gender, race, religion, social and domestic familial background and language. Indeed, in accordance with the human rights principle the nineteenth-century decision that English should be the national school language has been partially revoked to allow children from different linguistic backgrounds to be taught in their 'mother tongue'. But what about standards of achievement in subjects considered vital to the economic well-being of society?

Since the late 1950s these have been regarded as mathematics, the natural sciences and modern foreign languages. The struggle to realize the aims of the 1958 National Defense and Education Act goes on. It was expected that the federal funds made available under that Act would not only raise the level of teaching and learning in these key subjects but would also vastly increase the number of high school students studying them. The first aim was achieved. The second was not because the academics who revised syllabuses and made them academically more rigorous were almost exclusively interested in the education of college- and university-bound high school students. Bruner highlights the conference, of which he was chairman, at Woods Hole, Cape Cod (1959) attended by thirty eminent scholars, as the source of this interest in curriculum reform. Their findings stimulated projects which for some years had been encouraged by the National Academy of Sciences through its Education Committee. The best-known high school projects were directed by university mathematicians, physicists (PSSC), biologists (BSCS) and chemists (CHEMBOND). In general these projects were designed to improve the quality and rigour of science syllabuses by organizing their content in accordance with Bruner's assertion that it should be given coherence through the principles which inform the structure of a subject. High-powered scientists, like Jerrold Zacharias and Francis L. Friedman of the Massachusetts Institute of Technology who provided leadership in the development of high schools science syllabuses, agreed.

The number of high school graduates who had studied the natural sciences and modern languages did not increase as expected. Between the mid-1960s and the late 1970s the percentage of students taking chemistry in the first grade of the high school (ninth grade) dropped from 51.1 to 44.5; in algebra from 35.3 to 31.4; and in Spanish from 29.2 to 26.2. In the 1980s only a third of American high schools teach calculus and less than that number offer a course in physics taught by a qualified teacher. One third of America's 21,000 secondary schools do not offer enough mathematics to qualify their graduates for admission to accredited university engineering departments. Quite evidently when curricula allow considerable choice of courses to students and include syllabuses designed for the few rather than for all, such subjects will attract fewer and fewer students. It is a dilemma which faces all curriculum developers who are committed to freedom of choice as a human right, the general education of all young people which contains common elements and the maintenance of standards of achievement which satisfy university academics.

In the event, according to Gerald Leinward in *Education Today* (vol. 35, no 2, 1985) the American high school curriculum is soft. For example, in 1975 a college board survey showed that Standard Aptitude Test (SAT) scores taken by more than a million students in the final year of senior high schools had steadily declined over a period of ten years. The President's National Commission on Excellence in Education (*A Nation at Risk*, 1983) reported that the proportion of students graduating from high schools taking driver education had risen from 0.3 per cent in the mid-1960s to 58.6 per cent in the mid-1970s. The proportion taking 'training for marriage and adulthood' had risen from 1.1 per cent to 16.1 per cent over the same period. At the same time Leinward points out that 13 per cent of 17 year-olds are functionally illiterate: 40 per cent of them cannot draw inferences from written material and two thirds cannot solve mathematical problems that require several steps. Among minority group youngsters 40 per cent of the age cohort is functionally illiterate. On most standardized tests, despite recent improvements, the average achievement of high school students is lower than before Sputnik (1957). Indeed in the 1970s a Louis Harris Associates poll revealed that as many as 18.5 million Americans over the age of 16 could not read well enough to fill out simple forms in spite of the Adult Literacy Program which had been launched under the Economic Opportunity Act (EOA) of 1964 and subsumed in the Adult Education Act of 1966.

The way in which high school courses are organized makes remedial action difficult because students are granted a very free choice of 'electives' or options. Traditionally the high school course lasted four years; now the first year is taken in the last year of the junior high school – the rest in senior high schools. Courses are offered on a yearly basis. Each subject has its place in the four-year sequence. Chemistry is offered in the ninth grade. Physics is a twelfth-grade subject. Branches of mathematics – algebra, trigonometry, geometry – are offered in different years. The successful completion of a high school course which requires attendance at one lesson each day of the school week throughout the academic year merits a 'credit' in the subject. Examinations, powerfully influenced by the standardized testing movement, are run by individual teachers who assess student performance on a continuous basis. No national requirements have to be met for a student to 'graduate' from high school and, since the criteria teachers use to assess achievement levels differ, standards throughout the country vary considerably.

University admission requirements place some constraint on what schools offer. It should be recognized, however, that generally graduation from an accredited state high school gives a student the automatic right to enter an institution of higher learning run by the state. Simply to graduate a student is expected to take four courses each year and accumulate sixteen credits. On the basis of Conant's recommendations some of these should be drawn from the social sciences, the natural sciences and languages. Many well-known universities, such as Harvard, require that out of the sixteen credits gained for graduation twelve must be taken from all three areas. National standardized tests place students on a normal distribution curve and the test results together with a high school graduation certificate determine the university a student is able to enter. Again entrance requirements vary greatly and, even when schools pay attention to them, if they are to ensure that their students are admitted to a university of their choice it is easy to see how many American high school students, while finding a university place, may not have reached a satisfactory level of achievement in what in most countries are regarded as basic subjects.

Against this somewhat dismal picture of a mass system of high school education must be recorded the enormous achievements of the American system which has over the last 100 years responded to the demand for education from a rapidly growing, highly mobile and culturally diverse population. It should be remembered that during the first decade of the twentieth century millions of immigrants entered the United States of whom on the most simple tests (Can you read? Can you write?) one fourth were illiterate. Tests in the early 1950s showed that since 1900 illiteracy had steadily declined. Female illiteracy rates had dropped faster than the rate for males. In 1950 differences between rural and urban youngsters were not great but between members of the white and non-white populations (particularly among those over 45) the differences were enormous. Even so, in spite of the fact that a mass system of higher education has been created in the USA and the content and standards of university courses vary greatly, excellence has not been neglected. Many of the world's outstanding universities are located in the USA.

College and university curricula

It is this variety and the freedom of American academics to move away from European curriculum stereotypes which make the American university system unique. Typically a first degree course lasts four years and leads to a bachelor's degree. Each academic year is divided into two semesters lasting eighteen weeks or into four quarters each of nine weeks' duration. Most universities run summer schools for students wishing to complete their degrees more quickly or to take extra 'credits', and for postgraduate students many of whom are schoolteachers whose salaries depend on the qualifications they possess. One credit hour is granted for one hour's attendance per week over a semester or quarter. Frequently courses carry a rating of three credit hours. An undergraduate has to complete a minimum of 120 semester hours, i.e. usually five courses a semester, in order to qualify for a degree. Where the academic year is divided into quarters, 180 credits hours are needed to complete a first degree. The significance of this system is that knowledge is divided up and tested in small packages, teaching is intensive and assessments, made on the sole authority of an individual teacher and entered on the student's transcript, are immediate. The safeguard against teacher patronage, or personal dislike, lies in the number of courses which have to be taken and the number of professors involved in evaluating each student.

Usually first degree courses move from a fairly general first year when the freshman takes courses in the natural sciences, the social sciences and the language arts, to an increasingly higher degree of specialization. The number of credits to be taken in a subject in order to 'major' in it depends on university and departmental requirements. The number of credit hours in a 'major' subject may occupy as much as 75 per cent of the four-year course. Students may take enough 'credits' in a second subject to be awarded a 'minor' in it. Primary school teachers frequently 'major' in education. The course includes a period of supervised teaching practice in the last year for which credits are earned.

Professional training in law, medicine and some other fields is usually pursued in special 'schools' (or professional departments) and follows the award of a first degree in arts or science. Students preparing to teach in senior high schools must 'major' in the subject they propose to teach and take some education courses, including practice teaching, before qualifying for a state senior high school teacher's certificate. Such a certificate allows its holder to teach only the subject or subjects listed on the certificate. Usually a high school certificate is granted on the basis of the subject in which a teacher has 'majored'.

One of the great strengths of the system of higher education, all of which comes under the umbrella of the universities, lies in the variety of semi-professional courses which can be taken. Since 1900 the shift from degrees in the traditional arts and science subjects to degrees in journalism, nursing, counselling and so on has been very great and shows how adequately university academics have responded to demands for well-educated persons with a range of skills to fill responsible positions in a complex industrial society. To be sure, criticism of American higher education has concentrated principally on professors of education. Criticism of high schools has concentrated on the curriculum. Yet as Brian Holmes pointed out in his 1956 Boyd H. Bode memorial lectures at Ohio State University, *American Criticism of American Education*, none of the critics of education has dared to suggest that to remedy the situation Americans should abandon their faith in universal education and revert to a traditional selective system of schooling based on a theory of inherited individual differences in which a few subjects are offered at the second and third levels of education only to those capable of benefiting from them (as was the case in England prior to 1988) or by expecting all pupils to cover a national encyclopaedic curriculum during their period of compulsory education (as in the USSR).

The debate continues

Nothing better exemplifies the willingness of Americans to criticize their own system while at the same time retaining such faith in it than the opening statement of *A Nation at Risk*. It reads:

> Our Nation is at risk. Our once unchallenged pre-eminence in commerce, industry, science and technological innovation is being overtaken by competitors throughout the world ... the educational foundations of our society are presently being eroded by a rising tide of mediocrity ... If an unfriendly power had attempted to impose on America the mediocre educational performance that exists today, we might have viewed it as an act of war.

Whether or not the judgement is justified is debatable. It is the prerogative of Americans to criticize their own institutions. Unfortunately it is an assessment which foreigners may too readily accept. It is clear, however, that Americans are unwilling to seek answers to their real or imagined present-day educational problems in traditions which their forefathers abandoned or in theories advocated today by their ideologically opposed international competitors. They will respond to the present crisis, if such it is, by attempting to provide education for all, regardless of the consequences, on a lifelong basis and will accept without regret exponential increases in scientific knowledge. American educationists will discriminate far less than most of their international colleagues between what knowledge is worth including in school curricula and what is not. They will continue to include in second- and third-level curricula subjects which elsewhere are regarded with suspicion or relegated to lower-status institutions. To be sure, within this mass system there remains great inequality of provision. History should not be ignored. The constitution makes it unlikely that a national curriculum will be laid down to equalize provision. Under the constitution each state is responsible for its own education system. Most of them delegate to local school bodies authority to determine curricula. Without greater uniformity of curriculum content throughout the USA the proclaimed ideal that all men and women have a right to equal education will not be achieved. But the opportunities a mass system provides mean that inequality is no greater, and in many cases less, than elsewhere. It is unlikely that the power of the federal government will be radically increased.

Nor is it likely that elitist psychological theories will be adopted to solve the crisis. To be sure, the assumption on which the testing and measurement movement is based, which suggests that about 25 per cent of those tested are above average in attainment, about 50 per cent are average and about 25 per cent are below average, is unlikely to be abandoned. Standardized tests, constructed on this assumption, to measure achievement in the light of stated cognitive and affective objectives will continue to influence curriculum development.

It is hardly conceivable that Americans will overtly accept that only a small proportion of young adults is capable of benefiting from a university education. If 'All American Youth' have to be accommodated in universities then the traditional notions of what constitutes a university and what knowledge is worthy of inclusion in university courses will have to be further modified and the content of courses at this level will be adjusted to meet the needs of those attending universities. Those not interested in well-established subjects or not capable of studying them successfully will not be excluded from the system. The system will change. Whether these trends will lead, in a mass system, to the neglect of high-level work at the frontiers of knowledge is very doubtful. There is no reason to suppose that in other systems of mass education, e.g. Japan and the USSR, more and better fundamental research is carried out. Ideologically Soviet theory and Japanese practice will not be acceptable to Americans. In the modern world American criticism of American curricula should not be taken too seriously. Their theories offer the only viable means for curriculum development in situations where education is accepted as a human right, scientific knowledge is expanding at an unprecedented rate and schools are seen as making an important contribution to manpower needs.

Further reading

Aiken, Wilfred, *The Story of the Eight Year Study* (London: Harper, 1942).
Altbach, Philip G., and Berdhal, Robert O., *Higher Education in American Society* (Buffalo, NY: Prometheus, 1982).
Aronowitz, Stanley, and Giroux, Henry, *Education under Siege: the Conservative, Liberal and Radical Debate over Schooling* (South Hadley, Mass.: Bergin & Garvey, 1985).
Ashby, Eric, *Any Person, Any Study: An Essay on Higher Education in the United States* (New York: McGraw-Hill, 1971).
Baker, Adriane A. de Kanter, *Bilingual Education: A Reappraisal of Federal Policy* (New York: Lexington, 1983).
Bayer, Ernest L., *College: the Undemocratic Experience in America* (New York: Harper & Row, 1987).
Bennet, William J., *First Lesson: A Report on Elementary Education in America* (Washington, DC: US Department of Education, 1986).
Bestor, A. E., *Educational Wastelands (The Retreat from Learning in our Public Schools)*, 2nd edn (Urbana, Ill.: University of Illinois Press, 1985).
Bloom, Allan, *The Closing of the American Mind* (New York: Simon & Schuster, 1987).
Bloom, Benjamin S. *Taxonomy of Educational Objectives* (London: Longmans, 1956).
Broudy, Harry S., *et al.*, *Democracy and Excellence in American Secondary Education: A Study in Curriculum Theory* (Chicago: Rand McNally, 1964).
Bruner, Jerome S. *The Process of Education* (New York: Random, 1963).
Childs, John L., *American Pragmatism and Education* (New York: Henry Holt, 1956).
Coleman, James S., *Equality of Educational Opportunity* (New York: Arno, 1979).
Conant, James Bryant, *The American High School Today* (New York: McGraw-Hill, 1959).
Conant, James Bryant, *The Comprehensive High School* (New York: McGraw-Hill, 1967).
Conant, James Bryant, see Harvard Committee ... in a Free Society, *The Harvard Report*.
Counts, George S., *Dare the Schools Build a New Social Order?* (New York: John Day, 1932–5).
Counts, George S., *Education and American Civilization* (Westport, Conn.: Greenwood, 1974).
Cremin, Lawrence A., *The Transformation of the School 1876–1957* (New York: Knopf, 1961).
Cremin, Lawrence A., *Traditions of American Education* (New York: Basic Books, 1977).

Cusick, Philip A., *The Egalitarian Ideal and the American High School* (New York/London: Longmans, 1983).

Dewey, John, *The School and Society* (Chicago: University of Chicago Press, 1900).

Dewey, John, *The Child and the Curriculum* (Chicago: University of Chicago Press, 1902).

Dewey, John, *How We Think* (New York: Heath, 1933).

De Young, Chris A., *et al.*, *American Education*, 7th edn (New York: McGraw-Hill, 1972).

Eliot, Charles W., *Educational Reform: Essays and Addresses* (New York: Century, 1909).

Fellman, David, *The Supreme Court and Education*, 3rd edn (New York: Teachers College, 1976).

Franklin, Barry M., *Building the American Community: The School Curriculum and the Search for Social Control* (Studies in Curriculum History, No. 4) (London: Falmer, 1986).

Haertel, Thomas James, and Levin, Henry M., *Comparing Public and Private Schools*, Vol. 2: *School Achievement* (London: Falmer, 1987).

Harvard Committee on the Objectives of a General Education in a Free Society, *General Education in a Free Society* (the Harvard Report with an introduction by James B. Conant) (Cambridge, Mass.: Harvard University Press, 1944).

Harvard Education Review, *Equal Educational Opportunity* (Cambridge, Mass.: Harvard University Press, 1969).

Hemming, James, *Teach Them to Live* (London: Longmans, 1957).

Henderson, George, *Introduction to American Education* (Norman, Okla: University of Oklahoma Press, 1978).

Holmes, Brian, *American Criticism of American Education* (Columbus, Ohio: College of Education, Ohio State University, 1957).

Hutchins, Robert M., *The Higher Learning in America* (New Haven, Conn.: Yale University Press, 1936).

Hutchins, Robert M., *Some Observations on American Education* (Cambridge: Cambridge University Press, 1956).

Jencks, Christopher, *Inequality: An Assessment of the Effect of Family and Schooling in America* (Harmondsworth: Penguin, 1973).

Kilpatrick, William Heard, *The Project Method: The Use of the Purposeful Act in the Educative Process* (Teachers College Bulletin 1918) (Columbia, NY: Teachers College, 1918).

Kliebard, Herbert M., *The Struggle for the American Curriculum 1893–1958* (London: Routledge, 1986).

Koerner, James D., *Reform in Education: England and the United States* (London: Weidenfeld & Nicolson, 1968).

Meyer, Adolphe E., *An Educational History of the American People* (New York: McGraw-Hill, 1967).

National Commission on Excellence in Education, *A Nation at Risk* (Washington, DC: US Department of Education, 1983).

National Society for the Study of Education, *The Elementary School in the United States*, 72nd yearbook (Chicago: University of Chicago Press, 1973).

National Society for the Study of Education, *Issues in Secondary Education*, 75th yearbook (Chicago: University of Chicago Press, 1976).

Parkhurst, Helen, *Education on the Dalton Plan* (London: Bell, 1930).

Ravich, Diane, *The Troubled Crusade: American Education 1945–1980* (New York: Basic Books, 1983).

Rickover, H. G., *American Education: A National Failure* (New York: Dutton, 1963).

Salomone, Rosemary C., *Equal Education under Law, Legal Rights and Federal Policy in the post Brown Era* (New York: St Martin's, 1986).

Sedlak, Michael W., *et al.*, *Selling Students Short: Classroom Bargains and Academic Reform in the American High School* (New York: Teachers College, 1986).

Taba, Hilda, *Curriculum Development: Theory and Practice* (New York: Harcourt Brace & World, 1962).

UNITED STATES

Congress of the US, *Trends in Educational Achievement* (Washington, DC: Congressional Budget Office, 1986).

Valentine, John A., *The College Board and the School Curriculum* (New York: College Entrance Board, 1987).

Warner, W. Lloyd, *et al.*, *Who Shall Be Educated? The Challenge of Equal Opportunities* (London: Kegan Paul, 1946).

Woodring, Paul, *The Persistent Problem of Education* (Bloomington, Ind.: Phi Delta Kappa Educational Foundation, 1983).

Chapter Five

Marxist-Leninist ideology – curricula in the USSR

It remains to be seen what influence General Secretary Gorbachev's new policies will have on education in the USSR. Already in 1988, some of the research work of the Academy of Pedagogical Sciences Institute of General Education had been much criticized in the Soviet press. Previously criticism of education had been voiced publicly by leading members of the Communist Party or the academy. For example, in 1958 after several years of debate and experimentation Mr Khrushchev stated very succinctly in a memorandum to the Presidium of the Central Committee of the Communist Party of the Soviet Union (CPSU) that 'The chief and basic defect in our secondary and higher educational establishments is the fact that they are divorced from life'. He went on that, in spite of their obvious successes, 'Our ten year schools . . . are at present not accomplishing the task of training the young people for life and are only training them for entering college'. Two years later, in 1960, at an All-Russian Teachers' Congress he declared that 'We are now fulfilling two particular tasks: the creation of the material and technical basis for communism and the education of a new type of man'. His analysis and statement of purpose remain true in spite of the new climate of opinion which in 1988 was clearly apparent to regular visitors to the Soviet Union. Since the October Revolution in 1917, stress has consistently been placed on the role of education, and particularly the curriculum, in the creation of a New Soviet Man. Under the leadership of General Secretary Gorbachev the aims and objectives of Soviet education are not likely to change radically.

Who shall be educated?

Certainly the aims of Soviet education have survived fluctuations in policies designed to meet changing circumstances. For example, the creation of a communist society and citizens who contribute to its well-being has been based on the extension of education as a human right. In spite of difficulties, in the first Soviet Constitution of 1918 and subsequently in those that followed in 1924, 1936 and 1977 the right of Soviet citizens to education was proclaimed. The achievement of this ideal of equality of educational opportunity regardless of sex, race, nationality, class, linguistic background, domestic circumstances and place of residence has informed Soviet policy since 1917.

The first task facing the Soviet authorities was to eliminate illiteracy. Lenin regarded it as crucial and advised young communists to go out into the rural areas to tackle illiteracy among adults to re-enforce efforts made in regular primary schools. According to the 1897 census, illiteracy in Tsarist Russia was appalling. In Central Asia, for example, literacy rates were as low as 2 to 3 per cent. By 1935 illiteracy had been conquered. There remained, however, many peoples in the far north, the north-east and Central Asia who had no written language. Soviet policy has been to create languages for these minority groups and the constitutional right of parents to have their children taught in the language of the home is designed to ensure that every child in a multilingual nation is educated.

Post-revolution conditions, when millions of homeless orphans roamed the streets and did not attend school, created other problems. Under these circumstances A. S. Makarenko developed principles which he applied in the colonies he ran for young deliquents in the Ukraine. In several very famous books he describes the pedagogical methods he employed. They are full of common sense. Two general principles, however, induced from these accounts continue to influence theory in the USSR. The first is that a strict regime informed by kindness results in self-discipline. The second is that education takes place best through community activity, i.e. through a collective. In view of these principles the place of individual creativity in the education of children is frequently debated. It has recently occupied the attention of research workers.

Efforts to include everyone in a mass system of education are sustained by widely held psychological theories which contrast sharply with those advanced by Plato whose theory of inherited individual differences undoubtedly informed the system of education inherited by the Soviet authorities.

On the other hand, in nineteenth-century Russia materialist views emerged which stressed the influence of external conditions on the development of an individual's psychological activity. Russian physiologists laid the foundations of a psychology which points to the importance of the material environment on the development of the cortex. I. P. Pavlov is the most notable Russian precursor of physiological theories which characterize the work of Soviet educational psychologists. His pioneering work was finally rehabilitated when in 1950 at a joint meeting of the USSR Academies of Science and Medical Sciences his position in Soviet psychology was re-examined. Renewed importance was then given to the contributions made by L. S. Vygotsky, whose work had been banned shortly after his early death in 1934. Central to Vygotsky's theory is the assumption that psychological phenomena are integral parts of brain reflexes. His discovery that instruction played a leading role in psychic development removed the limitation placed on the abilities of children by 'behaviouristic' views that man is an animal which simply responds to external stimuli. Pavlov's 'second signal system' implies that in its process of development the cortex enables the nervous system to analyse, select and synthesize stimuli in ways which allow the organism to anticipate events. Consequently men and women can control their environment and do not simply respond to it.

The longitudinal research carried out by L. V. Zankov, D. R. El'konin and their colleagues after 1952 went beyond Vygotsky's view that teaching outpaces development. Zankov stressed process and the independent activity of the pupil. El'konin emphasized content and the role of the teacher. Aspects of the research were criticized in the USSR after 1962 but it furnished a theoretical framework within which subsequent curriculum reforms are discussed. The research confirmed official policy that every child, unless suffering from severe brain damage, can be educated along with its peers in the same pedagogical environment. Of course the creation of the right kind of environmental stimuli to build up the cerebral cortex is paramount in an 'education for all' which takes account of the child's physiology, its material environment and the contribution of teachers to development.

Within this theoretical framework most children are expected to be able to enter a regular school, remain in it and succeed but a number of severely brain-damaged children, e.g. children with Downs Syndrome, have to attend special schools. Even so they are encouraged to complete the regular school curriculum over a longer period of time than normal.

For this reason Soviet medical personnel and educators make every effort to identify children with brain damage. Early signs of it are investigated with great thoroughness and diagnosis is a continuous process. Tests are used to classify children on a scale of idiots, imbeciles and debiles on scores which bear some relation to non-Soviet IQ test scores. The tests, however, are not used to exclude pupils from the general common school but as one approach to the identification of brain damage. In the Institute of Defectology tests are devised and administered to improve diagnostic and therapeutic techniques. Work in the Soviet Union, based on a physiological approach to learning, is impressive. It is materialistic, clinical and in the final analysis optimistic. It suggests that all but a few children should be able to enter regular schools and succeed.

A unified school system

Under the circumstances the creation of a mass system of education in the Soviet Union is a remarkable achievement. The elimination of illiteracy was a formidable task. The Second World War resulted in the loss of millions of lives. War damage was horrific. During the war some socialist principles were abandoned in the interests of survival. Fees were reintroduced and the State Labour Reserves, set up in 1940, offered very short manual training courses closely linked with factories. Coeducation was abandoned so that boys could be prepared for industry and the armed services and girls educated as wives and mothers. As a result the central principle of Soviet education, that free general education should be provided for all in a unified school during the period of compulsory education, was held in suspense.

After 1945 aspirations remained high but during the first postwar Five Year Plan (1946–50) emphasis was given to healing war-inflicted wounds and raising national production figures to prewar levels. The work of schoolchildren in production, however, ceased and the main efforts of the authorities were directed to developing a compulsory system of education, establishing universal secondary education, developing technical and vocational schools, and expanding secondary specialized and, higher education, pre-school and out-of-school provision.

A unified common compulsory school is the cornerstone of the system which emerged. Until enrolments in kindergartens, which grew exponentially after 1945, reached a point when the authorities could safely lower the age at which children were required to attend school, that age was 7. Now it is 6. The period of attendance in a unified school increased over the period of Soviet power. For some time it was four years, then seven and after the mid-1970s eight years. A leaving age of 17 – after a ten-year general school – has been the aim of the government since it was included in the third Five Year Plan (1938–42). By the late 1980s this aim had almost been realized, particularly in the urban areas, when more than 60 per cent of the 15–17 year-olds were in full-time education.

The unified school is organized in stages. First-level education, lasting three years, is part of an incomplete eight-year or complete ten- or eleven-year secondary school. In 1970, shortly after the four-year first level of education had been reduced to three, 2.3 million pupils were enrolled in 'primary schools' as such. By 1980, the figure had dropped to 0.6 million. Effectively primary education is now provided for all in unified schools. Some kindergartens now offer first-grade syllabuses. After the first level of schooling pupils remain in eight-year incomplete secondary schools most of which in the urban areas are part of a ten- or eleven-year complete secondary school.

However, at the end of compulsory education many pupils leave general schools for work or go on to a vocational school or secondary specialized school. Post eight-year school courses vary from two to four years depending on the expertise needed. Since the Khrushchev reforms many vocational schools have added a general component to their courses and by 1985 almost 1.5 million students leaving the vocational or technical schools (PTUs) had a certificate of general education.

New secondary-vocational-technical schools (SPTUs), which used not to prepare pupils for general school-leaving certificates, provide courses in a wide range of specialized occupational skills. By 1990 these schools should enrol more than 50 per cent of pupils in the ninth grade. Technical schools which admit pupils from ten-year schools and provide one-year courses for a skilled occupation have become less popular. Instead vocational and specialized secondary schools offering a general certificate and specialized vocational training are much in demand, no doubt because they leave open for students the choice between taking up a skilled job or going on to third-level education. The ten- or eleven-year complete secondary school continues to attract pupils whose major ambition is to enter an institution of higher education.

Three types of institutions offer higher education courses. The universities, of which Moscow and Leningrad are the most famous, enjoy the most prestige. Polytechnics offer high-level technological education in an enormous number of specialized subjects. Pedagogical institutes prepare students for teaching positions in the upper stage of the unified school. Many teachers employed in the first stage of education are trained in secondary schools for teachers but the tendency is for more and more of them to complete a course in higher education before entering the teaching profession. Some pedagogical institutes prepare teachers for many academic subjects; others, like the Maurice Thorez Pedagogical Institute in Moscow, concentrate on the preparation of language teachers. Characteristic of all pedagogical institutes, however, is the attention paid to the subjects which are to be taught. The high proportion of time spent in teacher-training courses on them testifies to the fact that Soviet curricula are heavily knowledge-centred.

Parallel to this well-developed full-time system of education are part-time and correspondence courses. The scope of such provision reflects the desire of people not able to complete a stage of full-time education to improve their qualifications and the commitment of the authorities to fulfil their intention to provide education as a human right on a lifelong basis.

Recent estimates suggest that some 50 million people are in full-time institutions of education and another 50 million are undergoing some kind of education to improve themselves while in employment. In most respects the Soviet system is by intention and in practice moving towards a mass system of provision.

What knowledge is of most worth?

In this unified system continuity is important. It is provided, as in most countries, in accordance with curriculum theories designed

107

to reconcile the needs of individuals and society with the demands of knowledge itself. Expansion has created curriculum problems. Over the years Soviet curriculum theory has changed little. It was and is designed to create a 'New Soviet Man' and promote communism through the correct interpretation of worthwhile knowledge. The all-round upbringing of Soviet boys and girls should be informed by a communist ideology, high moral standards, spiritual enrichment and harmonious physical and mental development. All subjects in the school curriculum should be taught with these child-centred objectives in mind. The pre-eminence of the ideological component in the creation of a new type of citizen has rightly been emphasized by Soviet educationists in order not to perpetuate but to eliminate those deeply held beliefs passed on after the revolution by a generation of persons brought up under capitalism. Raising the political consciousness of all pupils is central to their all-round upbring-ing. It was again emphasized during the 1980s when politicians and educationists were aware of external ideological threats. History and studies in the writings of Marx, Engels, Lenin and the basic documents of the Communist Party and the Soviet state have long been recognized as valuable educational instruments. A new course in the fundamentals of the Soviet state and legal system was introduced in 1975 into the eighth grade. In this course, as in the *Communist Manifesto*, more is said in accounts of communist morality about what is wrong with capitalist moral and spiritual beliefs and with the hegemony in capitalist systems of their ruling classes than about the specifics of collectivism, internationalism (except that it is an internationalism of the working classes) and Soviet patriotism. It is as though, covertly, Soviet educationists recognize the virtues of some Russian traditional beliefs. Worth-while knowledge, and how it is treated, lie at the heart of Soviet child- and society-centred curriculum theories. On the authority of Lenin, a good communist should learn more than slogans but repeat through education the whole socioeconomic and historical experience of mankind.

This criterion justifies at all levels an encyclopaedic curriculum in the French tradition. Knowledge which contributes to the all-round intellectual, moral, physical and aesthetic development of individual pupils and promotes worthy civic attitudes should be continuously updated in response to scientific, technological and cultural progress. The elements of science should, therefore, be introduced at a fairly early stage and over the years of formal study the content of education should be distributed rationally in accordance with the structure of knowledge. The recent explosion of knowledge has led to overloaded curricula making selection of data from the history of every subject necessary.

The fact that the curriculum in Russian language schools includes a maximum of seventeen subjects, or, where the language of instruction is not Russian, eighteen because Russian is a compulsory second language, testifies to the continuation in Soviet second-level schools of the eighteenth-century French curriculum tradition. Lenin himself maintained that the building of a socialist culture entailed drawing on the achievements of Russian and world culture and putting them to the service of working people. Such a process would require the creation of a new intelligentsia, the elimination of the capitalist class consciousness of Tsarist Russia and the creation of a new socialist consciousness. In this way Lenin and his successors identified the contribution the socioeconomic and historical experience of mankind should play in the content of Soviet education.

Child-centred criteria of selection find their most obvious expressions in discussions about pre-school curricula. In close co-operation with the family, kindergartens are expected to protect the health of young children, develop their practical skills and a respect for work, see to their aesthetic development, prepare them for the eight-year school and ensure that they respect their elders and love socialism, their local region and their motherland. Syllabuses have been worked out with these aims in mind. Qualified medical staff attend kindergartens. Much of the learning is through a combination of work and play. Environmental studies, musical training, reading and writing, graphic studies and arithmetic help to prepare them for school. Children learn to respect work by helping to keep their schools clean, neat and tidy. A hotly debated issue is whether or not kindergartens can effectively introduce to 6 year-old children what was previously taught in the first grade of the eight-year school.

Curricula in the three-year primary stage are more subject-centred. This stage of education was reduced from four years in a decree issued in 1966 which was implemented somewhat later. The encyclopaedic content of education was retained on research which showed that young children could internalize abstract principles and apply them more widely than had previously been thought possible. The reform placed pressure on kindergartens to concentrate more on cognitive than on other aspects of development.

Zankov was critical of this knowledge-centred approach to the content of primary education. His research suggested that the curriculum was overloaded and that too little attention was paid to the all-round upbringing of children. One recommended improvement was the introduction of special subjects designed to instil norms of behaviour and promote the moral, aesthetic and physical well-being of individual children. Educationists in favour of these deliberate attempts to introduce elements of a child-centred curriculum and new methods of teaching were at pains to point out that they had no wish to interfere with the basic subjects or to repeat the errors introduced in the 1920s by the founders of pedology. This discussion of methods and the differences of opinion arising from Zankov's research suggest that the relative merits of child- and process-centred curricula on the one hand, and knowledge-centred curricula on the other hand, have long been aired among Soviet educationists.

In the second and third stages of the incomplete eight-year and the complete ten- or eleven-year school, the school curricula are encyclopaedic and, as in the primary stage, overloaded with factual information. Undoubtedly the explosion of knowledge has made it difficult, if not impossible, to sustain in practice Lenin's requirement that the whole experience of mankind should be included in school curricula. Principles of selection have been worked out. As reported by V. V. Kraevskij and I. V. Lerner in *The Theory of Curriculum Content in the USSR*, Soviet educationists have asked:

(1)   How much content should each syllabus contain?

(2)   How should the course in any subject satisfy the requirements of general education?

(3)   How should a course in any subject be drawn up to ensure the attainment of educational goals?

(4)   What knowledge, procedures and skills can be acquired through a particular subject in relation to the goals of general education?

In relation to these general questions more specifically the intention is to answer two major questions, namely: 'What minimum content should have been acquired by all students at the end of secondary school?' and 'What kind of curriculum will best serve the educational goals of a typical Soviet school?'

Answers lie in an analysis of the social experiences which should be passed on from one generation to the next. Knowledge is the first element of social experience. Skill acquisition is the second element. On the basis of this practical problem-solving activities of a previous generation simple 'knowing' can be translated into 'being able to do something'. Creativity, the third element in social experience, is vital if new problems are to be solved and reality is to be transformed. These elements are not vastly different from those identified as important in the transmission of experience in Western European and North American schools.

The psychological theory of Vygotsky and the pedagogical findings of Zankov sustain the view that selection from the social experience of mankind might imply identifying problems in the solutions to which skills like reading, writing and mathematics and creative abilities are important. Among the latter the ability to transfer knowledge from one situation to another, to see new problems in old situations, to see alternative solutions to problems and to solve new problems when confronted with them by using established knowledge and practical skills, are important. Features of these proposals are similar to Dewey's problem-solving approach but Soviet educators are anxious to point out the differences between his theories and theirs. A major difference lies in the social context in which problems are identified and solutions proposed.

The special requirements of each subject also provide criteria on which to select minimal knowledge. According to Kraevskij and Lerner, the activities associated with each subject should determine the composition of the curriculum in terms of a total pattern of subjects. Presumably some activities, like laboratory work, are common to several subjects. Teaching methods, learning processes, the personality of teachers and the learning capacity of pupils help to determine what activities should be selected as essential ingredients in curricula. Practical activities include self-help, help to others, workshop and gardening experience, improving facilities and conserving nature. Social activities include participation in social events, helping children to organize themselves, dealing with family life, interpersonal relations, leisure and health. Again this list bears a close resemblance to the range of problems American progressive educationsts identified

111

as the source from which criteria for selecting curricula content should be drawn.

Fundamental to Soviet curriculum theory, which distinguishes it from American theory, is the way content is interpreted. Soviet writers acknowledge that Dewey expressed views about the relationship between theory and practice and between education and work which pedagogically have merit. They reject the capitalist values which, for Dewey, should inform these relationships. Yet since the Revolution Soviet educationists have, like Dewey, struggled to break from the European tradition that school and university knowledge is intrinsically worthwhile.

Soviet polytechnical theory has its origins in Marx's *Capital* in which he wrote:

As Robert Owen has shown us in detail, the germ of the education of the future is present in the factory system; this education will in the case of every child over a given age, combine productive labour with instruction and gymnastics, not only as one of the methods of adding to the efficiency of production, but as the only method of producing fully developed human beings.

Soviet polytechnical curriculum theory is a theory of general not vocational education. It insists that the building-up of a socialist consciousness is more important than training young people to produce goods and services. Compared with Platonic theories which encourage sharp distinctions to be drawn between general education and vocational training Soviet polytechnical theory is very novel. Because it is so original it is frequently misunderstood and is the subject of endless debate.

Debates about polytechnical curriculum theory

Krupskaya did much to show how polytechnical theory could contribute to the upbringing of children and the creation of a communist society. Polytechnical education implies that education, in its widest sense, should be combined with production and the economic life of society. Krupskaya herself laid down some still accepted curriculum guidelines as early as 1920.

Much of what Krupskaya said is reiterated today. To bring her views into line with modern industry polytechnical education today should teach young people about present-day conditions and the consequences for workers of automation made possible by electrification. For example, developments in the chemical industry and in nuclear energy imply the disappearance of certain skills and their replacement by others. Under these circumstances, in a socialist economy, workers should be given the knowledge and skills to guarantee high-quality, low-cost products.

In theory a polytechnical curriculum should make the distinction between unified general labour schools and specialized vocational schools unnecessary. Over this issue Soviet educators have disagreed. The literature is replete with suggestions that the purpose of polytechnical education is simply to increase the number of trained workers for Soviet industry rather than provide all pupils with a good general education. The debate continues.

M. N. Skatin summarized Soviet experience between 1917 and 1958. A resolution adopted by the Central Committee of the Communist Party in September 1931 stated that the polytechnical curriculum should provide a good basis in mathematics, physics, chemistry and biology linked with a study of production. In the 1930s appropriate textbooks in these subjects were designed to prepare cadres of specialists to meet international threats. Labour instruction was cut out of the curriculum in 1937. These changes reflect a return to traditional Western European practices but with an emphasis on the natural sciences.

After 1945 interest in Marx's fundamental curriculum principle revived. At the Nineteenth Congress of the Communist Party in 1952, directives were issued for the development of polytechnical instruction in the general education schools. Four years later the schools came in for serious criticism. Again Congress agreed that Soviet schools should familiarize pupils with the main branches of production and link instruction with socially useful work. A new system of polytechnical education was tried out in a few experimental schools run by the Academy of Pedagogical Sciences and then in 1956–7 in another 350 schools. According to I. A. Kairov in *Polytechnical Education in the USSR*, edited by S. G. Shapovalenko, only after wide-ranging discussions was it safe for Khrushchev in 1958 formally to submit to the Presidium of the Central Committee of the CPSU a memorandum on strengthening the ties of school with life. The memorandum, which appeared in *Pravda*, was accepted. Subsequent theses prepared by the Central Committee of the USSR Council of Ministers were adopted by the Central Committee and discussed in some 200,000 meetings, attended by 13 million people, in the Russian Republic. Similar meetings were held all over the USSR. Even popular support for proposals which were adopted in the 1958 law failed to ensure that the proposals succeeded in practice. Since then curriculum reform has occupied a central position in Soviet educational debates.

Specific proposals in the 1958 law included starting socially useful work from the third grade in the eight-year school. It was to occupy two lessons a week out of between twenty-six and thirty-four. After the eight-year school the majority of pupils were to go into full-time employment. In the complete secondary school emphasis was given to general education but twelve lessons a week in the last three years of schooling were to be spent studying production in nearby enterprises.

Responses to these proposals varied. Some administrators interpreted the reform to mean that the number of vocational courses should be increased. Relatively few teachers understood the educational implications of the proposals. Other teachers simply did not wish to abandon old habits to learn new tricks.

During the first few years after 1958 it was not unusual to hear these reservations expressed by Soviet teachers and administrators even in the presence of foreign visitors. By the mid-1960s Soviet educationists were admitting publicly that the Khrushchev reforms had not succeeded. Major shifts in policy occurred. Instead of attempting to make the curriculum of the general, academically orientated, ten-year school one that would prepare young people for both productive life and higher education the authorities proposed that in specialized technical secondary schools it should be possible for students to complete their general education, learn a trade and qualify to enter an institution of higher education.

Given the prestige enjoyed by academic subjects the new secondary-vocational-technical schools (SPTUs) seem to have worked, because though some 2,554 lessons are spent on the vocational-technical cycle with production training, of the 1,684 general education cycle lessons (a number which compares favourably with that in the ninth and tenth grades of the general seconday schools) some 870 lessons are devoted to mathematics and the natural sciences. A range of subjects plus aesthetics, military training, physical education and options complete an encyclopaedic curriculum. Hence the popularity of the SPTUs.

Encyclopaedic polytechnical curricula

Throughout the unified school Soviet curricula are encyclopaedic. In the first three grades emphasis is placed on the native tongue but a range of subjects such as history, geography and some science is prescribed. In certain schools a modern foreign language, the most popular is English, is introduced to 8 year-old children in the second grade of schools. In the Russian republic the second grade have twelve weekly lessons of Russian which represents 50 per cent of the curriculum. Mathematics takes up a further 25 per cent of the time. Since the Twenty-Sixth Party Congress in 1981, when officially the compulsory starting age was lowered to 6, the encyclopaedic first-stage curriculum has been the subject of renewed controversy.

Overloading is regarded as a health hazard and has been criticized. Traditionally, 7 year-old pupils attend four lessons on each of six days a week and have up to an hour's homework each day. Secondly, it has been argued that many concepts introduced into the curriculum are beyond the capabilities of many children. For example, the algebra added to arithmetic in the curriculum was conceptually too difficult for many children. Then the effect of introducing grade 1 material into the last year of kindergartens is very controversial. Pre-school educationists claim that it is denying children their childhood and assert that their expertise in the upbringing of young children is at risk. Conventional primary stage teachers, on the other hand, maintain that kindergarten school teachers do not have the expertise to teach 6 year-old pupils in 'O' classes what is expected of them in the first grade.

The debate is between educationists who believe the primary stage curricula should be child-centred and process-orientated and those who wish to reduce overloading by introducing more abstract concepts into the programme. In neither case are traditional methods of teaching appropriate. Over a period of twenty-eight years, the impression of a visitor to primary stage classes in the USSR is that teaching is subject-centred. Discipline is firm but kindly and pupils eagerly respond to methods of teaching based on the structure of the subjects taught.

At the next stage of the unified school, from the fourth through the eighth grade, curricula in all republics are by intention similar, although the authorities in each republic have the right to adapt them to meet regional needs. This freedom finds its most obvious expression in the constitutional right of parents to choose the language in which their children are educated. In Latvia, for example, Lettish (Latvian) is the medium of instruction at all three levels of education if parents wish their children to be taught in their mother tongue. A similar choice is open to parents living in other non-Russian-speaking republics. All pupils, if not Russian-speaking, must learn Russian.

Options also allow for curriculum variations from school to school. The accumulation of scientific knowledge in recent decades makes it impossible to include all of it in a curriculum for everybody. At the same time students have to be prepared to take the entrance tests conducted by high-status institutions. Options were introduced in the last years of the complete secondary school curriculum to allow the most able students to add to their basic knowledge of the natural sciences, mathematics and geography by following courses based on the most up-to-date information and new concepts. The number of options in the seventh and eighth grades is strictly limited. In the ninth, tenth and, in non-Russian-speaking republics, the eleventh classes, potential natural and social scientists and mathematicians are prepared for competitive university entrance examinations. Less able students may be offered additional lessons in basic subjects like Russian and mathematics. Wholesale curriculum selection in the complete secondary school is not, however, the norm and options, introduced in the 1970s, are not typical.

For the most part all pupils are expected to follow the same subject-centred encyclopaedic curriculum for eight years and in the complete secondary schools. The following subjects are spread rationally over the second level of schooling: Russian language and literature, mathematics, history and the Constitution of the USSR, geography and economic geography, biology, chemistry, physics, astronomy, a foreign language, mechanical drawing, physical culture, art and music.

As in Western European school systems, the historical development of each subject determines syllabuses and the sequence in which knowledge is presented. For example, physics syllabuses in the Soviet Union include statics and dynamics, followed in historical sequence by heat, light, sound, magnetism, electricity, electronics and nuclear energy. In the same way the chemistry syllabus includes all the data accumulated during the historical development of physical, inorganic and organic chemistry. The same principles apply to the establishment of syllabuses for mathematics and biology. School mathematics is divided into

116

arithmetic, algebra, geometry and trigonometry in accordance with the logical structures of each branch of mathematics. The development of history, world, economic and social geography syllabuses is based on similar criteria.

The content of each subject is divided so as to be distributed throughout the eight-year school in a rational manner. In the lower grades elementary physical phenomena, physical quantities and their measurement constitute the physics course. In the complete secondary schools, modern physics courses include electricity, quantum theory, atomic structure, radioactivity and atomic energy. The chemistry course covers five years (from the seventh through the eleventh grade). In the eight-year school important chemical phenomena are taught followed by systematic courses in inorganic and then organic chemistry. In the early classes nature study covers the rudiments of physical geography and information about air, fire, water and the soil. In the fifth to the eighth class elementary courses cover botany, zoology, human anatomy, physiology and hygiene. In the ninth grade pupils follow courses in general biology and the principles of Darwinism.

History syllabuses are very comprehensive. In the first three years pupils are given some general historical notions. In the fourth year they are introduced to stories from the history of the USSR, about daily life before the revolution, about the revolution itself, the civil war, foreign intervention, the building of socialism and the 1941–5 war. Then follows world history with an emphasis on economic development and the class struggle. Systematic geography starts in grade five and includes the economic geography of foreign countries and the USSR.

All pupils are expected to complete the same eight-year curriculum and *all* students preparing for admission to higher education are expected to follow the whole range of subjects. No wonder a major criticism made by Soviet educators is that curricula are overloaded and students are overworked.

Selection from the historical experience of mankind is necessary. In history, selection is made of events in world history which illustrate the main principles of the historical struggle of the working classes. Physics is one of the most important subjects because of its wide applications in the modern material world. Selection is made on the basis of the principles which have informed the productive life of mankind. In biology selection is based on the principles which are related to agriculture, health care and fishing. Chemistry has a wide range of applications in ferrous and non-ferrous metal industries, oil and coal processing and the pharmaceutical industry. They provide criteria on which the content of chemistry courses is selected. Geography syllabuses are based on a selection of principles which show the relevance of geographical conditions to the organization of socialist production.

If the principles of selection are clear, differences of opinion exist. These became very obvious when in the 1960s major curriculum reforms were demanded in the Soviet Union. Criticisms appeared in the Soviet press. Curricula were held to be out-of-date. The most severe criticism was directed at mathematics and the natural sciences. History syllabuses were criticized as repetitious. Literature it was argued paid too much attention to the analysis of literary works. The critics proposed to revolutionize the curriculum – or at least to make sure it included recent material. Physics, for example, should be based on quantum theory and relativity. Euclidean geometry should be replaced by linear algebra. Molecular biology should form the core of biology syllabuses. And so on.

A. Markushevich, a professor of mathematics at the State University of Moscow, has described how curriculum debate was conducted in the USSR during the 1960s. In 1964 a joint committee was formed by the Academies of Sciences and Pedagogical Sciences to look into the content of education. Five hundred scholars took part and within a year draft proposals were sent to all the scientific, cultural and educational organizations. There were more than 2,000 responses to the draft. Many teachers confessed they would have to relearn their subjects if they were to teach the new syllabuses. Critics from institutes of the USSR Academy of Sciences asked the authors to moderate their recommendations. A revised version of the original draft was accepted by the party and the government. It was published in journals to permit wide discussion. Further work was done on the mathematics and physics syllabuses before they were approved by the Ministry of Education for implementation. The task was completed in 1976.

This major attempt to introduce modern concepts in school curricula illustrates how distinguished scientists and educationists co-operated in formulating proposals not all of which were accepted by practising teachers. To be sure, formal approval was given to the document 'About further improvement of the work of the secondary schools' by the ministry but, as in the USA, the

leading participants in the formulation of new curricula were
leading university academics and educationists. There is no doubt
that many scholars and schoolteachers were opposed to radical
curriculum reform. Some academics wanted to include the most
up-to-date knowledge and principles of science. Educationists
opposed such innovations on pedagogical grounds. Doubtless,
debate will continue. After resisting change on the authority of
Lenin for so long, a central issue now is how to reduce the
enormous amount of factual information crammed into the
ten-year school while introducing the most recent concepts and
knowledge.

These debates have implications for methods of teaching. They
are discussed in the Unesco/IBE publication *Teaching Methods in
the Soviet School* by I. D. Zverev. If the stated principles are
successfully operationalized it will be possible for Soviet scientists
and educationists to draw up coherent syllabuses which do not
violate Lenin's dictum. It is less likely that radical proposals to
introduce child- and process-centred curricula will overcome the
opposition of teachers who are accustomed to an encyclopaedic
subject-centred curriculum.

The polytechnicalization of the curriculum is by no means a
dead issue. The difficulties of reaching consensus on what is
meant by a polytechnical curriculum and how it can be realized in
practice will not prevent debates about it going on among
scientists, scholars, industrialists, politicians, teachers and parents.
The originality of the concept as an organizing curriculum
principle compared with Western European practices guarantees
this.

At the same time it must be said that the many extra-curricular
activities designed to create a 'New Soviet Man' may contribute
more than the regular school curriculum to the achievement of
this long-standing aim. The Octoberists, the Young Pioneers and
members of the Konsomol or Young Communists have a significant role to play in ameliorating the emphasis in the general
Soviet curriculum on academic subjects presented in the light of
their logical structures and historical developments. Pioneer
Palaces provide an antidote to formal academic education on the
one hand, and specialized vocational training on the other.

Attempts to break the stranglehold of teachers on the content of
education are resisted in the Soviet Union with no less vigour and
success than in other countries where teachers have traditionally
decided 'What knowledge is of most worth?' The fact that the

119

situation is not vastly different in countries committed to centralized democratic systems of control from that in countries where
administrations are decentralized is worthy of much closer
analysis. Mr Gorbachev's reforms are not likely, in practice, to
provoke a curriculum revolution.

Further reading

Asratyan, E. A., *I. P. Pavlov, his life and work* (Moscow: Foreign Languages
  Publishing House, 1953).
Black, Cyril E., *The Transformation of Russian Society* (Cambridge, Mass.:
  Harvard University Press, 1960).
Bronfenbrenner, Urie, *Two Worlds of Childhood* (London: Allen &
  Unwin, 1971).
Chauncey, Henry (ed.), *Soviet Preschool Education*, Vol. II: *Teacher's
  Commentary* (New York: Holt, Rinehart & Winston, 1968).
Constitution (Fundamental Law) of the Soviet Socialist Republics (Mos-
  cow: Novosti).
Deineko, M., *Public Education in the USSR* (Moscow: Progress, 1964).
DeWitt, N., *Soviet Professional Manpower, Training and Supply*
  (Washington, DC: National Science Foundation, 1955).
Dunstan, John, *Paths to Excellence and the Soviet School* (Slough: Nelson,
  1977).
Hans, Nicholas, *The Russian Tradition in Education* (London: Routledge,
  1963).
Holmes, Brian, 'Education in the Soviet Union', in Edward Ignas and
  Raymond J. Corsini (eds), *Comparative Educational Systems* (Itasca,
  Ill.: Peacock, 1981), pp. 325–83.
Inkeles, Alex, and Geiger, Kent, *Soviet Society* (London: Constable, 1961).
Klein, Margaret S., *The Challenge of Communist Education: A Look at the
  German Democratic Republic* (New York: Columbia University Press,
  1980).
Koutaissoff, Elisabeth, *The Soviet Union* (London: Benn, 1971).
Kraevskij, V. V., and Lerner, I. Y., *The Theory of Curriculum Content in the
  USSR* (Paris: Unesco/IBE, 1985).
Krupskaya, N. K., *Works on Education*, Vol. 4 (Moscow: R.S.F.S.R.
  Academy of Pedagogical Sciences, 1959).
Kuzin, N., and Kondakov, M., *Education in the USSR* (Moscow: Progress,
  1977).
Lenin, V., *On Socialist Ideology and Culture* (Moscow: Progress, 1978).
Malkova, Z. A., 'Secondary education in the world today', *International
  Yearbook of Education*, Vol. XXXIX (Paris: Unesco/IBE, 1987).
Markushevich, A., 'The problems of the content of school education', in
  Brian Holmes and Raymond Ryba (eds), *Curriculum Development at*

the Second Level of Education, Proceedings of the Comparative Education Society in Europe, Fourth General Meeting (London: 1969), pp. 43–50.

Marx, K., Engels, F. and Lenin, V. I., *Marx, Engels, Lenin: On Communist Society* (Moscow: Progress, 1978).

Marx, Karl, *Capital*, two volumes (Moscow: Foreign Languages Publishing House, 1954).

Maxwell, Robert (ed.), *Information USSR* (New York: Macmillan, 1962).

Matthews, Mervyn, *Education in the Soviet Union* (London: Allen & Unwin, 1982).

Medinsky, Y. N., *et al.*, *Makarenko: His Life and Work* (Moscow: Foreign Languages Publishing House, n.d.).

Rosen, Seymour M., *Education and Modernization in the USSR* (Reading, Mass.: Addison-Wesley, 1971).

Shapovalenko, S. G. (ed.), *Polytechnical Education in the USSR* (Paris: Unesco, 1963).

Soviet Union, *Soviet Union: Political and Economic Reference Book* (Moscow: Progress, 1985).

Sukhomlinsky, V., *On Education* (Moscow: Progress, 1977).

Tomiak, J. J. (ed.), *Soviet Education in the 1980s* (London: Croom Helm, 1983).

Tomiak, J. J. (ed.), *Western Perspectives on Soviet Education* (London: Macmillan, 1986).

University of London, Institute of Education, *Education in the USSR* reports of comparative education tours organized by Brian Holmes to the USSR (London: 1960 to 1986).

USSR, *Constitution (Fundamental Law) of the Union of Soviet Socialist Republics* (Moscow: Foreign Languages Publishing House, 1977).

USSR, *History of the USSR*, three volumes (Moscow: Progress, 1977).

Vygotsky, S., *Thought and Language*, trans. and ed. Eugenie Hanfmann and Gertrude Vakar (Cambridge: Mass.: MIT Press, 1962).

Zajda, Joseph I., *Education in the USSR* (Oxford: Pergamon, 1980)

Zankov, L. V., *et al.*, 'Teaching and development: a Soviet investigation, in *Soviet Education*, vol. XIX, nos 4, 5, 6 (February, March, April, 1977), White Plains, NY: M. E. Sharpe.

Zinovyev, M., and Pleshakova, A., *How Illiteracy Was Wiped out in the USSR* (Moscow: Foreign Languages Publishing House, n.d.).

Zverev, I. D., *Teaching Methods in the Soviet School* (Paris: Unesco, 1983).

Chapter Six

Curriculum dependence –
transfers between countries

What views of worthwhile knowledge do teachers and other educators defend in the less industrialized countries of Africa, Asia and Latin America? How far have they internalized the traditions of essentialism, encylopaedism, pragmatism, or poly-technicialism which were implanted by colonialism or by other kinds of political/economic penetration? How far do they refer instead to older, pre-colonial views of valued knowledge, derived, for instance, from Confucian, Hindu or Islamic traditions? To what extent are teachers willing to adopt and implement new curriculum proposals which aim to adapt education to the imperatives facing politically independent but economically underdeveloped countries?

The global impact of essentialism, encyclopaedism,
pragmatism and polytechnicalism

The USA, France, the Soviet Union and Britain have been not only the centres of distinctive curriculum philosophies. Each has had a major political influence on other parts of the world and, through this impact, educational practices based on the four major curriculum philosophies have been widely diffused. In the cases of Britain and France, educational practices spread with their colonial empires in the nineteenth and early twentieth centuries though French ideas were also received in many countries through the impact of the 1789 French Revolution. The USA and the Soviet Union have been influential in the period mainly since

122

1945 when, as world superpowers, they have competed to offer rival ideologies and, with them, educational ideas to the rest of the world.

THE ADOPTION OF THE ESSENTIALIST CURRICULUM OUTSIDE BRITAIN

In 1945, the British colonial empire included the Indian sub-continent, much of sub-Saharan Africa, parts of the Caribbean and a variety of islands, peninsulas and small states in the Indian and Pacific Oceans. The states of the Indian subcontinent broke from colonial rule in 1947 but political independence was not achieved in most other areas until the 1960s. By this time fully developed education systems had been created by the British which were closely linked at the upper levels to institutions in Britain.

While the colonial elementary school curriculum was based on the nineteenth-century British model with some local 'adaptations', colonial secondary and higher education much more closely mirrored the curricula of equivalent elite institutions in Britain. Secondary and higher education developed in tandem in most colonies especially after 1945. The universities dominated the secondary schools. The 1945 Asquith report not only proposed that colonial universities should follow the pattern of those of Britain but led to the establishment of an Inter-University Council through which universities in Britain determined courses, controlled entry and examination requirements and provided British teaching staff (Colonial Office, 1945; Maxwell, 1984). Even though locally relevant courses of study were sometimes introduced the principles of stringent student selection, specialization of study and a humanistic or pure science bias prevailed.

The essentialist principles were transposed directly to the colonies. The wider justification was similar to that used in England since the purpose was to prepare a leadership class in the colonies to govern eventually independent states with British-style political systems who would continue to have close cultural ties with the former metropolis.

Many former colonies were forced by poverty or powerlessness (equated often with small size as well as lack of economic resources) to rely on British educational aid after political independence so that British teachers continued to orientate curricula towards British patterns while local educationists were imbued with British views through training in institutions in

Britain. The mechanisms for maintaining a British educational philosophy were clear and strong.

The countries under the greatest political domination by Britain were often those with the weakest indigenous alternatives to British educational philosophy. While there had been well-defined schemes of tribal education in many African countries before and even during colonial rule (Fortes, 1938; Raum, 1940) these had been localized to particular areas and groups of people.

A second group of countries which had experienced British colonial rule had much stronger bases for eradicating the British educational influences. These countries included 'settler' colonies such as Australia, New Zealand and Canada which had achieved a high degree of internal self-government by the end of the nineteenth century. There were also countries in the Middle East such as Egypt which had been freed from British colonial education control by the 1920s, which also had a strong pre-colonial educational tradition based on Islam.

In this second group of countries, British essentialist ideas did sometimes continue to influence the curriculum particularly at the level of the general philosophies as in Australia. Elsewhere, educational ideas from other countries were influential such as those from the USA in Canada or from France in Egypt (while in New Zealand curriculum philosophy was closer to the encyclo-paedist tradition of Scotland than the essentialism of England). Residual English curriculum influences, however, are not entirely absent from any of these countries.

The post-colonial states of the Indian subcontinent – India, Pakistan and Sri Lanka – were a special case. British educational institutions were strongly established. But indigenous cultures provided the basis for powerful alternative philosophies of education. After independence in 1947, India and Pakistan were sufficiently large and powerful to propose radical changes to the British tradition. The special case of India will be considered in Chapter 7.

THE DISSEMINATION OF FRENCH ENCYCLOPAEDISM

When serious debates about the expansion of public education throughout the world began after 1945, the French colonial empire was confined to North Africa, to West and Central Africa, to Indo-China and to other scattered colonies in the Caribbean and the Indian and Pacific Oceans. The process of decolonization occurred between 1954 in Indo-China and in the 1960s in sub-Saharan Africa. By this time, full-scale colonial education systems had been established.

French colonial educational policy has been distinguished from that of Britain and other European countries such as the Netherlands by its strongly 'assimilationist' character. The argument has been that while the British colonial authorities tried to 'adapt' education to local conditions, the French intention was to 'assimilate' an elite of colonial subjects completely into French culture. The means was a system of education in most colonies which was a replica of that of France, both in organization and in what was taught (Mumford and Orde-Browne, 1937).

There is little doubt that assimilation occurred. The accounts of 'psychological colonialism' which formed part of the anti-colonialist movement in the 1950s and 1960s came very largely from authors with first-hand experience of French colonialism such as Frantz Fanon, Memmi, or Moumouni (Clignet, 1971). But the assimilationist process was not as complete as is sometimes assumed. The 'assimilés' at most periods of French colonial history and in most colonies were a very small minority of those receiving French colonial education.

Continued dependence on France is strong in West Africa. There are powerful institutional links where French teachers, forms of educational organization and curriculum materials are transferred to Africa and African students move to France for specialized training at higher levels. But this continuing dependence is a result of the poverty and small size of most former French sub-Saharan African territories and the active policies of fostering links which have been pursued by successive French governments since the early 1960s.

The informal borrowing of French educational ideas that has occurred in many areas of the world since the late eighteenth century had a quite different character. Belief in the efficacy of state planning of economic and social affairs had been accepted during the eighteenth-century Enlightenment in many areas of continental Europe. The 1789 revolution in France had added republican, nationalist and egalitarian elements to this rational centralism. The educational elements of these ideas were accepted in many areas of Europe after 1815 even when the political doctrines of republicanism were not.

A view that education should transmit a standardized body of knowledge unified by rational principles had support throughout Europe in the early nineteenth century from Russia to Greece and from Spain to Sweden. The encyclopaedist view was established, if not necessarily predominant, in almost every country except, perhaps, England.

Encyclopaedism was interpreted differently in various countries. In many European countries it is tempered by locally influential philosophies. In Scandinavia a Lutheran Protestant view has been expressed in the educational philosophy of Grundtwig in Denmark which connected the curriculum with local rural community cultures. In Germany, Kerschensteiner's Protestant Christianity emphasized the dignity of manual work and manual vocations in a Christian life. This philosophy underpins the relatively strong place given to vocational education in West Germany (Hearnden, 1976).

Encyclopaedic views of the universal value of a standardized curriculum and of the prime place of rationally organized subjects such as mathematics and natural sciences have remained powerful also in eastern European states including the Soviet Union which overtly have based their educational philosophies on Marxism.

The implications for poorer Third World countries of adopting an encyclopaedist approach will be explored in Chapter 8 in relation to the states of Latin America which adopted encyclopaedism freely in the early period of independence from Spain and Portugal in the nineteenth century but which, in the later twentieth century, have not achieved the economic development reached by other nineteenth-century nations in Europe.

THE IMPACT OF EDUCATIONAL IDEAS FROM THE USA

The USA has had relatively few colonies in which American educational ideas could be established. An exception was the Philippines. Since 1945, however, American informal educational influences throughout the world have been extensive. A comparison could be made with the French influence in Europe and elsewhere following the 1789 revolution.

The formal and informal channels of American educational influence can be separated. Informally, a number of American educational ideas and institutions have been borrowed by other industrial and non-industrial countries. More formal channels have included the impact of American aid agencies on education in a number of non-industrial countries throughout the world since 1945.

The pragmatic philosophy of Dewey was of interest to progressive educators in the 1920s and 1930s in Britain (see Chapter 2), the Soviet Union (see Chapter 5) and Latin America (see Chapter 8). There is no suggestion that these ideas were transferred by any other means than voluntary and spontaneous borrowing by the recipients. On the other hand, these ideas were never institutionalized as a predominant educational philosophy in any of these recipient countries. Similarly, the American comprehensive high school was taken as a model by other industrial countries from the 1940s as they began to consider the democratization of secondary schooling. But even in Britain where American practices were most widely invoked, there was considerable resistance to the American model and much attention to the criticisms of the American high school.

Perhaps the most widely experienced institutional transfer was the American pattern of organizing the curriculum of higher education. The democratization of higher education to include a wider range both of students and of subjects of study that occurred in many countries after 1945 followed an earlier American development. Patterns of organizing courses and assessment (multi-disciplinary studies, course units, continuous assessment) were taken from the USA and applied in other industrial countries including Britain (such as the Open University established in 1968) and France (seen in the reorganization of higher education in 1968). Suggestions that these institutions were enforced on non-industrial countries through American economic and political power should be tempered by examples of similar borrowing where such political influences were absent.

After 1945, the world-wide educational activities of the American agencies expanded in less developed countries. American government aid also grew as the provision of education was seen to be a major weapon in the world-wide strategy of disseminating American political idealogy. The AID scheme in Latin America was an example (see Chapter 8).

Perhaps the strongest American influence, however, has come not through the establishment of American educational institutions in other countries, but through the migration of many students from many other parts of the world to American universities, often aided by American foundations. Such experiences may have led to a stronger internalization of American educational values by future teachers and administrators, especially at higher education level, in many less industrialized countries. But there is also evidence of an uneven acceptance and application of American ideas by these students when they return to their home countries (Myers, 1984).

The case of Japan considered in Chapter 9 is interesting because American educational ideas were applied after 1945 in conditions similar to those of colonialism. But American political control lasted a short time and American proposals collided with long-established Japanese educational values. Even so, there were groups in Japan who were eager to support some American suggestions when they coincided with these groups' own perceptions of desirable change.

SOVIET INFLUENCES

Soviet models of education have also had a fairly brief history of world-wide influence. In the 1920s and 1930s, borrowing was informal, voluntary and spontaneous. But it was limited in scale. Educationists in countries which did not accept the Soviet political system treated its educational ideas with some reservation. However, since 1945 a number of countries both in Eastern Europe and in other parts of the world have undergone Marxist-Communist revolutions and, consequently, have looked to the Soviet Union for educational models, a process which has been intensified by the growth of Soviet educational aid schemes.

The introduction of the centrally planned economy in the Soviet Union after 1917 and the deliberate gearing of educational provision to such economic needs by Stalin in the 1930s was followed by other countries after 1945. French and Indian educational planning from the 1940s shows some similarity with that of the Soviet Union of the 1930s (see Chapters 3 and 7). The manpower planning approach to educational provision, which was widely adopted by less industrialized countries after 1945 (Youdi and Hinchcliffe, 1985), had been introduced first in the Soviet Union in the 1930s. Similarly, the establishment of specialized technical/vocational institutions of higher education in a number of countries in the 1960s and 1970s (including Britain and France) mirrored Soviet policies of the 1930s. Incidentally, both the manpower planning strategy and the policy of establishing specialized vocational higher education institutions were not adopted in the USA.

Systematic adoption of Soviet educational practices has been restricted largely to countries which have undergone Marxist-communist political revolutions. Most striking have been the states of Eastern Europe together with Cuba and China. In most cases, the borrowing of Soviet educational practices has been accompanied by the migration of students from these countries to institutions of higher education in the Soviet Union, which has had the second or third largest number of foreign students of all countries of the world after the USA. In less industrialized countries, educational personnel have been transferred from the Soviet Union or other Eastern bloc countries. The processes of educational transfer from the Soviet Union to other countries after 1945 have not differed greatly from those by which American practices have penetrated Third World countries.

The outcomes of educational transfer from the Soviet Union have been mixed. The philosophy of polytechnical education has been widely accepted in policy statements in socialist countries. But the implementation of this policy has met difficulties in many countries. On the other hand, it is claimed that the idea of polytechnical education is applied more systematically in the curriculum of schools in the German Democratic Republic than it is in the Soviet Union (Castles and Wustenburg, 1979).

China provides a fascinating case of Soviet educational influence (Chapter 10). Following the 1949 revolution, Soviet educational ideas were widely accepted. But in the Cultural Revolution of 1966 an attempt was made to develop a quite different concept of socialist education. Persisting throughout these changes, however, there has also been a long-established indigenous Chinese cultural and educational tradition based on Confucius which may obstruct the implementation of socialist educational policies whether from the Soviet Union or of indigenous Chinese origin.

Cross-national curriculum transfers: dependence or autonomous choice?

The survey of British, French, American and Soviet international educational influences raises a number of questions about the nature of transfers of curriculum from one country to another. Are there particular aspects of the curriculum in which dependence is most frequently experienced? Are there areas in which there is often a relatively high degree of autonomy? Does the extent of dependence or autonomy in these specific aspects differ greatly in some less industrialized countries compared to others?

129

CURRICULUM AIMS AND OBJECTIVES

Since the end of the colonial empires, almost all countries in the contemporary world enjoy full national sovereignty and autonomy. In independent states, the aims of education and the aims of curriculum are formulated by indigenous agencies whether at national, regional, or local level. Broad curriculum aims in most countries emphasize the transmission of knowledge which is seen to be valuable for national or local economic development, social unity, political identity, or cultural autonomy. Very few governments, however weak and economically poor, would tolerate external interference and dictation in these areas. Indeed, many problems of curriculum implementation perceived by governments revolve round the failure of education systems to respond adequately to new curriculum aims proposed by these governments.

Foreign influences on the formulation of curriculum aims occur through the initiative or willing acceptance of national or local policy-makers who have internalized foreign philosophies of worthwhile knowledge or who accept the claims to special professional expertise of foreign 'specialists'. General aims may be locally determined but precise curriculum objectives may be imported within specialist techniques of curriculum planning or organized content packages (curriculum projects).

There have been many instances of the transfer of British curriculum projects to schools in former colonies in the 1960s and 1970s – particularly in subject areas such as English language, mathematics, or the sciences. These projects have incorporated broad curriculum aims, most frequently ideas that learning should start from the curiosity of children and should utilize their experience and environment.

Specific studies on, for instance, the introduction of the School Mathematics Project in Kenya (Lillis, 1985) have indicated that the imported projects were accepted, particularly in the 1960s, because of the professional positions of those who supported them. In former colonial countries, there was a strong residual influence of expatriate teachers and educationists who could facilitate transfer, which happened in the case of the School Mathematics Project in Kenya. But when the lack of consistency between the discovery-centred aims of the English School Mathematics Project and the more instrumental views of Kenyan educationists and educational consumers towards mathematics became clear, then the imported innovation was rejected.

Similar instances have been recorded in other post-colonial countries (Lewin, 1985). New externally derived curriculum aims or objectives are not adopted in the long term unless they are consistent with the views of indigenous policy-makers.

CONTENT

While curriculum aims are fairly fully under the control of national and local groups, the content of the curriculum may not be locally determined to the same extent. Some aspects of valued knowledge are created in and disseminated from a few metropolitan centres. The question then is what aspects of this worthwhile knowledge are totally controlled in metropoles and what may be brought under local control.

Distinctions have been made between universal and particularistic kinds of knowledge. For Berger and Luckman (1967) the dichotomy was of public and private forms. For Habermas (1974) there was a difference between 'technical' and 'practical' knowledge. 'Technical' knowledge underlies the organization of modern industrial states. It includes not only the scientific areas of knowledge which make a technological economy possible but also the economic, social and political concepts which inform the organization of a complex industrial society. Such technical knowledge tends to have a similar character throughout the world (McLean, 1985).

Much 'technical' knowledge is created and defined in advanced industrial societies and is imported with relatively little modification into less developed countries. Countries which make little contribution to scientific development are dependent on the foreign creative centres. These subject areas – not only mathematics and the natural sciences but also economics, medicine and knowledge about social planning (including educational planning) – are important in the curriculum in less developed as well as in developed countries.

But dependence is not total or uniform. In some less developed countries, local scientists have had considerable success in taking general principles created in the centre and adapting and applying them to specific conditions and problems in their own countries. In India agricultural productivity has been enhanced dramatically by the application of principles of plant genetics by Indian scientists (Schultz, 1982). However, in African countries, scientists have been less creative even in the application of general principles taken from elsewhere (Eisemon, 1981).

There have also been attempts to find alternatives to Western science – particularly in areas such as medicine which draw upon traditional culture and practices. Departments of traditional medicine have been established in some African universities which can create or collect knowledge which ultimately may find its way into the school curriculum. This process has been fairly slow and often resisted. But these developments together indicate that not even in the areas of technical knowledge is dependence total and unalterable.

'Technical' knowledge dependence has been the greatest in the curricula of higher education institutions. In schools, the content of mathematics and the sciences does not necessarily depend so directly on recent advances in scholarship in developed countries. Conventional mathematics at school level was as much part of traditional cultures of Middle Eastern and certain Asian countries as it was of those of Europe. Western science penetrates the curriculum of non-Western schools through the agency of local universities which have accepted this science and insist on its dissemination in schools.

The 'private', 'particularistic', or 'practical' form of knowledge is found in informal and intimate human relations. Such private knowledge exists in every society and social group however dominated and dependent its formal education system.

'Practical' or 'private' knowledge finds a place in school curricula especially in moral and social education. Religious studies, history, social studies, literature, art and music which are taught in schools to some degree are extensions of private or practical knowledge. In most countries they reflect the national or local heritages of the societies in which schools are found. The domination of Western history, literature, or religion in school curricula in non-Western dependent societies was largely confined to periods of direct colonial rule and the immediate post-colonial period. Most former colonial countries quickly began to indigenize the content of these areas of the curriculum after political independence (Lewin, 1985).

What survives is dependence in the ways of organizing knowledge – the methodologies of inquiry – in these 'particularistic' areas. History, as a subject in African universities after political independence, was given a new content which reflected the experience of colonial subjects rather than that of their masters but the way in which the subject was researched and organized remained much the same (Denoon and Kuper, 1970).

Some areas of curriculum content remain in an ambivalent position when they have a dual function in both the particularistic and universalistic areas of knowledge. Most prominent is the language of education. External languages, most commonly English and French, remain the medium of education because they give access to international 'technical' knowledge. Local languages have been developed (and in some areas were never challenged at some levels of education) because of their particularistic function. Whether the balance tilts towards the internal or external language depends on specific political, economic and social conditions in particular countries, especially the relative importance at each stage of education of acquiring international 'technical' or local 'particularistic' knowledge.

TEXTBOOKS AND OTHER SOURCES OF KNOWLEDGE

Western domination of the production of textbooks is frequently cited as evidence of continued curriculum dependence in Third World countries. Much knowledge which is used in curricula comes through mass-produced print and other media (such as film, television, video, radio, audio tapes, etc.). These materials are produced commercially whether they are mass circulation school textbooks or limited-run abstruse academic journals. If publishers in a few countries dominate production in many areas of the world, this is a function of commercial relationships which are largely outside the control of educationists.

Textbook dependence is most acute at higher education level and in subjects where there is an international communality of curriculum content. This particularly applies when the content is that of highly specialized branches of limited appeal subjects. Economies of scale dictate international distribution of the same books (and when the market is small in each country even translations cannot be made). Publishers with international markets and efficient production and marketing systems tend to predominate (Altbach, 1985).

Where there is mass consumption of textbooks – in schools and in popular subjects in higher education – local production is often possible. In practice metropolitan publishers often produce books for specific markets in less developed countries. To meet the demands of these markets, they have to respond to locally expressed needs. There may then be economic dependence on foreign publishers but not curriculum dependence because foreign publishers respond to locally expressed demands over content.

The scale of operation does not have to be very great to be economically viable and the technical difficulties of production are not sufficient to inhibit local and national production of textbooks. Most countries, except for the very smallest, can produce their own school texts efficiently and economically and most do. Indeed, there are numerous examples of texts being replaced rapidly when curriculum content is reformed. The major problem is the localization of textbook production within very small or very poor regions where resources of money and writers are limited.

However, many countries may not be able to compete effectively in presentation of materials. It has been suggested that, while most less developed countries have created their local television programmes, they have some difficulty in competing with the skills of packaging and presentation of the imported programmes (Rodwell, 1985). These slicker imported materials attract consumers. The same phenomenon may apply to school books. Indeed, within the USA, a few large-circulation school textbooks predominate in a vast country with fifty states which have legislative autonomy in education and over 16,000 school districts. Economies of scale and consumer preference for professionally presented works lead to the domination of relatively small numbers of mass circulation textbooks.

But in most countries, national or local education authorities have the right to dictate which books shall be or shall not be used in schools. This suggests that it is a matter of policy decision whether textbook production is localized. Locally produced materials may be more expensive and may be less attractive in presentation than internationally disseminated textbooks. But educational policy-makers usually can insist on local alternatives and have the means to produce them.

ASSESSMENT

Metropolitan forms of examination and assessment do persist in former colonial countries even after other areas of the curriculum have changed to meet local conditions. British secondary school examination boards – particularly of the universities of London and Cambridge – have continued to influence assessment in former colonial countries, especially in Africa and the Caribbean, even when the curriculum content of the examinations was localized and the formal control of the examination was taken over by national organizations. This influence was perpetuated through the use of British examiners and assessors who would tend to apply standards that are accepted in Britain. So local curriculum content may be organized for assessment purposes in ways which meet British norms of achievement.

There is also evidence that British-style examinations, particularly with an emphasis on depth knowledge in a few, mainly academic subjects, survive in countries which have a high degree of autonomy in other areas of the curriculum. So British-style upper secondary examinations survive in India, Pakistan and Australia even though formal links with British examination boards disappeared long ago.

Such assessment dependence may be supported by a number of conditions. Examination systems may not be changed easily when they determine access to higher education or to sought-after occupations. When competition is intense, it may be difficult to change the forms of assessment (Dore, 1976). Secondary school examinations in some countries are controlled by higher education institutions which may have closer contacts with and dependence on metropolitan institutions than the school systems of their own country.

A different kind of assessment dependence which has been noted in many less developed countries does not have a colonial origin. American 'objective' multiple choice tests and internal course unit assessment have been widely adopted in many countries, both industrial and less industrialized. With the democratization of access to education and diversification of curriculum, some traditional techniques of assessment have become administratively unfeasible – such as externally controlled written papers and/or oral examinations, which formed a major part of the continental European procedures. American assessment procedures may have been adopted because they particularly suit a movement to wider access and more diversified schooling which historically developed earlier in the USA but which has developed in most countries through internally perceived needs.

KINDS AND DEGREES OF CURRICULUM DEPENDENCE

There are clearly differences between the degree of curriculum dependence in separate aspects of the curriculum. Dependence may be greater in terms of content and to some extent textbooks than in the curriculum aims or teaching methods. There is also a greater degree of curriculum dependence at more advanced stages of education, at higher education and upper secondary level, than in primary education. This applies particularly in the content and textbook elements of the curriculum. This raises questions about whether mechanisms of dependence operate largely through higher education institutions in metropolis and periphery.

The extent of curriculum dependence does seem to differ greatly between countries in ways that bear little relationship to level of economic development. Dependence continues in sub-Saharan African or Caribbean countries that were under British or French rule. Yet both Australia and New Zealand, which have had formal independence for almost a century and have had relatively developed economies also for a long period, maintain curricula which show marked similarities to those of equivalent institutions in Britain.

On the other hand, as will be seen in Chapter 7, India and the other former British colonies of the Indian sub-continent have demonstrated a high degree of curriculum autonomy especially in the language media of education, in textbooks and in the adoption of a distinctly Indian philosophy of Basic Education. Even the higher education system has departed from the British model in some respects and the best institutions have had a reputation for advancing scholarship which is matched in few other poorer countries. In India it was an English conception of worthwhile knowledge which was accepted rather than the other elements from which curricula are constructed.

It will be seen in Chapter 8 that Latin American educationists complain of a greater degree of dependence in cultural and educational areas than strikes an outside observer who would be more impressed by the persistence of French and Iberian educational traditions. This dependence (mainly on the USA) is most noticeable at higher educational level and in areas such as national level curriculum planning than in school curriculum practice. Yet Latin Americans, who fiercely defend their cultural autonomy, resist and resent even limited educational dependence on other countries.

It is not always easy to identify the sources of dependence. In former colonial territories, it is usually clear. Curricula have been adopted from the former colonial power – either as a survival of colonial rule or through post-colonial influences. Another kind of 'neo-colonialism' can be observed in which influence is transmitted to independent states by metropoles that never had colonial power over them, particularly American influence in Latin America or the impact of the Soviet Union in China (see Chapters 8 and 10).

But there is also dependence on undefined or diffuse metropolés. Countries which are claimed to be dependent have such a relationship with geographically and politically unspecific concepts such as 'Western science' which may be controlled in industrialized countries generally but which cannot be located in any one country. Even the use of English language in education – frequently taken as a sign of dependence on Britain or the USA – is now geographically diffuse on an international scale. When Singapore reversed a movement towards the use of local languages and reasserted the centrality of the English medium, it was not re-establishing colonial links with Britain but strengthening an international language which had commercial advantages to a rapidly developing economy.

This complexity of the phenomenon of curriculum dependence suggests that explanations of dependence should be examined carefully to determine how far they can aid understanding of the processes.

How is curriculum dependence created and maintained

Three kinds of argument may be advanced to suggest how curriculum dependence occurs and how it is maintained. First, educational dependence may be seen as an outcome of the economic and political dependence of less industrialized peripheral countries on a highly industrialized metropolis. So education is seen as little more than a passive reflection of wider economic and political relationships.

Secondly, curriculum dependence may be seen largely in terms of intra-educational relationships. The educational and curriculum power structures which are found within countries also apply on an international scale. Some educationists and educational agencies in developed countries have been able to exert influence and control over the behaviour of their counterparts in less developed states. 'Educational dependence' may be relatively separate from political and economic relationships.

Thirdly, educational dependence may be a product of internal conditions within peripheral countries. Local educationists may accept dependent relationships in some countries and reject them in others because of the widely held norms or the educational power configurations in each country. This 'explanation' is consistent with the argument followed in other chapters of this book that educationists maintain deeply held beliefs about worthwhile knowledge which determine their responses to proposals for curriculum reform.

CURRICULUM DEPENDENCE AS A PRODUCT OF ECONOMIC DEPENDENCE

When the idea of educational dependence gained currency among educationists in the early 1970s, it was linked to a number of theories of economic dependency which had emerged in the 1950s and 1960s (see Carnoy, 1974; Altbach and Kelly, 1978; Berman, 1979; Arnove, 1980).

These theories had been proposed by Latin Americans but had become better known through the work of Andre Gunder Frank (see McLean, 1983). Frank (1967) made three propositions. Metropolitan capital investment 'underdeveloped' and impoverished Latin America because capital outflows (dividends) exceeded capital inflows and because metropolitan capital investment was concentrated on traditional areas of the economy such as plantation agriculture and mineral extraction. Metropolitan capital interests were managed and protected by local elites in the peripheral countries who identified with metropolitan interests against those of the mass of their own people.

Educational dependency arguments focused on the last of these propositions. Education was the means by which local elites were created and separated from the mass of the people. Through the content of education local elites were encouraged to identify with the values of the metropolis whose interests they supported. Reference was also made to anti-colonialist positions such as that of Fanon (1967) who analysed the psychological domination which was maintained over national indigenous elites in colonial areas through education.

However, the economic dependency theories used to support assertions about educational dependency themselves came under attack. Frederico Cardoso (1972), Bill Warren (1973) and others showed that, while economic dependency inhibited to some extent the freedom of action of governments of peripheral countries, it was not inconsistent with economic growth and development. Secondly, they argued that elites in peripheral countries, though they might be agents of metropolitan capital to some degree, also retained a high degree of autonomy in influencing (in the extreme by nationalization) the activities of foreign capital enterprises in their countries.

The attacks on crude economic dependency theories throw some doubt on the value of ideas of educational dependency drawn from them. Educational dependency could not so easily be associated with economic decline. Nor did it appear to create passive and submissive elites in peripheral areas.

The critics of economic dependency theory admitted that it would be applicable to those countries, mainly in Africa and the Caribbean, which continued to experience after political independence a domination of their economies by traditional primary products exports (under the control of foreign companies) and of their administrative systems (including education) by expatriate personnel. However, such countries have been in a minority in the Third World since the 1960s.

There is another criticism of the application of crude economic dependency theories to educational systems. With the ending of colonial rule, it is difficult to establish how foreign economic agencies could control, politically and administratively, the education systems of independent countries even if they were economically dependent. At most these economic pressures could operate indirectly.

There do seem to be rather greater degrees of educational and curriculum dependence in many countries than can be explained simply by theories of economic dependency. There is too great a variation in the degree of educational dependence between countries for such economic theories to give a satisfactory account of dependence throughout the world.

LINES OF EDUCATIONAL CONTROL

Curriculum dependence may be a product of purely educational relationships. Several models and theories suggest mechanisms of academic or educational 'imperialism' which exist relatively independently of wider political and economic relationships. Apex educational institutions tend to dominate subordinate ones both within countries and across national frontiers (McLean, 1984).

This domination may take two forms. High-status universities tend to dominate lower-status institutions of higher education (appointment of staff, creation of new knowledge, definition of dominant 'paradigms' of knowledge) (Mills, 1970). Higher education institutions tend to define, dominate and control the knowledge which is transmitted in schools through the influence they maintain over teachers, inspectors and curriculum designers (see Bernstein, 1977; Becher and Maclure, 1978).

When applied to relations between industrialized and less industrialized countries, these mechanisms can operate in the following ways. Academic staff in universities in peripheral countries look to high-status institutions in metropolitan countries for the definition of the knowledge they transmit. The connection is created by the placement of former students of the high-status metropolitan institutions on the academic staff of peripheral country universities (orginally expatriates but increasingly indigenous staff who have undertaken foreign study programmes). It is reinforced by the domination of the production of new knowledge (and of means of dissemination such as books and journals) by metropolitan institutions.

At school level, there are three major ways in which institutional educational dependency can work. University academics trained in metropolitan universities can have a major role in the definition of school curricula (especially in academic subjects in upper secondary schools). Teachers and educational administrators who design or implement curricula have been educated at national universities by academic staff trained in the metropolis and receive metropolitan conceptions at second hand. Educationists (administrators and curriculum designers) may take educational studies courses in metropolitan universities.

However, these general propositions should be treated as provisional hypotheses rather than as iron rules. Even university academics in peripheral institutions who were educated in high-status institutions may balance their obedience to their alma mater (from which they gain prestige and status) with local interests. Sometimes these links are weakened or broken (though peripheral institutions may continue to follow outmoded conceptions which date from before the break). There are cases of universities in peripheral countries becoming world-ranking institutions (though usually in fields related to the economy or environment of the country). In many countries, universities have staff who have been trained at different high-status institutions in different countries and no one group is able to establish a lasting dominance.

These propositions may have to be treated even more carefully when applied to school level. Very few classroom teachers in schools in peripheral countries (apart from expatriates in some of the poorest ex-colonial states) have had overseas educational experience. So lines of connection to classroom teachers are indirect. Primary education (and non-academic secondary, adult and non-formal education) are least affected by metropolitan connections maintained by universities. It is more likely, at these levels, that education will be relatively autonomous.

DEPENDENCE AND LOCAL POLITICAL, CULTURAL AND SOCIAL CONDITIONS

Two kinds of local and specific conditions may affect the degree to which curriculum dependence is experienced in different countries. First, there is the historic legacy of prevalent norms and institutions which may have a considerable impact on curriculum practice – strong pre-colonial traditions may reduce the impact of colonialism and strong colonial legacies may create a greater continuing dependence than current institutional connections appear to justify. Secondly, the internal political or professional interests of those involved in curriculum decision-making may encourage them either to accept or to reject dependence according to its perceived impact on these interests.

Curriculum dependence is often most acute in countries that have most recently escaped European colonial rule because this control had such a strong and lasting effect both on institutions and on prevailing values. Indeed these may persist without any continuing metropolitan post-colonial intervention. Educational consumers and educational policy-makers may still believe that the former, colonial ways of operating are better because of their internalized norms. The failure of American intervention in some former European colonies where the innovations challenged established colonial practices (like the American-style university at Nsukka in Nigeria) is an example. This may particularly apply to assessment and examination procedures where there is likely to be greatest suspicion of change (changing the rules of the game, reducing standards).

Conversely, pre-colonial norms and institutions may survive so strongly that they reduce the colonial impact. The influence of Islamic norms and institutions in Egypt or Pakistan and of Hindu norms in India has reduced the impact of colonialism and post-colonialism on views of worthwhile knowledge (except where the two were consistent). The revolution in Iran in 1979 and the revival of Islamic educational institutions in Pakistan indicate the strength of pre-colonial legacies. American influences in Latin America are not as powerful as those inherited from

France and Spain/Portugal in the curriculum at all levels of education.

Continued acceptance of dependence or its rejection may suit the wider political or narrower professional interests of those who affect curriculum decision-making. This has applied at a broad political level to language policies. The delicate political balance between groups in Nigeria has meant that English survives as the medium of education at every level. Non-Hindi speaking groups in India have fought for the maintenance of an official status for English because a Hindi monopoly would affect their occupational chances. Educational consumers in Africa may prefer a 'British' education because this is seen to give economic advantages. University academics may support practices associated with universities in the foreign country in which they trained because of the greater possibilities of professional advantage this may give them.

The importance of these local choices would seem to suggest that dependence is less acute than is sometimes thought. But once these choices are made to maintain external links, it does give greater power and influence to metropolitan organizations. Dependence may be chosen freely but this does entail a loss of autonomy which does have implications for policies of curriculum reform in less developed countries.

The following chapters examine in more detail a variety of cases of curriculum dependence and transfer. British educational influences in India were strongly entrenched through a long period of colonial rule. Yet in India, there are strong pre-colonial cultural norms which have a powerful impact and the government of India since 1947 has attempted to develop its own unique approach to curriculum reform. In Latin America, French encyclopaedism was imported freely and without political constraint after 1800 but curricula based on this view have been challenged from a variety of sources in the twentieth century as alternative models of development have gained currency. American influences in Japan were strongest for five years of military occupation after 1945. These influences have been modified both by strong indigenous Japanese educational traditions and by the imperatives facing a country which has become one of the world's most powerful economies. China in contrast remains a Third World country but with strongly persisting indigenous traditions of education. Soviet models of education were adopted as a consequence of the 1949 revolution. Since the 1960s, China has attempted to devise its own educational and curriculum strategies.

Further reading

Altbach, Philip G., 'Centre and periphery in knowledge distribution in the Third World: the case of India', in Edgar B. Gumbert (ed.), *A World of Strangers* (Atlanta, Ga: Georgia State University, 1985), pp. 69–90.

Altbach, Philip, G. *et al.* (eds), *Publishing in the Third World* (London: Mansell, 1985).

Altbach, Philip G., and Kelly, Gail P. (eds), 'Introduction', in *Education and Colonialism* (London: Longman, 1978), pp. 1–49.

Arnove, R., 'Education and world systems analysis', *Comparative Education Review*, vol. 24, no. 1 (1980), pp. 48–62.

Becher, Tony, and Maclure Stuart, *The Politics of Curriculum Change* (London: Hutchinson, 1978).

Berger, Peter L., and Luckman, Thomas, *The Social Construction of Reality* (Harmondsworth: Penguin, 1967).

Berman, E. H., 'Foundations, United States foreign policy, African education', *Harvard Educational Review*, vol. 49, no. 2 (1979), pp. 145–79.

Bernstein, Basil, 'On the classification and framing of educational knowledge', in Basil Bernstein (ed.), *Class Codes and Control*, vol. 3 (London: Routledge, 1977), pp. 85–115.

Cardoso, F. H., 'Dependency and development in Latin-America', *New Left Review*, vol. 74 (1972), pp. 83–95.

Carnoy, Martin, *Education as Cultural Imperialism* (New York: McKay, 1974).

Castles, Stephen, and Wustemburg, G. *Education of the Future* (London: Pluto Press, 1979).

Clignet, Remi, 'Damned if you do, damned if you don't: the dilemmas of colonizer–colonized relations', *Comparative Education Review*, vol. 8, no. 3 (1971), pp. 296–312.

Clignet, Remi, and Foster, Philip J., 'French and British colonial education in Africa', *Comparative Education Review*, vol. 15, no. 3 (1964), pp. 191–8.

Colonial Office Advisory Committee on Education in the Colonies, *Education Policy in British Tropical Africa* (London: HMSO, 1925).

Colonial Office, *Report of the Commission on Higher Education in the Colonies* (Asquith Report) (London: HMSO, 1945).

Denoon, D., and Kuper, A., 'Nationalist historians in search of a nation', *African Affairs*, vol. 69, no. 277 (1970), pp. 329–49.

Dore, Ronald, *Diploma Disease* (London: Allen & Unwin, 1976).

Eisemon, Thomas O., 'Scientific life in Indian and African universities: a comparative study of peripherality in science', *Comparative Education Review*, vol. 25, no. 2 (1981), pp. 164–82.

Fanon, Frantz, *The Wretched of the Earth* (Harmondsworth: Penguin, 1967).

Flexner, Abraham, *Universities: American, English, German* (New York and Oxford: Oxford University Press, 1930).

Fortes, M., *The Social and Psychological Aspects of Education in Taleland* (Oxford: Oxford University Press, 1938).

Frank, Andre G., *Capitalism and Underdevelopment in Latin-America* (New York: Monthly Review Press, 1967).

Habermas, Jurgen, *Theory and Practice* (London: Heinemann, 1974).

Hearnden, Arthur, *Education, Culture and Politics in West Germany* (Oxford: Pergamon, 1976).

Kelly, Gail P., 'Colonial school in Vietnam: policy and practice', in Philip G. Altbach and Gail P. Kelly (eds), *Education and Colonialism* op. cit., pp. 96–121.

Lewin, Keith, 'Quality in question: a new agenda for curriculum reform in developing countries', *Comparative Education*, vol. 21, no. 2 (1985).

Lillis, Kevin M., 'School mathematics in East Africa', *Compare*, vol. 15, no. 2 (1985), pp. 141–59.

McLean, Martin, 'Educational dependency: a critique', *Compare*, vol. 13, no. 1 (1983), pp. 25–42.

McLean, Martin, 'Educational dependency – two lines of inquiry', in Keith Watson (ed.), *Dependence and Interdependence in Education* (London: Croom Helm, 1984), pp. 21–9.

McLean, Martin, 'Knowledge and dependency', *Interchange*, vol. 16, no. 4 (1985), pp. 52–6.

Maxwell, I. C. M., *Universities in Partnership* (Edinburgh: Scottish Academic Press, 1984).

Mills, C. W., *The Sociological Imagination* (Harmondsworth: Penguin, 1970).

Mumford, W. Bryant, and Orde-Browne, G. St J., *Africans Learn to be French* (London: Evans, 1937).

Myers, Robert G., 'Foreign training and development strategies', in Elinor G. Barber, Philip G. Altbach and Robert G. Myers (eds), *Bridges to Knowledge* (Chicago: Chicago University Press, 1984), pp. 147–63.

Raum, Otto, *Chaga Childhood* (Oxford: Oxford University Press, 1940).

Rodwell, Susie, 'A world communications crisis', *Compare*, vol. 15, no. 1 (1985), pp. 53–66.

Schultz, Thomas W., 'The value of education in low income countries: an economist's view', in Bikas C. Sanyal (ed.), *Higher Education and the New International Order* (London: Frances Pinter, 1982), pp. 42–62.

van den Berghe, Pierre L., *Power and Privilege at an African University* (London: Routledge, 1973).

Ward, W. E. F., *Fraser of Trinity and Achimota* (Accra: Ghana Universities Press, 1965).

Warren, Bill, 'Imperialism and capitalist industrialisation', *New Left Review*, vol. 81 (1973), pp. 3–44.

Youdi, R. V., and Hinchcliffe, K. (eds), *Forecasting Skilled-Manpower Needs* (Paris: Unesco, 1985).

Chapter Seven

The curriculum in India: British traditions, ancient philosophies and independent alternatives

The colonial authorities first gave aid to educational institutions in India in 1781. The long history of colonial education allowed for British philosophies of education to become strongly entrenched. Yet the British colonial educational inheritance seems to have little relevance for contemporary India which in size, culture and economy is worlds apart from its former colonial metropolis.

India had a population of well over 700 million in 1983. It is one of the fifteen poorest countries in the world judged by per capita income (US$260 in 1983) and its population predominantly is involved in peasant agriculture. Yet India is also one of the top ten industrial producers in the world and 20 per cent of the population is urban, including the residents of eight cities with more than one million people each.

Colonial India was partitioned at independence in 1947 into Muslim Pakistan and Hindu India. But religious minorities have remained in India (Muslims, Christians, Buddhists and Sikhs). The national language, Hindi, is understood by a majority of the population but hundreds of other languages are also used by the peoples of India.

These economic and cultural conditions have produced insistent pressures for educational change in India. The low per capita income and the rural occupation of the majority of the population have both restricted the provision of educational opportunities and led to demands for education to be relevant to the improvement of the condition of the majority of the rural population. Yet significant urban and industrial development has prevented the adoption of a purely rural orientation to education.

The religious and especially the linguistic divisions of India have led to calls that education should mirror a large range of particularistic cultural aspirations. Yet the unity of the nation, especially in the light of its international non-aligned role, has demanded the creation of a specifically Indian identity through education. This identity is threatened not only by traditional cultural divisions but the persistence of alien cultural and educational patterns especially those drawn from Britain.

What knowledge

A diversity of knowledge traditions continues to be influential in India. There is the colonial legacy of British essentialism. There is the alternative which emerged from the nationalist movement in India – Mahatma Gandhi's idea of Basic Education. There are traditional, pre-colonial knowledge concepts derived from the religious traditions of Hinduism and, to a lesser extent, Islam and Buddhism.

The British essentialist tradition had been established in India at an early period of colonial rule. The intention that Indian education should be modelled on that of elite British institutions was signalled in Lord Macaulay's Minute of 1835. This suggested that the aim of education should be to produce Indians whose culture and values were thoroughly European and British (Macaulay, 1835). The main principles of essentialism in England, it will be recalled, were morality, individualism and specialism. Worthwhile knowledge was found largely in the humanities and was accessible only to social and political elites. These principles gave importance to the study of the literature, history and philosophy first of classical Greece and Rome and later of Britain and Europe. Macaulay's intention was that the same knowledge content should be offered in elite Indian education and should be governed by the same general principles.

These same principles, of course, could be applied to the selection of knowledge content of an Indian origin. The 'orientalists', against whom Macaulay's proposals were directed, argued that it was possible to introduce Indian languages, literature and culture into the curriculum without modifying the principles by which the value of this knowledge was judged.

The recurring criticism of British colonial educationists was that the subject content of the essentialist tradition was maintained but not its underlying ethos (Mayhew, 1926). An instrumental attitude prevailed in Indian education. The idea that the essentialist curriculum should develop qualities of service, commitment and respect for justice among future political and administrative elites carried little weight. There was little individualization of teaching at any level. Instead the ideas of stringent selection of future elites through examinations, of specialized study at an early stage and of the high status of the humanities were institutionalized without their strong moral and individualist rationales.

This utilitarian view may have allowed subjects such as the natural sciences and engineering very quickly to gain high status from the 1950s when highly selective institutions specializing in engineering, management and other vocational areas were established following industrialization plans in the 1950s. But the principles of early selection of students for elite education and of early specialization survived even when new subjects gained in status. And while students and governments may have viewed the content of the curriculum from a utilitarian perspective (especially related to economic opportunities), teachers at higher education level especially continued to stress the importance of humanistic, or at least 'pure', studies, which predominated even in courses which were intended to have a vocational orientation (Sancheti, 1986).

The radical alternative came from Gandhi. The Wardha Scheme of Basic Education of 1937 suggested that Basic Education should be available for all children aged 7–14. It would lead into work and adult life. The medium of such schooling should be local languages rather than English. So education was to start from local cultures. The curriculum should include the study and practice of traditional crafts such as spinning and weaving found in village communities (Nurullah and Naik, 1951).

Gandhi's proposals were made in the context of the mass nationalist struggle against colonial rule. The focus was on the daily life of peasants. English was rejected not only because it was the language of colonial rule but also because it was used largely by an urban Indian elite which was divorced from the mass of the people. The emphasis on traditional crafts, despite the injunction that they should be a means by which pupils would finance the cost of schooling, was consistent with a concentration on the daily lives of the mass of the population rather than the culture of alien rulers.

The Basic Education policy was adopted by many states in India after 1937 and by the Union government from 1947. But, despite this political endorsement, the Basic Education philosophy has never predominated in the curriculum of independent India, especially the craft training elements.

Pre-colonial views of knowledge were associated with Hinduism and Islam respectively. Two concepts of Hinduism had importance for attitudes to education – Kharma and Dharma. Kharma determines the rank in society in which an individual is born and reborn. Dharma is the function that an individual performs in relation to his or her rank. How well this function is performed determines whether the individual is upgraded or degraded in rank in the next life.

Kharma is consistent with caste divisions in Indian society (Brahmins – the high priests with access to the highest knowledge; Kshatriyas – rulers and warriors; Vaisyas – traders and agriculturalists; Sudras – the servile caste; and Harijans – outcasts). The Dharma of the highest castes involved spiritual meditation and enlightenment. As with the British essentialist tradition, there was an emphasis on moral knowledge which was intuitively acquired. The idea that certain bodies of knowledge were reserved for particular social classes was found in Indian Hindu traditions as well as in those of Britain (Basu, 1957).

But there were differences between Hindu and British traditions. The highest-status knowledge in Hindu traditions was spiritual and inner-directed while the essentialist view gave highest status to moral knowledge which was of value to the political ruler (in effect for the king rather than the priest). The value of politically useful moral knowledge was not internalized easily by Hindus who were educated in British-style elite institutions.

Hinduism was not dogmatic. It was noted for a capacity for compromise with a variety of knowledge systems and concepts even to the point of contradiction. British essentialist concepts – and the ideas of the place of the individual, the nature of society and the character of knowledge contained in them – did not meet immediate rejection by Hindus but attempts at reconciliation. The outcome was a superficial – and ultimately instrumental – acceptance of essentialist ideas in education without unequivocal and exclusive internalization.

149

Hindu epistemology was codified in the four Vedas before 1000 BC. They had a written source and authority. Educational institutions had developed around these knowledge traditions including universities attracting students from throughout Asia in the period AD 300–1100. Vedic knowledge was extended to include the study of mathematics, architecture and sculpture. But this Hindu tradition of education largely disappeared before British penetration of India in the eighteenth century. There were no powerful formal institutional bases upon which Hindu education could develop during and after the colonial period. The Hindu tradition from the eighteenth century was preserved in family-based attitudes rather than formal educational structures.

Some elements of Hinduism, especially its association with the caste system and its other-worldliness, were rejected by the nationalist movement in the late nineteenth and twentieth centuries. Gandhi promoted an educational philosophy which would give social opportunities for depressed castes and which stressed economic activities. Nationalist schemes of education were an attack on both British and Hindu traditions.

Islamic views of knowledge have relevance for contemporary India. While a minority of the population of India is Muslim, Islamic schools were well developed in the pre-colonial and early colonial period and had many Hindu students. Islamic education is part of the Indian heritage and historical experience.

Islamic epistemology is authoritarian and revelatory. True and valuable knowledge is handed down by God rather than created by man. Its sources are the Koran and a number of ancient and sacred commentaries on the Koran. The first and essential stage of Islamic education consisted of studying and learning the Koran.

The content of the Koran and other texts was largely moral – a number of precepts by which individuals could follow God's laws and intentions for humanity. Islamic philosophers such as Ghazali and Khaldun in the sixth century in North Africa had given a greater importance to rational studies of, for instance, mathematics and the physical sciences, partly in response to European knowledge. But this kind of knowledge was restricted to higher levels of Islamic education. In contrast, mass Islamic education was based on the transmission of moral knowledge which was revealed in sacred texts (Tibawi, 1957).

Islamic views of worthwhile knowledge were not inconsistent with British essentialism. Platonic views of worthwhile knowledge also gave emphasis to the moral purpose of education, to its source in certain texts and to intuitive rather than rationalist or empirical methods of learning. The conflict between Islamic authorities and British colonial education lay less in epistemological differences (which were not acute) than in the Christian aspects of British education. A much greater conflict was likely between Islamic views and the technocratic, utilitarian and secular character of education in post-independence India.

The conflict between views of worthwhile knowledge contained in British colonial education and those with indigenous origins has been acute over questions of whether Indian schools should transmit specifically Western knowlege (language, religion, literature, history and expressive arts) or that derived from Indian culture. But British essentialism and Hindu traditions (and to some extent those of Islam) have coincided in their emphasis on moral, humanistic and spiritual knowledge (though Islamic views are less elitist than those of essentialism and Hinduism). British essentialism has taken a firm root in India in part because colonial values coincided with those of indigenous traditions.

Attempts to make the curriculum both more democratically accessible as in Gandhi's schemes or more economically relevant (as in the pragmatic and polytechnical views which have had some influence in post-independence India) have been met by the obstacle of an elitist and humanist view of knowledge which derives mainly from British colonialism but which has some support in older indigenous traditions.

As in other countries, it has been teachers, both in schools and in higher education, who have been the strongest supporters of the retention of these traditional views of the curriculum.

For which students?

A British view of knowledge has prevailed in India in respect to elite education especially at upper secondary and higher levels. Yet political and educational aims since independence in 1947 have been to democratize educational access especially at elementary (and basic adult) levels. Success in providing mass elementary schooling in recent years has led to similar pressures to open up access to lower secondary schooling. The more access to education at lower levels is widened, the more difficult it becomes to justify an essentialist curriculum.

But the expansion of provision has not been even or universal. There is stringent selection of pupils for every level of education beyond the most elementary, whether this selection is carried out formally through examinations or informally through differing economic capabilities of pupils and their parents to support attendance at higher levels of schooling. In these conditions of savage selection and premature withdrawal, the upper levels of the education system still dominate the character of schooling at lower levels. Even if political will could challenge the continued dominance of the essentialist curriculum at lower levels of schooling, the nature of the selective process would act as a major obstacle.

ELEMENTARY EDUCATION

The 1950 Indian Constitution asserted that there should be universal, free and compulsory education for 6–14 year-olds within ten years. At that time full elementary schooling was provided for only 43 per cent of 6–11 year-olds. In the course of the 1970s, universal elementary education (for the 6–11 age group) was achieved in about half the twenty-one states. The average for this age group for India as a whole was 87 per cent in 1982 (India, 1984). But almost 40 per cent of 'scheduled' caste children and 56 per cent of those from 'scheduled' tribes were out of school in 1980 (India, 1980). Enrolment ratios for girls aged 6–11 (69 per cent in 1982) were lower than for boys.

Low levels of enrolment in elementary schooling were associated less with low initial entry rates of 6 year-olds to school than with high levels of drop-out and repetition. So, only 44 per cent of the relevant age group was enrolled in middle schools (Grades VI–VIII in 1982) (India, 1984). The major problems were to persuade those who initially entered school to complete the elementary school course and to help them to achieve levels of performance which could merit promotion to higher grades.

Elementary schools have not been controlled by federal government either during the colonial or post-independence period. Elementary schools developed through indigenous private initiative – usually on a fee-paying basis – in the eighteenth and nineteenth centuries. There had been also some Christian missionary schools but their impact has not been great.

When the colonial government began to fund elementary education in the late nineteenth century, effective control lay with district and municipal education authorities which provided most of the resources. Since 1947, each of the twenty-one states has had control of elementary education and theoretically is responsible for provision. In practice, the extent of provision is often a local matter and in many cases is left to private bodies which charge fees.

Little attention has been given to developing or reforming the elementary school curriculum. Widespread curriculum change has been obstructed by the effective control of elementary schooling at local level and the existence of large numbers of private schools together with the paucity of state funds and the low standing of teachers. The rapid expansion of enrolments in the 1960s and 1970s also meant that less emphasis was given to the content of elementary schooling than to its provision.

Grand aims for the elementary school curriculum have been formulated at federal level as in the 1980–5 National Plan:

The basic objective would stress curriculum as an instrument for inculcating humanistic values, capacity for tolerance, promotion of national integration, scientific attitude and temper and individual capacity for learning from the surrounding world. (p. 355)

But the detailed content of the elementary school curriculum has been determined at state or local level and has been much more limited. In many schools, little more than the three Rs is provided apart from some history and geography and, at middle school level, perhaps a second language and some science.

In practice, the curriculum of elementary schools has been dominated by examinations. Tests which are administered at school or district/municipal level determine promotion of children from one grade to the next and, except in all-through Basic schools, from the five-grade elementary school to the three-grade middle school. The examination to select students for entry to upper secondary education is more usually conducted by state authorities. Such final examinations are more likely to reflect the curriculum priorities of the upper secondary schools than the official aims of elementary or middle schooling.

These examinations are associated not only with high wastage and repetition rates but also with a rigidity and narrowness of teaching which may be confined to coverage of examination-orientated knowledge. They indicate a survival of the priorities of the colonial and immediate post-colonial governments where elementary schools were seen as feeders for secondary schooling even though a small minority of primary school pupils entered secondary education.

The British essentialist tradition of worthwhile knowledge hardly touched elementary schooling. But the failure to institutionalize a strong alternative philosophy – such as Basic Education – has meant that the dominance of the lower levels of education by elite education has not been challenged.

UPPER SECONDARY AND HIGHER EDUCATION

Upper secondary schools (two- or three-grade institutions) have been always directed towards the selection of an elite. The proportion of the 14–17 age group in these schools was only 21 per cent in 1979–80 (compared to 5 per cent in 1950–1) (India, 1981). Entry is controlled either by selective examinations or by the capacity of student's families to pay since in some states the majority of upper secondary schools is private.

Governments have always had elitist aims for these schools. But the purpose of selection has changed since independence in 1947. During the colonial period, secondary schools, modelled on the English public schools, were designed to create an administrative class. Since the 1950 National Economic Plan, there has been an emphasis on the creation of a scientific and technological professional class in line with plans to expand manufacturing industry. The only variation on this plan has been the policy since 1950 that a proportion of secondary places should be reserved for socially disadvantaged groups (especially 'scheduled' castes and tribes).

The curriculum of upper secondary schools has remained relatively static despite changes in purpose since 1950. Conventional subjects such as mathematics, sciences, history and geography are studied independently with a high degree of specialization. While the medium of instruction is usually an Indian language, English is often taught as a second language.

The upper secondary school curriculum is dominated by examinations. The Secondary School Leaving Certificate and the Higher Secondary Certificate are survivals of the colonial period and parallel the old English School Certificate and Higher School Certificate. School examinations are organized by universities. They concentrate on individual subjects and each student usually specializes in four of them. Assessment is external to the school.

The outcome is the reinforcement of a standardized academic curriculum.

Higher education institutions tend to dominate the character of the whole education system. There are over 100 universities or university status institutions in India. While only 4 per cent of the 17–23 age group attended university level institutions in 1979–80, Indian universities have vast student populations. Enrolments, since the late nineteenth century, have been much higher than governments have deemed desirable.

When universities developed in the nineteenth century, London University rather than Oxford or Cambridge was the model. Universities in India became federations of associated colleges with undergraduate teaching concentrated in the colleges and postgraduate work in the universities. These federations were held together by the control that the university authorities maintained over examinations. These examinations, which were usually external to the teaching institutions, dominated Indian higher education and the curriculum. Those subjects which could be examined by traditional written papers tended to attract the most students. Most frequently these were the humanities (Ashby, 1966).

The large number of students in higher education – over 3 million in 1979–80 – was also associated with large institutions, great variations of standards and high student staff ratios. Such conditions have made the traditional humanities the most feasible subjects of study for relatively poor and under-equipped students in poor-quality institutions with poor resources in which standards are enforced by external examinations for which failure rates are high.

The response of the Union government to the growth of poor-quality higher education, both before and after 1947, was to develop a few high-quality institutions often concentrating on scientific and technological subjects. These high-quality institutions, which are supported mainly by Union rather than state resources, often have a very high reputation in teaching and research. But the typical higher education student still follows predominantly humanities courses at poor-quality institutions.

The essentialist view of worthwhile knowledge has been reinforced in a limited and distorted form in India by the pattern of educational provision. The savage selection procedures at every level of the education system have strengthened an elitist view of worthwhile knowledge – that it is accessible only to a minority. A highly specialized curriculum at higher levels has not been amenable to change when such change would involve parallel changes in selection procedures. Humanities have retained a strong place in the curriculum of upper secondary and higher education when these subjects have offered greater opportunities for success for poor students in poor institutions.

Curriculum debates

Curriculum debates have focused on three issues. There has been the content and organization of elementary education related especially to the question of Basic Education. There has been the question of the relevance and implications of a 'manpower planning' approach to the content of higher education. There has been also continuing discussion about the place of traditional languages and cultures in the curriculum. In each area there has been a conflict between new curriculum proposals adopted by the Indian government since 1947 and the continued adherence of teachers, particularly university academics, to a view of worthwhile knowledge which was derived from the colonial period.

'BASIC EDUCATION'

Gandhi's Basic Education policy has been official government policy since 1947 and by the mid-1960s almost one third of elementary schools were designated as 'Basic Education' schools. It is still seen as a solution to problems of educating children who will remain as adults in rural communities and whose skills, knowledge and initiative are required to develop these communities. But despite the origins of the 'Basic Education' policy in the Indian nationalist movement and its apparent relevance to contemporary problems, its implementation in India has been limited.

The implementation of Basic Education has met with a number of obstacles. First, most elementary schools (and, indeed, the complete educational experience of most children) have only covered five grades (ages 6–11). These schools have not been able to orientate the curriculum to manual occupations because of the lack of time in a five-year course and the immaturity of students who leave at the age of 11. Similarly, there have been few links between elementary schools and adult education schemes of the kind which could have encouraged attention to manual occupation in the curriculum. Despite national policy rhetoric after 1947 adult education has not developed.

Second, broad government economic strategies have not emphasized the local, rural, self-reliant activities to which Basic Education schemes could relate. The Five Year Plans from 1950 stressed industrial development. Even the government agricultural initiatives of the 1960s – the 'Green Revolution' – concentrated on the application of advanced technology (fertilizers, irrigation, genetically improved strains of seeds) by central agencies rather than local initiatives. The manual skills associated with Basic Education – particularly occupations such as spinning and weaving – seemed irrevelant even to rural economic development.

Third, while the people of India remain predominantly rural, the poor populations of large cities such as Calcutta were not touched by the original rural conception of Basic Education. It is the youth of these cities to whom more recent government policies have been directed especially in the manual training schemes for young people beyond the age of 14 who will work in urban occupations (India, 1980). The areas of economic and social concern which the Basic Education movement addressed in the 1930s and beyond have shifted to some extent from rural to urban areas and from children (aged 6–14) to young adults (aged 14–20 or 25). These work-orientated programmes for young adults entail a more conventional curriculum of literacy and numeracy for pupils in elementary schools.

Another barrier to the implementation of the Basic Education philosophy has been the popular aspirations for social mobility through education. Terminal elementary schooling offers few opportunities for individual social mobility. Elementary education is widely regarded only as a preparation for entry to secondary and higher education which offer greater chances for entry to salaried occupations. Popular pressure is for elementary schooling which is most fully articulated with secondary and higher education.

These obstacles reinforce the resistance or hostility of academics and teachers to a Basic Education curriculum. Their beliefs in the value of a humanities-based education and in a hierarchical relationship between higher and elementary education do not accommodate the idea of an autonomous phase of Basic Education which is guided by a different philosophy. The local community orientation of the Basic Education curriculum is not compatible with traditional views of valued knowledge.

ELITE EDUCATION AND TECHNOLOGICAL DEVELOPMENT

The government industrialization strategy since the 1950 Five Year Plan has been state intervention to plan and control much industrial activity, particularly in areas such as steel, coal, heavy engineering and chemicals. Government intervention to align the education system to the 'manpower' needs of these industrial enterprises was a concomitant of financial support and managerial control.

The educational changes designed to meet these economic aims concentrated largely on the highest levels of the system. Research and high-level teaching institutions were created in areas such as science, technology and management. Nine such institutions have been declared by government to be of national importance. These high-level foundations have had a high reputation and generous financial support from the Union government. They have attracted very able students who subsequently enter high-level managerial positions (Sancheti, 1986). These institutions also have produced research of internationally recognized excellence which has relevance to India's economic development, as, for instance, in the 'Green Revolution' (Schultz, 1982).

But the revolution at the top has not percolated to lower levels of the education system. The largest group of students, especially in less prestigious universities, have continued to take humanities courses of study. In 1979, almost 50 per cent of students in higher education followed humanities courses compared to 25 per cent science courses and less than 10 per cent engineering and medicine combined.

Proposals from the Union (federal) government that science teaching should be strengthened and expanded by, for instance, the provision of 'science' kits (India, 1980) have been obstructed by the poor economic situations of most schools and their students and by the continued rapid expansion of upper secondary and higher education in response to popular demand.

Government has also placed emphasis on the development of manual craft teaching (for skilled industrial occupations) at secondary level. But this innovation has been limited to a few areas (India, 1980) and to the older (and numerically limited) secondary 'trade' schools. Such institutions are expensive and have not been widely spread.

The technological orientation of a few centres of excellence at higher education level has been isolated from the rest of the education system. Attempts to extend technical education more widely have failed. The supremacy of the essentialist tradition has not been challenged.

INDIGENOUS LANGUAGE AND CULTURE

There were debates in India, both before and after independence, about the introduction of indigenous Indian culture into the curriculum to replace that of British colonial rulers. Two main arguments have been advanced for the indigenization of the content of the curriculum. First, it is argued that the content of education should reflect the culture of the student and the student's community. Otherwise, the transmission of an alien culture in school creates psychological and social conflicts for students. Second, it is claimed, the school curriculum should help to create and develop a sense of national identity and solidarity in newly independent states. Indigenous languages, history, arts, geography and other subjects in the school curriculum can contribute to cementing national unity.

In India since 1947, religion has not been a major issue in the school curriculum when 84 per cent of the population is Hindu and, of other religions, only Islam (11 per cent) has a very substantial number of followers. Hinduism has been a family-centred religion. The demand for a Hindu-based public education has not been strong.

The question of the indigenization of the content of most conventional school subjects has been resolved reasonably successfully. Though colonial education might have been associated with a curriculum of English and European history, literature and arts, since independence the content of most syllabuses has been drawn from the Indian culture and environment. This movement was aided not only by the indigenization of schoolteachers and examination boards but also of publishing. Since 1961 the National Council for Educational Research and Training has produced model school textbooks in which the content reflects Indian conditions (Singh, 1985).

The language question has been prominent since the beginning of colonial rule and still affects debates about the curriculum. Elite schools and universities which prepared students for salaried posts in the colonial administration used English as the medium so English was predominant in prestigious institutions at the time of independence.

Non-European languages had been used in some areas of education throughout the colonial period. The traditional colleges which received some encouragement from the colonial authorities since the late eighteenth century used Sanskrit (the classical written language) for Hindus and either Persian or Arabic for Muslims. These languages had developed literatures. But they were not vernaculars used in everyday life. The popular Indian languages were used to a large extent in elementary education though there were also pressures to adopt English to prepare students for entry to higher level institutions.

The Indian nationalist movement from the nineteenth century put great emphasis on the use of Hindi as the language of administration and of education. But Hindi was the mother tongue of only about 30 per cent of the population in 1947, mainly in North India. There were around 800 other languages used as mother tongues though the fourteen Indian languages recognized by the 1950 constitution (apart from the classical written language of Sanskrit) covered most of the population.

The main opposition to the use of Hindi came from the speakers of languages such as Tamil (7 per cent) in the south or Bengali (8 per cent) in the east. Non-Hindi speakers feared that the adoption of Hindi as the national language of independent India would give an advantage to Hindi mother-tongue speakers in the competition for state employment (das Gupta, 1970). Some non-Hindi groups supported the continuance of English as a 'neutral' official language, especially the speakers of Dravidian languages such as Tamil, the linguistic structures of which were quite different from Hindi.

The solution adopted in the 1950 constitution was to make Hindi the official language of India but to allow the use of English in all-India matters for an interim period up to 1965. The other languages recognized in the constitution could be used officially at state level.

In education, the 'three language formula' was adopted in 1956. Elementary education is conducted in the mother tongue of pupils as far as possible but the state language and Hindi may be introduced as subjects. Secondary and, to some extent, higher education institutions use the state language and, if this is not Hindi, then Hindi should be taught as a second language.

This language formula has respected local and individual cultural identities. It has been aided by the size of the populations involved. Almost all of the officially recognized languages have at least 10 million speakers and most have a substantial traditional literature. The problems of using in schools languages which have few speakers and a limited literature have not been encountered in India to the extent found elsewhere.

But there are difficulties for curriculum development arising from this language policy. Students in middle and upper secondary schools especially may spend considerable time and effort in learning languages which may have different linguistic structures and sometimes different scripts. This has been associated with a mechanical approach to learning in Indian education. The linguistic demands on pupils may deepen their alienation from the content to be learned.

English has survived as an unofficial *lingua franca* both among elites in the wider society and in prestigious educational institutions. However, this survival may be linked to other factors besides the strength of the colonial tradition. It reflects the resistance of non-Hindi areas to the use of Hindi as a *lingua franca*. It results also from the emphasis on high-level scientific and technological education contained in government policies since 1950. The literature available for such studies is most easily accessible in English and imported books and journals are significant at this level (Altbach, 1985).

It is sometimes claimed that the English language is the channel by which British educational traditions and influence are maintained in former colonies. This assertion does not stand up in India. Most education occurs in Indian languages and this indigenization of language medium has been accompanied by localization of curriculum content. The survival of the essentialist view of worthwhile knowledge in Indian education has not been a result simply of the persistence of the use of the English language.

Curriculum control and management

What conditions support the continued predominance of a British essentialist curriculum in Indian education despite pressures on the one hand to introduce Basic Education and on the other to relate the content of education to the demands for scientific and technological relevance? This question may be explored in terms of the positions taken by various groups and organizations that influence the curriculum. As in previous chapters, the official structure of curriculum decision-making may be contrasted with the actual power of various influential groups. But another element which should also be considered in the case of India is the influence of foreign organizations so that the issues of dependence, discussed earlier, may be examined.

THE OFFICIAL STRUCTURE OF CURRICULUM DECISION-MAKING

India has a federal system of government. There is a division of power between the federal or Union government based in New Delhi and the governments of each of the twenty-one states. Some of the major issues of curriculum change in India may be explored in the Union versus state division.

Each of the states has a parliament elected by universal suffrage and a strong bureaucracy including a state education department. State parliaments may enact different educational laws so that, in 1980, twelve had legislation making elementary education compulsory while the others did not. Over 75 per cent of the finance of public education is provided by state governments. The states have formal control over the curriculum of elementary and secondary schools which is strengthened both by their legislative power and their control over financial resources.

State governments determine the curriculum of elementary and secondary schools through legislative and administrative decision. The subjects for study for each grade are decided by state education departments. State textbook agencies determine which books shall be used, usually by commissioning and publishing the textbooks themselves or, less frequently, by licensing those of commercial publishers (Altbach, 1985). School examinations are nominally controlled by state examination boards except those concerning internal promotion within schools which are a matter usually for individual schools or local districts and municipalities. Teachers are employed by state education departments and are thus subject to supervision in their teaching by state officials.

The influence of the Union government is limited. It produces broad advisory documents contained, for instance, in the quinquennial Economic Plans or special reports such as that of the 1964 Education Commission (Kothari Report). Such documents often deal with curriculum matters. Despite the central government subsidy to state education (which is mainly designed to help poorer areas to catch up with the better-off), these recommendations cannot be implemented without active state government support.

The Union government does have specific powers in limited areas. The Union government is responsible directly for financing and administering six central universities (out of 132 in India) and a number of other institutions of higher education such as the five institutes of technology and certain institutions which have been deemed to be of national importance. As a result, the Union government controls the most prestigious institutions at the highest level of the education system but these bodies provide education for a tiny fraction even of higher education students.

Union government influence over other aspects of education is achieved indirectly. A University Grants Committee was established in 1956 to co-ordinate policy towards universities throughout India. This co-ordinates federal funding for all universities though it has less direct control over state universities. The division of power between government and university interests in this body is not clear.

Technical education is co-ordinated by the All-India Council for Technical Education and 60 per cent of the funds for this sector are provided by the Union government. There are also national councils which advise and provide model schemes on educational research and training, science education and teacher education. These model schemes, particularly model textbooks, are adopted and copied frequently by state education departments.

The Union government also exerts control over higher education and school examinations in the nine Union territories which do not enjoy the full autonomy of the states. The Union government also controls some 300 Central Schools throughout India which is its only direct involvement in school-level education.

THE POLITICS OF THE CURRICULUM

As in other countries, the main groups who engage in struggles to determine the curriculum of schools in India include politicians and administrators at both central and regional level in educational and non-educational departments of government. There are also the teachers, both in higher education and in schools. There are the consumers – students and their families. There are also employers. In India particular attention may be paid to central government as a source of potent demands for curriculum change and to university teachers as the main defenders of the essentialist view of worthwhile knowledge.

Politicians at both Union and state level in India wish to adapt the education system so that it can contribute to economic development. They hope that education can foster feelings of national or regional identity and they look to education to maximize social opportunities.

Since 1947, the Union government has been committed to a strategy of centrally planned and nationally self-reliant economic development. This has been expressed in the Five Year Plans which have set out educational priorities in the light of economic goals and of the process of 'manpower planning' which has been pursued since 1947 (Verma, 1985).

The priority of government has been to develop high-level scientific and technological education and middle-level technician and technical craft training. This has been implemented through Union government support for prestigious higher education institutions and for post-middle school institutions (such as industrial training institutes) specializing in areas relevant to industrial development.

These Union government initiatives have helped to make scientific and technological studies the most pretigious courses in higher education. At the highest levels, the old dominance of the humanities has been supplanted by a view giving higher status to scientific subjects. But the separation of Union government initiatives from those of the states (or in some cases the incapacity of the Union government to enforce its views on the states) as well as the very small number of students attending prestigious Union institutions of higher education has meant that this scientific and economic emphasis has not permeated the majority of educational institutions, even including most universities.

Politicians at state level may or may not support Union government priorities depending on the political orientation of state governments and on powerful regional and local interests. Obstructive and particularistic attitudes may prevail at state level. State-level politicians may be responsive to popular demands for more education but they hope to provide it as cheaply as possible. Grand schemes for education related to industrialization may have less appeal at state level especially when the states are not involved in the schemes for centres of scientific excellence. The domination of funding of scientific and technical education by the Union government gives state politicians the excuse to opt out of this programme.

Educational administrators at state level (for it is at state level that most educational administrators operate) have not been noted for innovative attitudes to education and the curriculum. The bureaucratization of administration discourages lower-level administrators, including inspectors, from supporting attempts at change. The tradition of subordination and routinization, which is broken only by the occasional emergence of dynamic leaders, has a highly conservative effect (Eisemon, 1984). State-level politicians and educational bureaucrats are not the main ideological defenders of the educational status quo. They are relatively passive preservers of administrative traditions.

It is the university teachers who have been seen as the main proponents of an essentialist view of worthwhile knowledge in the school curriculum. Their attitude of support for the humanities in the curriculum has been associated with the isolation of Indian academics from international developments in higher education (Shils, 1969). They preserve views which were dominant among their Western colleagues many years earlier. It has been suggested also that the view of worthwhile knowledge derived historically from Britain is supported by many academics because this is associated with the more general social status of universities and university teachers (Eisemon, 1984). In this case, respect for the essentialist view of knowledge may be maintained in a wider section of the Indian social and political elite. But it is the university teachers who are its active defenders in the education system.

The influence of university teachers over the school curriculum is maintained by a number of means. The most significant is the control that these academics have over the examinations that allow entry to universities. The specialized orientation of these examinations then affects the curriculum at lower levels of education since the utlimate purpose of schooling for many teachers is to help their students to attain university entrance.

The curriculum control of university academics is reinforced by a number of conditions. Central government, as in other countries, often calls upon them to make recommendations on the organization of schooling. The weakness of state governments in curriculum matters, reflecting not only lack of positive policies but also the high proportion of private secondary schools and undergraduate colleges in many states, gives power to university academics almost by default.

University academics have also held considerable influence over the curriculum because a strong schoolteacher curriculum lobby has not emerged to challenge them. Elementary school teachers have been constrained by their low status and pay from being a positive force in curriculum politics. Secondary school teachers are restricted by the dominance of external examinations and are under pressure from students to conform to examination requirements. But, as in other countries, secondary school teachers often share the curriculum preferences of the university academics who taught them.

Students at secondary and higher education level in India have been noted for their activism. Student action has been directed frequently at the administration of examinations and is expressed either in individual cheating or in mass protests. However, this activism tends to reinforce existing curriculum content since even the slightest change in examination practices is met with protest. The social rewards for educational success measured by examination performance are so great that the participants in the competition strongly resist changes in examinations or in the curriculum content the examiners test which may worsen their prospects in the competition.

Foreign influences have had a relatively marginal impact on Indian education since 1947 especially compared to other ex-colonial Third World countries. Most sectors of the educational system have been completely independent of foreign aid since 1947. There are very few expatriates working at any level of the education system and few Indians go abroad for further study when compared to the size of the Indian population.

Foreign influences in recent years have been greatest in the elite Union-controlled higher education institutions where teachers and researchers maintain international contacts. Some of these institutions were established through co-operation with foreign agencies – particularly universities, governments and foundations. Patterns of course organization may follow the imported model and foreign texts are used. Indeed, the policy of developing scientific education to achieve industrialization entailed close contact with foreign educational agencies in highly industrialized countries.

These foreign-influenced elite institutions have had relatively little impact on the rest of the education system of India. Most innovations that have occurred since 1947 – such as the development of the use of Indian languages, or the localization of the content of many school subjects, or, indeed, the Basic Education policy – have been Indian in origin and execution. The size and diversity of the Indian education system as much as a deliberate policy of achieving self-reliance since 1947 have made foreign borrowing unnecessary.

On the other hand, residual influences of former colonial educational practices have remained strongly entrenched. This is seen particularly in the predominance of British colonial views of an essentialist curriculum. Such a survival reflects, however, the maintenance of attitudes over generations and the self-interest of certain groups working within the education system in maintaining the educational status quo rather than a continuing dependence.

Conclusion

The Indian education system has provided both a model and a warning to other Third World countries that have experienced British colonial rule. It has been seen as an example to copy since India has created a small number of excellent and creative educational institutions at the highest level which have been geared to economic needs. The content of the curriculum has been changed to reflect Indian culture. Indian languages have been used in education both to reflect local culture and to create national unity through a national Indian language. Perhaps most significantly, reliance on foreign aid has been avoided. Except at the very highest levels, Indian education is self-sufficient.

The development of education in independent India has provided a warning in that mass elementary education (and mass adult education) was achieved very slowly and still has not become universal. The curriculum of secondary and most higher education is dominated by academic subjects which have little relevance to the future occupations of most students. The idea of Basic Education emerged in India but its implementation has been very limited.

Above all, the persistence in India of views of worthwhile knowledge associated with the colonial regime in a country which has achieved a high degree of educational autonomy from foreign influences and which has enormous human resources to achieve educational change suggests that the colonial curriculum philosophy may not disappear in other countries simply because external dependence is removed.

167

Further reading

Altbach, Philip G., 'Centre and periphery in knowledge distribution in the Third World: the case of India', in Edgar B. Gumbert (ed.), *A World of Strangers* (Atlanta, Ga: Georgia State University, 1985), pp. 69–90.

Ashby, Eric, *Universities: British, Indian, African* (London: Weidenfeld & Nicolson, 1966).

Basu, A., 'Hinduism and Buddhism', in George Z. F. Bereday and Joseph A. Lauwerys (eds), *The Yearbook of Education 1957* (London: Evans, 1957), pp. 93–112.

das Gupta, J., *Language Conflict and National Development: Group Politics and National Language Policy in India* (Bombay: Oxford University Press, 1970).

Eisemon, Thomas O., 'Scientific life in Indian and African universities: a comparative study of peripherality in science', *Comparative Education Review*, vol. 25, no. 2 (1981), pp. 164–82.

Eisemon, Thomas O., 'Autonomy and authority in an Indian university', *Compare*, vol. 14, no. 1 (1984), pp. 59–67.

India, *Sixth Five Year Plan 1980–1985* (New Delhi: Government of India Planning Commission, 1980).

India, *India: A Reference Manual* (New Delhi: Ministry of Information and Broadcasting, 1981).

India, *Statistical Manual* (New Delhi: Ministry of Information and Broadcasting, 1984).

Macaulay, Lord, 'Minute on education in India', *Calcutta University Commission 1917–1919 Report*, Vol. 6 ([1835], pp. 8–17).

Mayhew, Arthur, *The Education of India* (London: Faber & Gwyer, 1926).

Nurullah, Syed, and Naik, J. P., *A History of Education in India* (Bombay: Macmillan, 1951).

Sancheti, Neelu, 'Educational dependency: an Indian case study in comparative perspective' (PhD thesis, University of London, 1986).

Schultz, Theodore W., 'The value of education in low income countries: an economist's view', in Bikas C. Sanyal (ed.), *Higher Education and the New International Order* (London: Frances Pinter, 1982), pp. 42–62.

Shils, Edward, 'The academic profession in India', *Minerva*, vol. 7, no. 2, (1969) pp. 345–72.

Singh, Tejeshwar, 'Publishing in India', in Philip G. Altbach *et al.* (eds), *Publishing in the Third World* (London: Mansell, 1985), pp. 111–30.

Tibawi, A. L., 'The philosophy of Muslim education', in George Z. F. Bereday and Joseph A. Lauwerys (eds), *The Yearbook of Education 1957* (London: Evans, 1957), pp. 80–92.

Verma, M. C., 'Review of skilled-manpower forecasts in India', in R. V. Youdi and K. Hinchcliffe (eds), *Forecasting Skilled-Manpower Needs* (Paris: Unesco, 1985), pp. 194–210.

Zachariah, Mathew, 'Education for status improvement: the use of positive discrimination for scheduled castes in India', in Philip G. Altbach, Robert F. Arnove and Gail P. Kelly (eds), *Comparative Education* (New York: Macmillan, 1982), pp. 290–315.

Chapter Eight

Curriculum in Latin America – French encyclopaedic traditions, recent North American influences and 'popular education' alternatives

All Latin American states* fall into the World Bank's category of middle-income economies. None has the absolute and all-engulfing poverty of the lowest-income countries of Africa and Asia but none has yet crossed the boundary into full-scale industrialization. Economies are based upon extraction of minerals and cash crop agriculture for export yet there are pockets of industry. Populations are largely urban; in many countries between 70 per cent and 85 per cent live in towns. In every Latin American country there is a substantial gap between the relative poverty of the mass of the population in rural and urban areas and the life-styles of the professional middle classes who enjoy European and North American standards. Throughout Latin America, the present condition tends to be described as 'under-development' and the aim is 'development' to the standards of industrialized countries.

---

* Latin America is usually defined as comprising those states of Central and South America and the Caribbean which were historically colonies of Spain or (in the case of Brazil) Portugal. The examples given in this chapter are drawn mainly from the eight largest Latin American states: Argentina (population 27 million in 1985), Brazil (135 million), Chile (12 million), Colombia (29 million), Cuba (10 million), Mexico (80 million), Peru (20 million) and Venezuela (17 million).

Latin American countries share a common culture and common historical experience. Their populations are Spanish or Portuguese in origin with varying degrees of mixture with indigenous Indian peoples, the descendants of former African slaves (mainly Brazil) and twentieth-century immigrants from Europe (especially Italy). Apart from Portuguese in Brazil, Spanish is the common language and in most countries, except Peru and Mexico (where Indian languages are spoken by substantial minorities), practically the only language. All have been independent republics since escaping from Spanish or Portuguese control, in most cases in the first thirty years of the nineteenth century.

The education systems of the various Latin American countries also have much in common both in structure and dominant education philosophies. Debates about what kind of education is the most desirable follow a similar pattern in the different countries.

Educational debates centre on three issues. First, there is felt to be a need to create integral nation-states which can achieve the degree of development found in Europe and North America. It was to meet this aim that French models of education were so widely adopted in the nineteenth century. This aim remains prominent though the idea of development has shifted from the political definitions of national identity, administrative efficiency and democratic institutions towards an economic concern with industrialization and the enjoyment of its material fruits.

Second, there is a concern to make education more fully available to the majority of the population. In the nineteenth century, development was to be achieved by the creation of a dynamic and modernizing elite. Education concentrated on elite training. Later twentieth-century concerns have been to provide equality of educational opportunity. This aim has led to demands for an educational philosophy which is appropriate to mass education.

Third, there has been a concern to respect the autonomous development of communities of ordinary people. More recent 'popular education' schemes have emphasized local choice and local identity rather than the centralization and uniformity associated with the French encyclopaedic pattern.

What knowledge?

Three views of worthwhile knowledge predominate in contemporary Latin America. An encyclopaedic view was adopted along with other French institutions in the early nineteenth century. Encyclopaedism has been challenged in recent years as the institutionally dominant view by curriculum theories imported from the USA especially those stressing behavioural objectives. There has also been a popular education movement which emphasizes knowledge which will develop a community solidarity among the mass of the people. Encyclopaedism still predominates but is threatened by these other two movements from opposite ideological wings.

The encyclopaedist view entered Latin America as a result of the wars of liberation of the late eighteenth and early nineteenth centuries. The new republics derived little from the former colonial connection. The monarchies of Spain and Portugal were seen to be ideologically bankrupt as were the social and political systems that accompanied them. Education had been provided largely by missionaries whose first concern had been conversion of native peoples. When the missionaries were expelled they left few educational institutions. Secondary and higher education were undeveloped.

French ideas were adopted wholesale by the revolutionary republican elite. Their members had been deeply influenced by French revolutionary and enlightenment ideals whilst in exile in Europe planning the wars of liberation. The new republics were governed by an educated, professional middle class whose members were seen to have the function of modernizing new nations like the Jacobins of revolutionary France. The new ideas involved the introduction of a centralized and professional state administration which would carry out plans for modernization. The education system was developed to train new cadres of leaders and administrators. Emphasis was placed on the development of secondary and higher education. The new institutions were modelled on those of France. The content of secondary and higher education as in France was determined by central authorities and consisted of a standardized curriculum.

The encyclopaedist view was adopted because it appeared to offer the best training for future administrators and professionals. There was a tendency to adopt the form of the encyclopaedist view – a standardized and uniform curriculum and central control

– rather than the guiding intellectual principle of rationalism. The utility principle had some influence in states where a professional middle class was seen to be the agent of progress. So vocational studies predominated at higher levels (though vocational studies, as in France, were approached through general, academic subjects). But this vocationalism, even in the late twentieth century, concentrated on traditional high-status occupations, most particularly medicine.

Latin American state education systems were established before mass elementary education developed in France and other European countries. Distinctive philosophies of elementary schooling did not emerge. Instead elementary schooling was seen as a relatively unimportant stage which merely prepared pupils for the crucial levels of secondary and higher education.

There was a desire to borrow and copy foreign models motivated by beliefs that the best institutions were those which came from abroad rather than being developed at home – a tendency repeated in the later twentieth century in relation to the USA. Dependency in Latin America tended to mean a psychological subservience of national elites towards what were seen to be the most civilized or later the most developed countries in the world first in Europe and later in North America.

The behaviourist attack on encyclopaedic dominance came with increased penetration from the USA particularly after 1960. The curriculum objectives approach as proposed by its most influential exponents such as Bloom involved the specification of cognitive and affective aims and the design of the content and methods of teaching to achieve their implementation. In Latin America after 1960 (or at least in those countries with strong educational connections with the USA) curriculum guides issued by ministries of education were drawn up according to behavioural objectives. Broad cognitive or social aims were specified and then the content was organized according to these objectives. Textbooks were also written to conform to these plans and assessment on a yearly or weekly basis related to the objectives.

This widespread movement may be exemplified by elementary school science courses introduced in Chile in 1965. The courses and textbooks were structured round cognitive objectives such as observation, classification, measurement and communication. Information and experiments in science were offered to develop these skills. Affective objectives were later introduced in material stressing how the qualities of honesty, impartiality and collaboration could be developed in the process of scientific research (King, 1986). It may be noted, however, that this pedagogy involved nationally standard textbooks containing standard information and even standard questions for student assessment.

The adoption of a behavioural objectives model of curriculum planning differed substantially in some ways from older practices but was not completely inconsistent with the encyclopaedist tradition. The differences were that the specification of curriculum content was determined by social and psychological aims rather than by the rational structures of the subjects to be taught. There was an element of American pragmatism in this change. But the specification of objectives was not done at school or class teacher level relating to the particular needs of small groups of students. Curriculum objectives for particular subjects were decided at national level and the relevant content was also applied uniformly at national level. Standardization and uniformity, consistent with the encyclopaedist tradition, remained. What had changed was the substitution of intellectual, subject-based objectives by broader social and psychological aims.

The popular education movement did, however, diverge very sharply and completely from the encyclopaedist tradition. Central to its philosophy was a rejection of standardized knowledge handed down from above. Instead valuable knowledge was what emerged from the reflections of ordinary, poor people about their experience and their condition. Pedagogy involved the search for deeper understanding by ordinary people sharing their experience in conditions of communal solidarity.

The drive behind the popular education philosophy and movement was the great gulf between the national elites of the republics and the mass of poor rural and urban shanty-town dwellers. Latin American republics had adopted a strategy of reform from top downwards. This strategy had not worked especially since, for most of the nineteenth and twentieth centuries in most countries, the original parliamentary government system was replaced by socially conservative or reactionary dictatorships.

The popular education movement did not derive from indigenous cultural, religious, or linguistic traditions which contrasted with the alien cultural patterns of the elite as in many Third World countries in Africa or Asia. Only in Peru and, to a much lesser extent, Mexico did social class divisions tend to coincide with linguistic, cultural and racial divisions – a division between Indian-

and Spanish-origin peoples (van den Berghe, 1978).

In Latin America as a whole, except perhaps in highly Euro-peanized Argentina, popular education philosophies were based on a community identity of shared poverty of peoples who shared language (Spanish or Portugese) and religion (Catholicism) with the elite though in some states a sizeable proportion was more likely to be racially distinguished by its *mestizo* caste (European mixed with Indian or African) from the exclusively European-origin elite.

There had been governmental attempts to bridge this gulf between masses and elites through education in the nineteenth and early twentieth centuries. Sarmiento who was in charge of government schools in Argentina between 1856 and 1861 and was later president of the republic looked to the USA and Horace Mann for models of a genuine mass education system. There was official interest in Dewey's ideas of a curriculum for mass schooling in Brazil in the 1920s and 1930s. But these develop-ments were isolated in the overall history of governmental neglect both of popular education and mass social improvement for most of the nineteenth and twentieth centuries.

Internationally the best-known exponent of Latin American popular education may be Paulo Freire. But this movement began much earlier than Freire and was reflected in practice in a wide range of Latin American countries. Mariategui in Peru in the 1920s put forward schemes for education for liberation which had much in common with Freire in the 1960s and 1970s. Schools on these lines had been established in Bolivia at this time though as short-lived experiments (Avalos, 1982). Freire was the publicist of an established movement with deep roots.

Freire stressed that true education would be for liberation. When the mass of the poor understood and could articulate their social and political position they could then change it (Freire, 1972). Conventional education (on encyclopaedic lines) was rejected as a 'banking' concept whereby a socially meaningless or oppressive body of knowledge was transmitted from above. A liberating pedagogy would start from the experience of the poor and education was a process of helping the poor to articulate this experience.

Yet there was more to popular education than a politically revolutionary programme which only a few would or could adopt. Popular education was based on shared affection and social reciprocation among groups of people, so the key concepts were friendship, affection, giving oneself, forgiveness. The content of education was almost irrelevant since what mattered in education was social reciprocity and solidarity (King, 1986). There were close relationships between popular education movements in Latin America and the popular and reforming wing of the Catholic Church. In these cases, schools were churches and churches were schools.

The popular education movement was expressed in a myriad of small-scale private educational initiatives through much of Latin America, sometimes involving primary school children but often focusing, like Freire, on adults. Governments, as in Mexico in the 1970s, attempted to incorporate a popular education philosophy in governmental adult education programmes (Posner, 1985). But these official adventures no more captured the popular education movement than political revolutionaries did in other circumstances.

The relative strengths and impact of these competing views of worthwhile knowledge – encyclopaedic, behaviourist and populist – on the education systems of Latin America can be explored initially in an examination of educational structures and patterns of provision.

For which students?

Three points characterize educational provision in Latin America. First, primary education expanded in the 1950s and 1960s so that it became available for the majority of children. But the upward movement of enrolment rates became stuck at around 75–80 per cent of the age group in 1970 and they have not moved significantly since then in most countries. A large minority (in some countries the majority) of children do not complete elementary schooling.

Second, schooling at secondary level has grown so that almost half the age group is enrolled in most countries. Provision has expanded sufficiently for governments to try to reorientate the aims of secondary education away from exclusive preparation for higher education and towards the education of pupils who will fill middle- and lower middle-level occupations. But the growth has not gone beyond a critical stage where the majority of students and their parents cease to see secondary schooling mainly as preparation for university entrance.

Third, there has been a massive expansion of higher education which has meant that between 10 per cent and over 20 per cent of the relevant age group attend institutions of higher education, a proportion which is greater in most Latin American states than in many countries of Europe including Britain. A large proportion of total educational expenditure is devoted to higher education. Most students do not gain posts traditionally seen to be commensurate with higher education.

These pressures have encouraged governments to adopt policies which attempt to make the primary school curriculum responsive to the interests of the local community so that the neglected primary education drop-outs are brought back into the system. Throughout Latin America there have been government attempts to produce 'diversified' upper secondary schooling which will weaken the university/secondary school link. Attempts have been made also to introduce new short-cycle forms of higher education which will provide alternatives to the traditional university.

Each of these new policies involves some attack on traditionally dominant encyclopaedist views of worthwhile knowledge. However, there are constraints contained in both popular demand and institutional conservatism which threaten the achievement of each of these policies. These constraints prevent a major reduction in the encyclopaedic influence.

ELEMENTARY SCHOOLING

Elementary education has been perhaps the sector most neglected by governments in Latin America throughout the nineteenth and twentieth centuries. Though legislation making elementary schooling compulsory was introduced in most states in the nineteenth or early twentieth centuries, the actual provision of places did not make this enforceable until the 1960s. When attempts were made to make primary schooling universal, the traditional weaknesses of the system made this objective difficult to achieve.

Nineteenth-century legislation in most states made elementary schooling the responsibility of central government. In practice, provision was often left to municipalities and districts in contrast to central or regional government provision of secondary and higher education. Local responsibility for the establishment and financing of elementary schools produced uneven provision especially in poorer rural areas and in rapidly growing urban shanty towns.

Inadequate financing was matched by poor-quality teaching. Colombia, Mexico and Venezuela had less than 50 per cent qualified primary school teachers in 1960 while Brazil, Chile and Peru had less than 70 per cent (Gimeno, 1983). Even qualified primary teachers had low status and conditions. In most countries, primary school teacher training was provided in secondary school level institutions which, however, attracted mainly students who had failed to gain acceptance to the general, academic *liceos*.

After the conference organized by Unesco in Santiago de Chile in 1962, Latin American countries committed themselves to the achievement of universal primary schooling by 1970. But from a position of about 50 per cent enrolment in the 1950s, the actual proportions of primary-age children in school by 1980 in most countries was between 75 per cent and 80 per cent. Only Argentina and Chile, the two countries with traditionally the highest levels of educational development in Latin America, together with Mexico, Peru, and Cuba (which had a strongly supported mass schooling campaign in the 1960s), had achieved near universality.

The deficiencies of elementary schooling in Latin America in the 1980s are no longer those of physical provision. Only in remote rural areas, where three- or four-grade schools still exist, is full primary schooling unavailable. In all major countries, except Brazil and Colombia, most primary school teachers have had full training, which now occurs at upper secondary level (or in short-cycle higher education) in most countries. Almost all children enter primary schooling. Underprovision is concentrated on the drop-outs who fail to complete primary education. In the mid-1970s, between 30 per cent and 40 per cent of entrants failed to complete full primary education with Brazil (70 per cent) and Colombia (63 per cent) significantly worse than the others (Gimeno, 1983).

It has been argued that the high wastage rate in primary schooling is a product both of the poverty of parents who cannot sustain their children throughout full primary schooling and of the nature of the curriculum which discourages many from continuing. Primary school curricula have been determined by national ministries of education in most Latin American countries even where the actual provision of places is a local responsibility.

Curriculum content has been standardized. There has been an emphasis on pupils acquiring knowledge of conventional academic subjects to a standard required for entry to traditional secondary schools. Pupils who fail to reach certain levels of attainment are required to repeat grades and it is these grade repeaters who constitute a high proportion of drop-outs, largely from poorer and socially marginal families.

The weaknesses of the traditional primary curriculum can be associated with the survival of an encyclopaedic philosophy. Three kinds of reform strategies have been proposed. There have been injunctions that teacher training should pay more attention to helping teachers to understand the social backgrounds of poorer pupils, as in the 1971 education law in Brazil. This approach does not question the content of the curriculum but emphasizes the need for teachers to try to discover and overcome social obstacles to its acquisition by pupils.

Second, some governments have tried to institutionalize the 'popular' education movement which allows local communities to determine the content of the curriculum by reference to local cultures. The outstanding example of this approach was under the radical military government of Peru after 1968. However, even under more conservative governments, there has been a myriad of popular education initiatives undertaken outside the auspices of government by voluntary organizations, frequently under the umbrella of the Catholic Church.

The third strategy has been a more limited version of the Peruvian reform which has been widely adopted by governments in the 1970s and 1980s. The 1972 Peruvian education law aimed to replace the five-grade primary school by nine-grade 'Basic Education' for children aged 6–15. 'Basic Education' would provide a complete schooling for the majority of children before they entered work. The second element of the reform which was adopted elsewhere was that the curriculum would be specific to individual schools, would reflect local cultures and economic needs and would be constructed in consultation with parents and the local community.

The 'Basic Education' strategy has been adopted in other countries, as in, for instance, the 1980 education law in Venezuela. It has drawn support from international bodies such as Unesco and is based originally on Gandhi's schemes of the 1930s (see Chapter 7). It does represent a major attack on the encyclopaedic tradition of the curriculum in that central determination and uniformity of curriculum content are rejected and the domination of primary school learning by the requirements of higher-level institutions is challenged.

But, as in India, there are major obstacles to the implementation of Basic Education. Educational administrators and teachers have not easily relinquished the encyclopaedic view of a standardized and externally orientated curriculum. Parents hope to use primary schooling to allow their children to enter secondary and higher education which brings higher social rewards. Large numbers of socially marginal people have little faith in governments and turn instead to popular education movements which are often in conflict with government.

SECONDARY SCHOOLING

Before the 1960s, secondary education consisted mainly of academic schools which prepared students for university entrance after a course of around six or seven years. These schools were selective both formally in academic terms and informally in terms of social class. The course terminated in examinations for the state certificate of *bachillerato* which gave access to universities.

The content of the academic secondary school curriculum in most Latin American countries has consisted largely of standardized syllabuses and time allocations for subjects such as Spanish, mathematics, sciences, classics, foreign languages, history and civics. In the nineteenth century, classics, as in France, had the highest prestige but in the course of the twentieth century, mathematics and sciences, again as in France, have become the most prestigious because they give entry to the highest-status university faculties of medicine and engineering. Non-academic studies, except nominally physical education, have had little place in general secondary schooling.

With the expansion of primary education in the 1960s, access to the *liceos* became more open. By 1970, over 85 per cent of pupils completing primary schooling entered *liceos* or their equivalent in most large Latin American countries (Colombia was the exception with 53 per cent) (Gimeno, 1983). Furthermore, the examination for the *bachillerato* became a matter of internal school assessment in most countries so that the proportion of *liceo* graduates qualified for higher education also expanded.

The growth of secondary education increased the number of applicants to universities. The reaction of governments was to introduce a 'diversified' sector of upper (or second-cycle) secondary education. Technical and commercial branches were introduced alongside the traditional academic branch in the 1960s. The intention was to direct student ambitions away from traditional university entrance towards specific skilled worker and technician-level occupations.

The technical and vocational branches of upper secondary education did not take as many students as was hoped. Apart from Argentina, where 58 per cent of all secondary enrolments were in vocational education in 1983, and Brazil (44 per cent), only between 5 per cent (Venezuela) and 21 per cent (Colombia) attended commercial and technical courses at upper secondary level in the larger countries (Unesco, 1985). These schools sometimes suffered from a lack of qualified teachers and suitable equipment. More often they were rejected by students because they did not offer the same chances of social advancement as the general *liceos*. Students who did attend technical/vocational courses were more likely to come from lower social-class backgrounds and to have higher rates of grade repetition and drop-out than those attending general *liceos*.

The introduction of technical/vocational branches of upper secondary education in Latin America was not necessarily in conflict with the encyclopaedic view of knowledge. The Latin American reforms of the 1960s were very similar to those of France where *lycées professionels* were developed to provide technical/vocational education (see Chapter 3). Reference could be made to the utility principle of encyclopaedism where rational and theoretical knowledge could and should be applied to practical vocational ends. The Latin American technical/vocational branches of upper secondary schooling, like their French equivalents, had a curriculum which included both general academic subjects and those with vocational relevance.

The technical vocational schools of Latin America prepared for occupations which were not growing sufficiently in numbers or in material rewards to attract students. Students in Latin America preferred to enter universities to compete for prestigious posts in medicine and engineering even though the chances of completing these studies for many were not very great.

HIGHER EDUCATION

The encyclopaedist tradition in Latin America is largely enshrined and protected in the universities from where it is transmitted downwards in the education system. Universities in Latin America have patterns of organization similar to those of France before 1968. But the universities have gained a particularly strong position in Latin American politics and society which is not matched by their counterparts in metropolitan France.

In universities, the faculties have been professional not only because they prepare for specific occupations (though the older professions of medicine, law, engineering, or teaching) but because the teachers have often been working practitioners in the fields who teach in universities on a part-time basis. But, as in France until the reforms of the 1960s, professional titles of degrees have hidden the considerable general academic content of these courses. The bulk of studies in engineering courses before the final years consists of the study of conventional mathematics, physics and chemistry, just as a law degree includes much politics and economics.

The professional nature of university courses and the part-time status of many staff has been associated with an exclusively teaching function for universities. The creation or reinterpretation of knowledge have not been seen as major functions of universities. This relative intellectual stagnation of universities may be linked to the lack of dynamism and creativity in the definition of knowledge in the whole education system and to the continuing tendency to borrow from other countries.

Latin American universities are still mainly divided into the traditional vocational faculties of medicine, engineering, law, letters, pharmacy and others. Each faculty generally has a high degree of autonomy within the university and the faculty deans are the most powerful figures after the university rectors.

Since the Cordoba Declaration of students and teachers in Argentina in 1919, universities in Latin America have claimed a high degree of autonomy in relations with government. In addition, many important posts including those of deans and rectors are elected by staff and students. Universities are highly politicized and their politics spill over into national politics both through student and staff campaigns and through the national political ambitions of senior university staff such as deans and rectors.

The autonomy of universities from the state and the autonomy of faculties within the universities have made university reform very difficult to achieve. The traditional courses survive in an encyclopaedist curriculum as well as more vocational studies.

University autonomy has also meant that governments have found it difficult to control a massive growth of university student numbers. In 1970 the proportion of the age group enrolled in higher education in the largest countries varied between 4.8 per cent (Colombia) and 14 per cent (Argentina). The equivalent range in 1982 was 10.4 per cent (Chile) and 25.8 per cent (Argentina) (Unesco, 1985). The freedom to enter universities for all holders of secondary school leaving certificates, together with popular demand and the resistance of universities to government control, has meant a dramatic and unmanageable growth of university enrolments.

The new students generally have taken the same courses as their predecessors. In Latin America as a whole only the new field of social sciences (21 per cent) has more students than the traditional high-status courses of engineering (15.9 per cent) and medicine (13.7 per cent). In contrast humanities had 8.2 per cent and law 8.4 per cent of students in 1976 (Gimeno, 1983). But massive enrolments have led to enormous failure and wastage rates so that in some countries and some universities as few as 5 per cent of students initially enrolling in faculties such as engineering graduate at the end of the five-year course.

Government reactions have been either to attempt to control enrolments or to create new kinds of higher education institutions. Where enrolments are successfully controlled, as in Brazil, large numbers of private universities have emerged to cater for weaker and usually poorer students. Where public universities have been swamped by students, as in Venezuela, the rich send their children to expensive and usually more efficient private institutions at home or abroad.

New kinds of institutions have been modelled on short-cycle education in Europe. The polytechnic and university institute kind of institutions providing two- or three-year courses in specific vocational fields have been established in some Latin American countries. But they have not succeeded in attracting students who still prefer to take their chance of entering the very difficult competition to complete a degree in medicine or engineering.

New organizational structures have been established within universities such as departments and institutes. The intention has been to use smaller units than the faculty to give cohesion to academic staff and greater control over students. There has been a movement away from a largely part-time academic staff to full-time permanent posts. Staff have been sent abroad for further study and these qualifications are increasingly used in determining promotion. Behind these changes, which are often carried out in collaboration with foreign universities especially in the USA (Gonzales, 1981), is the aim to produce more efficient institutions with more dedicated staff and closer staff/student relations.

The failure to reform universities has undermined attempts to change the curriculum of other sectors of the education system of Latin American countries. Universities still offer encyclopaedic courses where standardized general academic curricula lead to traditional professional qualifications. Students aim to enter universities to gain access to posts in the traditional professions. Secondary and primary school curricula are still mainly orientated to university admission.

Curriculum control and management

The main questions are, first, what groups and agencies support curriculum reforms in Latin America especially those designed to relate education to local community identities or to changes in national economies. What are the strengths of these reform movements and what are their chances of success?

Second, which groups and agencies support the continued dominance of the encyclopaedic curriculum? What is the basis of their power and their ability, to the present, of maintaining an encyclopaedic dominance? As in other areas considered in this book, this question focuses on the powerful views of worthwhile knowledge held by educational officials, university academics and schoolteachers.

These questions have been associated in the past in Latin American states with questions of centralization. The concentration of power on government in the national capital may have been an important factor in the preservation of the influence of the encyclopaedic view of the curriculum. Attempts at decentralization in many Latin American countries in the 1970s may allow this assertion to be examined more fully.

But the curriculum has been influenced by groups and agencies outside the formal and official administrative structure. The influence of political parties, of industrial and economic organizations, of universities and of foreign aid agencies each needs to be considered. As in earlier chapters, analysis of the control of the curriculum may focus on both official structures of administration and informal politics.

Latin American countries, without exception, have had a tradition of centralized government and centralized administration of education. Since the 1960s there have been attempts to transfer decision-making to regions and, to a lesser extent, to local communities, which have had varying degrees of success.

Centralized government has been justified by reference to French revolutionary concepts of the reforming and radical state since the Latin American republics were established in the early nineteenth century. Major reform initiatives in all areas of government have come from the centre. An ideology of social transformation directed by central government has been strengthened by 'corporatist' movements such as that of the Mexican revolutionary government after 1917 or the Perónist government in Argentina in the 1940s. It has been reflected in other movements such as the radical military government of Peru after 1968. The 'corporatist' ideology emphasizes the unity of the centralized state and its pre-eminence in directing change above sectionalist movements such as political parties, trade unions, or the church (Stepan, 1978).

Central administration of education has had two elements. First, there is the power of the legislative wing of government. Most of the larger Latin American states have had histories of dictatorship, usually based on military authorities, punctuated by periods of parliamentary and democratic government. Of the seven largest countries Colombia, Mexico and Venezuela have enjoyed elected government throughout the period since 1960. Argentina, Brazil, Chile and Peru have had both elected governments and military control within this period.

However, under both military and elected governments, the powers of presidents have been great. Major laws and educational reforms have been associated with presidents (or sometimes military juntas) rather than with parliaments. Even in the long–standing democratic systems of Colombia, Mexico and Venezuela, major initiatives tend to come from presidents rather than from parliaments. Presidential power and the political importance of presidential political charisma tends to re-emphasize the centralization of decision-making.

Secondly, there is the residual power of centralized ministries of education. Few ministers of education have been associated with major initiatives when dramatic political initiatives are the prerogative of presidents. But the officials of ministries maintain a continuity in countries where few presidents, whether elected or military, last more than five years (the constitutions of Mexico and Venezuela prevent consecutive presidential terms). These officials tend to maintain a passive and conservative approach to educational matters.

Traditionally, ministries of education have decided all matters relating to the provision and content of education. The siting of schools and colleges, the appointment of teachers, the subjects, syllabuses and textbooks of the curriculum and the nature of examinations of primary and secondary education typically have been under the control of centralized ministries of education.

There are important variations of this complete centralization. In Brazil, and to a lesser extent Colombia, control of primary and secondary education has been devolved to regions for a considerable period of time. In these federal systems, governors and state/regional education ministers or secretaries have had responsibility for the provision and content of education below higher education level. This model of deconcentration to regions was adopted formally by most larger Latin American countries in the 1970s. However, in most countries, regional governors and education officials still defer to central decisions on matters of the content of education. There has been a stronger tradition of regional decision on allocation of educational resources than on curriculum matters.

Some educational reforms – especially those related to the creation of Basic Education schools since the early 1970s and, to a lesser extent, the diversification of secondary education in the 1960s – have implied local decision-making in the content of the curriculum. But, with traditions of highly centralized control, local communities or the principals of schools have been reluctant to use these powers (Hanson, 1986).

A major exception to the system of centralization has been universities. Co-ordinating bodies with titles like the National Commission for Universities have mediated between universities and government. But these bodies have tended to concentrate on issues of finance and student numbers. Universities in general have been free to decide their own curricula. Governmental control of the content of higher education has been achieved largely through creating new, less independent institutions such as the 'experimental' universities of Venezuela or the university and polytechnic institutes. These institutions usually offer more technical subjects than older universities. But they rarely have been able to attract students in as large numbers as the older 'autonomous' universities.

Governments have intervened indirectly to influence both the curriculum of higher education and the attitudes of educational planners by creating institutions to finance foreign study. Agencies such as CNpq in Brazil or the Ayacucho Foundation in Venezuela have been influential because they have had an impact on the types of courses that educationists can follow in foreign institutions. But the influence of these scholarship bodies is mediated also by the policies followed by foreign institutions and by the sponsoring universities in their own countries.

Private education is only partly under governmental control. In most countries of Latin America, private schools and universities have to be licensed by government. But there is little control over their curricula except where they prepare for state examinations. Private education covers a large spectrum from informal 'popular' education movements which are outside effective government control to secondary schools and universities which cover both high-status institutions patronized by the wealthy and, more often, lower-standard schools and universities which cater for a demand which state institutions have been unable or unwilling to meet.

However, these formal structures of administration hide many unofficial influences which have a much greater impact on what curricula are adopted in schools and higher education.

THE POLITICS OF THE CURRICULUM

In Latin American as in other less industrialized countries, the major groups which effectively influence the curriculum include politicians and political parties; industrialists and other economic interests; educational officials at central, regional and local level; teachers, including those in higher education; parents and students; and, specifically in these less industrial countries, foreign aid agencies.

Political influences on education in Latin America are considerable because of the politicization of so many aspects of Latin American public life. There has been a tradition that teachers and education officials are appointed because of their membership of the same political parties as their sponsors at state governor or national cabinet minister level. A system of political appointment and political patronage is rife. Changes in the political hue of government, whether by presidential election or military takeover, can have a dramatic effect on the tenure of office of officials even at fairly junior level. So in Venezuela, the government-controlled 'experimental' universities and the traditional 'autonomous' universities differ only in that the senior staff (deans and rectors) in the former change each five years after national presidential elections while in the latter they change every three years after internal university elections which are often based on national political allegiances of the candidates.

The politicization of the educational service tends to strengthen curriculum conservatism and centralized control. Education officials change frequently. Few challenge central authority when their own positions are based on the patronage of officials at central or regional level. Instability of tenure of office by individuals is matched by a continued acceptance of standardization and centralization of educational practice.

Some national political initiatives do change the curriculum. The 1972 Basic Education law in Peru was the outcome of the policy of a radical military government. The adoption of a free market economic ideology in Chile by the military government after 1971 led to the handing-over of much vocational education to industrial enterprises which re-orientated their curricula to suit immediate training needs, or even to become economically productive enterprises (King, 1986). The rise to power of Castro in Cuba in 1959 led to a major educational revolution through political action which brought schools and colleges into line with polytechnical theory and practices of Eastern Europe.

Less powerful political regimes have not carried out such major changes. Politicization of many areas of public life has meant that educational reforms proposed by one group are opposed in principle by agencies dominated by other political parties. The law proposing diversified upper secondary education in 1969 in Venezuela was opposed by teacher groups because the law was seen to have the support of conservative and industrialist political interests of the Christian Democrats while the teachers, who had no objection to diversification on educational grounds, had Social Democrat allegiances. Similarly, the much-vaunted Ministry of Intelligence of the Christian Democrat government in Venezuela after 1979 was demoted to an obscure section of the Ministry of Education, with two administrative officers, after the Social Democrat presidential victory in 1984 (McLean, 1985).

In these conditions, education officials at national and regional level as well as teachers rarely try to challenge established curriculum practice, unless they are working outside the framework of government in the 'poular' education movement. If they wish to effect change, then they wait for a political change at national level which may bring policies of which they approve. But, since these policies are established at national level, they rarely undermine the tradition of central control except where central government politicians or officials wish to divest themselves of troublesome educational problems to regional or local level. Basic Education policies may be seen as attempts by central government to divert unpopularity for restricting opportunities for elite education to local authorities.

Higher education teachers often have more influence on policy. This is not, as in Britain, because the universities control school curricula since it is the state qualification, the secondary school graduation certificate, which gives automatic right of entry to most kinds of higher education and not university stipulations. The autonomy of universities and the links between university and national politics allow university teachers to develop their own educational ideas and then to attempt to implement them when they gain national political power.

Conversely, higher education teachers commonly resist curriculum change which they themselves have not initiated. Resistance occurs on the basis of their power as an interest group in national politics, though the rhetoric of this opposition often makes reference to the ideal of university autonomy. Governments often fear that a conflict with universities (both teachers and students) may have grave political consequences. It is worth noting that substantial curriculum change was initiated by government in Chile after 1972 because the universities had been politically crushed.

While several curriculum innovations, particularly curriculum organization principles derived from the USA, penetrated Latin America through the medium of university teachers with study experience in the USA, teachers in higher education as a whole tend to be conservative in curriculum matters. They are among the most powerful supporters of the retention of the encyclopaedic view of knowledge.

Secondary school teachers, especially university graduates, tend to identify with university interests particularly since, in most countries, university teachers are appointed through open competitions in which a high proportion of candidates are secondary school graduate teachers. Secondary school teachers have little reason to challenge the views of knowledge supported by their university colleagues.

Elementary school teachers, in contrast, have a socially depressed status in most of Latin America. Low rates of pay, poor conditions of work and low educational preparation (very rarely above secondary level) inhibit initiatives in curriculum matters by elementary school teachers. It is unlikely that any representations they might make on curriculum matters would carry much weight. On the other hand, elementary school teachers can and do resist government attempts to make them work harder or show greater skill which are contained in, for instance, the curriculum proposals of Basic Education schemes. The poor conditions of elementary school teachers encourage them to do little more than follow the nationally determined syllabuses.

Parents and students, as in other parts of the world, vote with their feet. The great popular demand for traditional secondary and higher education which give access to traditional high-status professions and the unpopularity of new institutions such as diversified upper secondary schooling or Basic Education have tended to reinforce the educational status quo. Ultimately politicians with a penchant for introducing radical educational changes are constrained by such popular demand.

There have been many claims that Latin American education has been greatly influenced by foreign practices, especially from the USA in the period since 1960. Certainly, the US government directed much educational aid to Latin America following the 1961 Alliance for Progress which led to attempts to introduce American practices especially in higher education (Gonzales, 1981). North American foundations gave much weight to academic interchanges between North and South America (Myers, 1984). The result can be seen in the spread of North American curriculum practices which have been described above.

These borrowings have not been a consequence primarily of economic dependence. Latin American politicians have deliberately chosen North American solutions to internal educational problems, sometimes in order to give the impression that they are the inevitable consequence of development (with the USA as the model) rather than the outcome of local political choice. The highly publicized and prominent use of North American curriculum objectives gives a greater apparent sophistication and

socioeconomic relevance to the traditional standardized encyclopaedic curriculum. The introduction of North American forms of
internal organization for universities deals with the problems of
massive expansion of university enrolments while avoiding the
opposition which might accrue to nationally created policies.
Dependence is often a means by which national politicians ensure
that potentially unpopular reforms are accepted. There is a
residual tendency in Latin America to believe that foreign practice
offers the best model for reform. National politicians frequently
exploit this belief to have their policies adopted by dressing them
in foreign clothes.

Conclusion

The encyclopaedic tradition was adopted in Latin America under
particular and specific conditions. The outcomes have been
different compared to other parts of the world. Yet certain
elements of the education systems of Latin America can be seen to
be quite different from those of other less industrialized countries, especially those which were under British influence, because of this encyclopaedic tradition.

Latin American education offers a universalist curriculum
especially at secondary and higher level which avoids the narrow
specialization prevailing in many former British colonies. There is
a substantial entry to higher education in line with continental
European traditions. A vocational sector of secondary schooling
has been established rather more thoroughly than in areas
influenced by Britain. The highest-status subjects with the highest
enrolments in higher education are not the humanities but the
physical and biological sciences (in the faculties of engineering
and medicine). All of these characteristics may be attributed to the
long-standing influence of an encyclopaedic view of worthwhile
knowledge.

The continuing centralization and uniformity of the curriculum
is also consistent with the French encyclopaedic tradition. But it is
re-enforced by a centralist ideology in Latin America which is
perhaps stronger and more pervasive than in metropolitan
France. The encyclopaedic curriculum is the product of more
than a residual cultural tradition dating to the nineteenth-century
establishment of the Latin American republics. It is consistent also

191

with rigid centralist political traditions in Latin America which offer great barriers to localization of curriculum choice.

The socially divisive effect of the encyclopaedic tradition in education in Latin America is also the product of specific conditions in the subcontinent. The poor in Latin America are those left behind in the process of modernization associated with political centralism. There has been no great economic revolution to match that in government so that modernization based on rational centralized government has not benefited large sections of society. These people have been excluded also from the benefits bestowed by a rigidly centralized education system. The *marginales* have turned to alternative politics and it is likely that they will turn also to alternative forms of educational organization.

Further reading

Avalos, Beatrice, 'Neocolonialism and education in Latin America', in Keith Watson (ed.), *Education in the Third World* (London: Croom Helm, 1982), pp. 141–70.

Freire, Paulo, *Pedagogy of the Oppressed* (Harmondsworth: Penguin 1972).

Fuenzalida, Edmundo F., 'The contribution of higher education to a new international order', in Bikas C. Sanyal (ed.), *Higher Education and the New International Order* (London: Frances Pinter, 1982), pp. 124–44.

Gimeno, Jose Blat, *Education in Latin America and the Caribbean* (Paris: Unesco, 1983).

Gonzales Gilbert, G., 'Educational reform and the University of Colombia, *Comparative Education*, vol. 17, no. 2 (1981), pp. 229–46.

Hanson, E. Mark, *Educational Reform and Administrative Development: The Cases of Colombia and Venezuela* (Stanford, Calif.: Hoover Institution Press, 1986).

King, Kenneth, 'Science and technology images and policies in the ambits of education, training and production in Chile', *Compare*, vol. 16, no. 1 (1986), pp. 37–63.

Lewis, Oscar, *The Children of Sanchez* (London: Secker & Warburg, 1962).

McLean, Martin, 'The international student trade from tied monopoly to open market: some global perspectives and a study of Venezuelan students in Britian', in David Smawfield (ed.), *International Academic Interchange and Cooperation in Higher Education* (Hull: University of Hull, 1985), pp. 81–101.

Myers, Robert G., 'Foreign training and development strategies', in Elinor G. Barber, Philip G. Altbach and Robert G. Myers (eds), *Bridges to Knowledge* (Chicago: University of Chicago Press, 1984), pp. 147–63.

Posner, C. M., 'The new Latin-American pedagogy and the decentralisation of knowledge', in Jon Lauglo and Martin McLean (eds), *The Control of Education* (London: Heinemann, 1985), pp. 53–9.

Stepan, Alfred, *The State and Society: Peru in Comparative Perspective* (Princeton, NJ: Princeton University Press, 1978).

Unesco, *Statistical Yearbook* (Paris: Unesco, 1985).

van den Berghe, Pierre L., 'Education, class and ethnicity in southern Peru', *Education and Colonialism* (London, Longman, 1978), pp. 270–98.

Chapter Nine

Western technology –
Japanese spirit

In little more than 100 years Japan's system of education has been subjected to critical review on at least three occasions. The outcome of the first of these after the Meiji Restoration in 1868 was the establishment of an educational system which was based on a French system of administration, emerging American-British pragmatism, through the influence of Samuel Smiles's *Self Help*, and the German philosophy of Hegel (in its modern form that of Heidegger). Yet at the same time the inner spirit of the system remained Japanese exemplified in the Imperial Rescript published in 1890 which provided the ethical basis of education until the second major reform movement after 1945. The rescript called upon the Japanese people to be loyal to the emperor and empire and to respect the constitution. It became an essential part of school curricula and emphasized filial piety and loyalty. Its cermonial reading in schools together with lessons in morals (*Shushin*) undoubtedly helped to preserve deeply held Japanese traditions during a period of rapid economic transformation based on Western technology.

It was to the interpretation given during the 1930s by the ultra-militarists to the rescript and *Shushin* that the Americans objected after the Second World War when under the Supreme Commander of the Allied Powers (SCAP), the victorious General MacArthur set out to democratize Japan by introducing a liberal constitution and, on the informal advice presented by a United States Education Mission to representatives of the Japan Ministry of Education (*Monbusho*), by reforming education. The Mission considered that education for life in a democracy should rest on the worth and dignity of the individual. It proposed that the content and methods of instruction should foster freedom of inquiry and that textbooks should not be prescribed. Teachers should be free to adapt the content of education to the abilities of children in their various environments. It recommended that the content of school subjects should be reconsidered in order to increase co-operation between Japan and the rest of the world. The aim, shared by parents, students and teachers, of passing examinations should cease to dominate the system. Finally coeducational schools should actively seek the co-operation of the family, the neighbourhood and other social institutions in the all-round development of individual children. Emphasis was placed on the principles enunciated in the charters of the United Nations and Unesco.

Scholars disagree about the role of SCAP in the reform of education in Japan which culminated in principles provided in the 1946 constitution and the Fundamental Law of Education enacted in 1947 which states that the central aim of education should be 'the full development of personality. Striving for the rearing of people, sound in body and mind, who shall love truth and justice, esteem the value of the individual, respect labor and have a deep sense of responsibility, and be imbued with an independent spirit, as builders of a peaceful state and society.'

Whether or not SCAP re-enforced development trends which were already under way in Japan, there can be no doubt that the reforms proposed during the occupation were very much in line with American and indeed world opinion. Education as a human right was implicit in the English 1944 Education Act. The *classes nouvelles* in France reflected a similar philosophy and many progressive educationists in the USA wished to make education 'child-centred'. The speed with which during this second period of reform the Japanese authorities expanded educational provision and made it available to all regardless of gender and social position is astounding and is in sharp contrast to the difficulties faced by people who wished to reduce the power of the central Ministry of Education, Monbusho, and those who wished to introduce child-centred or process curriculum models and get rid of the dominance of examinations throughout the system. Indeed it is to some of the ideas proposed immediately after the war that members of the government's National Council on Educational Reform, set up in August 1984 to advise the Prime Minister, returned in their final report published in English in December 1987.

In a series of reports the council reduced the main issues related to the 'necessary reforms with regard to government policies and measures in various sectors, so as to secure such education as will be compatible with the social changes and cultural developments of our countries', from eight to three. These were how to individualize and increase the flexibility of curricula, how to internationalize Japan and how to establish a system of recurrent or lifelong education. In view of the country's 'economic miracle' it may seem surprising that Nakasone's government considered a major reform of the educational system was urgently needed. Some commentators assert that the Prime Minister hoped that the council would recommend a return to a more traditional system than that which had evolved after 1945. Others deny this. In the event it is clear from the report prepared by a council consisting of more than twenty members drawn from various walks of life that there was little consensus on what precisely should be done to prepare a mass system of education to meet the challenges of the twenty-first century. Indeed in it are found both conservative and radical solutions to problems identified as arising from rapid changes in the economy and ways of life and the failure of aspects of education to respond adequately to them. There is no suggestion, however, that the principles in the 1947 Fundamental Law of Education should be abandoned or that the size of the system should be reduced.

Who shall be educated?

SCAP officials had no difficulty in persuading the Japanese authorities to accept that education was one of the human rights. The new (1946) constitution proclaimed in Article 26 that 'All people have the right to receive an equal education corresponding with their ability, as provided by law. The people shall be obliged to have all boys and girls under their protection receive ordinary education as provided by law. Such compulsory education shall be free.' The period of compulsory education was soon raised from six to nine years and schools were organized so that six-year primary schools were followed by three-year lower secondary and then three-year upper secondary schools. Kindergartens were expanded and in 1949 many post-secondary school institutions were upgraded to universities. Since then the number of national, local and private universities has risen to 460 in 1985. Junior colleges were provisionally introduced in 1950 and made permanent in 1964.

The result is that, in 1985, 63.7 per cent of 5 year-old children were enrolled in kindergartens – the majority of which are private. Virtually all children of compulsory school age (99.9 per cent) were attending elementary and lower secondary schools which cover the period of compulsory attendance. On average 94.1 per cent of all pupils finishing compulsory education were going on to upper secondary schools in that year with a slightly higher percentage of girls than boys. Over the years the percentage of the age cohort going on to higher education has risen phenomenally from 10.1 per cent (4.6 female) in 1954 to 37.6 per cent (34.5 per cent female) in 1985.

In this mass system of education private schools, colleges and universities play an important role. Private kindergartens enrol more than 72 per cent of the 2 million children attending pre-schools. Enrolments in private elementary, lower secondary and special schools for the handicapped are very small, i.e. less than 1 per cent in elementary schools (0.5 per cent) and special schools (0.8 per cent). The percentage of pupils enrolled in private lower secondary schools is 2.9, and 7 per cent of the students in technical schools attended private institutions (1984). The Reform Council encouraged the growth of private elementary and lower secondary schools with the intention of introducing more variety into the system. Private universities enrolled more than 73 per cent of the 2 million students in universities and numbered 328 out of a total of 460 universities. Between these extremes, of the 5,427 upper secondary schools in Japan more than 23 per cent are private and 28 per cent of senior high school students attend private schools. Almost 90 per cent of the junior colleges are private. There is little doubt that without these private institutions it would have been difficult, if not impossible, for education to be provided on such a universal scale in such a short time. It is also clear that the private schools and colleges do introduce variety into a system which operates under guidelines laid down by the Ministry of Education, Science and Culture.

The difference in fees between public and private schools, colleges and universities is considerable. In 1983 parents spent annually 87,298 yen to send their children to public kindergartens. Private kindergartens cost 195,325 yen. Similar differen-

197

tials exist at the second and third levels of education. No tuition fees are charged for public elementary and lower secondary schools but the estimated household expenditure per pupil (on books, stationery, school trips and so on) amounted to nearly 48,000 yen and 96,000 in public elementary and lower secondary schools respectively. Tuition fees amounting to over 5,000 yen are charged in upper secondary schools compared with the 8,000 yen charged by private upper secondary schools. Tuition fees for private universities are more than twice the fees charged by national universities and additional costs such as registration fees increase the differentials.

In spite of the cost of private education many private upper secondary schools enjoy a higher status than some of the public high schools. In some cases more than 3,000 candidates apply and take entrance examinations·for 650 places in private upper secondary schools. There can be no doubt that public per capita subsidies keep the cost of private education to parents down and contribute to their popularity. For the same reason, since the ministry may well provide a proportion of capital costs, some private schools and universities have fine new buildings, and are better equipped with more modern technology than comparable public institutions. Teaching staff may also receive higher salaries. At the same time many private institutions have large bank loans and some people running them fear the financial consequences of the anticipated demographic trends which suggest that in the near future age cohorts will be very much smaller.

At the moment, however, in spite of the fact that the Japanese system is more nearly a mass system than any other in the world except that of the USA, it is extremely competitive. The reason is obvious. The educational background of students determines their future career, status and power – a phenomenon criticized by the National Council on Educational Reform which stated that qualities other than educational background should be taken into account in evaluating the worth of individuals.

Competition is maintained by a series of highly selective entrance examinations to upper secondary schools, universities and indeed large companies which recruit new employees from favoured universities. Once an employee finds work in a big company, tradition has ensured that he or she remains with the company and is promoted as a consequence of long and faithful service. It is clear from the report of the Reform Council and comments made about it that there is little consensus in Japan about the present close links between educational achievement, as measured by examinations, and employment. The council criticized the examination system but its members could not agree on what should be done. Some maintained that one national university entrance examination should replace the many examinations held by private universities. Others considered that there should be no national examination and that every university should conduct its own entrance tests as it deemed necessary. American-style scholastic aptitude tests were considered.

Meanwhile upper secondary school graduates enter for a national examination in five subjects which vary in accordance with the desired field of study. To guard against failure to gain admission to a universty, candidates almost immediately take as many as seven private university entrance examinations which consist of three papers. On the arts side Japanese, English and a paper from the social sciences – Japanese or world history – are required. Students wishing to concentrate on the natural sciences are usually required to take papers in English, mathematics and a natural science. Waseda University in Tokyo, one of the oldest and most famous private universities, had over 34,000 candidates for its entrance examination in 1988 of whom not more than 9,000 were admitted. Candidates who pass the first national examination may enter for a second set of entrance examinations run by individual national universities of which Tokyo University is the most famous. In Tokyo, the national university has to compete with long-established private universities such as Waseda and Keio. Outside Tokyo the reputation of the other national universities is usually considerably higher than that of the new private universities so that the competition to enter a national university is fierce. Each of them decides at the second stage what kind of entrance examination it should set. In some cases no more than two papers are required at this stage.

This kind of 'examination hell' – to which frequent reference is made in the literature – has given rise to innumerable cram schools (*Juku*) whose specific task is to prepare students for entrance examinations at all levels – including, some people say, for very highly regarded private kindergartens. It is reported that members of the Reform Council were invited to recommend that the *Jukus* be recognized as a legitimate part of the national system. Whether they are or not, it seems unlikely that they will disappear since educational qualifications count for so much in Japanese society.

What knowledge is of most worth?

Parents, students, industrialists and teachers may well consider that the knowledge needed to enable pupils and students to pass one of the series of entrance examinations is in practice most worthwhile. Certainly these examinations play an important role in determining the emphasis placed on required subjects which at the point of entry to a university include the Japanese language, English and mathematics. Theory, however, does not legitimize such specialization but is still a subject on which there are conflicting opinions. In marked contrast to the ease with which the Japanese authorities accepted education as a human right after 1945, curriculum reform has been constantly debated. The pre-war system of education undoubtedly had some of its origins in European and American practices but it was run on the basis of deeply held traditions. Loyalty to the emperor and the nation and filial piety were basic obligations which informed the spirit of what was taught. As stated, it found expression in the Imperial Rescript, in moral education and, during the militarist and ultra-nationalist period, in the Cardinal Principles of the National Entity of Japan (*Kokutai no Honqi*) issued in 1937.

Moral education became the centre of a violent struggle between Monbusho and radical members of the teachers' unions. At first union leaders were supported by SCAP in demanding that the formal teaching of morals should be abolished and replaced by social studies. When the political climate changed during the Korean War the Americans transferred their support from the communist-led teachers' union to the Ministry of Education. After the occupation the position of moral education in the curriculum dominated violent debates. Even now the recommendation in the Reform Council's report that moral education should be strengthened reflects that the battle had not been decisively won even by 1988.

The teachers' union and left-wing academics continue to support American-inspired curriculum innovations. The ministry has tried to reverse some of the curriculum changes introduced during the occupation by proposals to include vocational subjects in upper secondary school curricula and a return, at all levels, to the so-called 'basic' subjects. Both views find expression in the council's final report.

A brief historical account of the curriculum debate provides clues to the dilemmas faced by the Reform Council. In 1950, for example, the Ministry of Education raised the issue of 'morals' as a separate course of study. In 1951 the Japanese government appointed a committee to evaluate the American-inspired re-forms. It recommended that more emphasis should be given to vocational studies in the upper secondary school partly because industrialists criticized the single-line American system for failing to supply trained manpower needed by the country. The commit-tee proposed that a five-year vocational secondary school should be established to include three years of lower secondary and two years of upper secondary school. Courses of study should not be uniform but should be revised for both general and technical schools. Another reversal of policy was suggested, namely, that the government should prepare textbooks.

The 1988 Reform Report returned to these issues by recom-mending vocational courses, a six-year lower and upper secon-dary school and ways in which the ministry should assess and authorize textbooks without asserting that it should prepare them.

During the 1950s some of these recommendations were car-ried out by the ministry against the determined opposition of the Japan Teachers' Union. Its leaders were particularly opposed to the reintroduction of 'morals education' as a separate course of study. So fierce was the reaction to its proposal that the ministry postponed action and in 1955 recommended that it should be incorporated in social studies. The Advisory Council for the Curriculum set up by the ministry, however, argued that the teaching of morals through social studies had not been effective and could not be made either systematic or consistent through the study of 'problems' many of which, in a complex world, were trivial. 'Morals' as a separate and compulsory subject was reintro-duced into school curricula in 1958.

A contribution was made to the debate by the late Professor M. Hiratsuka and his colleagues at Kyushu University who devised and carried through a comparative study of moral education in Japan, England, France and Germany. The research team, helped by three European scholars, came to the conclusion that in prewar moral education too much attention had been paid to the acceptance of patterns of behaviour in accordance with the age, status and sex of exemplary persons and what they said, and too little attention had been paid to 'principles' as guides to be-haviour.

The research undoubtedly influenced the establishment of a new moral code drawn up in 1966 by the General Advisory

Council which stressed as appropriate virtues in the ideal human being, respect for life, health and safety, appearance, language, property, punctuality, freedom and justice. The subject (*Doutoku*) introduced as compulsory in school curricula undoubtedly attempted to reconcile some traditional Japanese virtues with contemporary Western international values. On this specific question the Reform Council had relatively little to say in its 1988 report but it did emphasize the need to 'internationalize' education in Japan. In mentioning the need to strengthen moral education in schools it failed to grasp as firmly as it might have done a major issue, namely ways of encouraging the majority of Japanese people, and not only their international businessmen and diplomats, to see themselves as part of a world community.

Instead attention was directed to the difficulties faced by children returning to Japan who had been educated abroad. The command of Japanese of many of these 'returnees' is far less good than that of pupils who have never left Japan. In one public elementary school on the outskirts of Tokyo an intelligent 'returnee' confessed that while she knew only 500 *kanji* characters most of her classmates who had not been overseas could read and write 1,000 characters. In this school, Ohizumi Elementary School, forty-five 'returnees' are taught separately as a group. Many of them fail to pass the entrance examination for the popular lower secondary school associated with the elementary school. By the same token throughout the system as a whole 'returnees' cannot easily compete successfully in competitive entrance examinations and the Reform Council recommended that a number of places should be reserved specifically for 'returnees'.

Already in 1988 some schools with a special interest in the fate of these children intend to run separate examinations at a different time of the year for 'returnees'. In this way such pupils and students will not have to reach the same high level of competence in Japanese as the majority of candidates. The aim of these new policies is, however, simply to bring the level of achievement of 'returnees' up to that of students who have not studied abroad and to make it easier for them to re-enter the Japanese system of education. Little attention, except in a few schools like Bunri High School near Tokyo, is paid to developing the international outlook of *all* pupils. The need to do this in the universities was recognized by the Reform Council. International

student, scholar and teacher exchanges are now actively encouraged and are on the increase.

These problems have a long history but curriculum debate in
general has taken place at regular intervals. A series of ministry-
inspired revisions of curricula took place during the decade when
the battle over 'morals' was at its height. The elementary school
curriculum was revised in 1951, 1955 and 1958. By 1961 curricula
were again laid down in ministry regulations. In this year another
elementary school curriculum was promulgated for adoption in
elementary schools. By 1962 new courses were in operation in
the lower secondary schools, and geography and history were
again taught in the elementary and lower secondary schools –
inclusions which ran contrary to American prohibitions.

The teachers' union opposed all these attempts by the ministry
to abandon the curriculum reforms favoured by the Americans. It
was not entirely successful because the ministry appealed to the
deeply held beliefs of many, if not all, teachers and parents.
Moreover, teachers had been accustomed to accepting ministry
regulations and finally the entrance examinations stressed the
acquisition of 'basic' knowledge. Criticism of the ministry's inflex-
ibility is hardly justified in the light of the freedom, particularly at
the upper secondary level, granted to local authorities and
schools to offer a variety of courses within ministry guidelines.

Curricula in the final quarter of the twentieth century

Apart from stating that curricula should be more flexible and that
more emphasis should be placed on the mental and physical
development of individual children in their social environment
the Reform Council failed to make specific suggestions about how
best Japanese curricula could be revised to meet the challenge of
the twenty-first century. It made clear, however, that it did not
consider the school the only educative agency and that the family,
neighbourhood and community had roles to play in the development of individual children. These views echo the recommendations made by the US Education Mission and have the support of
many Japanese educationists. The difficulties are seen in terms
either of the stranglehold of the Ministry of Education, Science
and Culture or of the university entrance examinations. A closer
look at what curricula are prescribed reveals that there is truth in

both claims. Schools, for example, operate under a considerable number of national regulations. On the other hand public schools probably do not use as fully as they might the flexibility which regulations permit.

For example, the school year lasts thirty-five weeks and the number of curriculum 'hours' per year for each subject is specified. The minimum number of days for kindergarten education is 220 a year and four is the usual number of classroom hours per day. In the elementary school a class 'hour' lasts forty-five minutes. In the lower secondary and upper secondary schools it lasts fifty minutes. As pupils move up the elementary school the number of lessons per week increases from twenty-five to twenty-nine. In each year of the lower secondary school the number of lessons each week is thirty.

The proportion of time spent on the Japanese language, arithmetic and physical education in the elementary school varies between 60 per cent in the first year to just over 48 per cent in the sixth and final year. In lower secondary schools more than 46 per cent of the first-year curriculum is devoted to Japanese, mathematics, science, and health and physical education compared with 16.5 per cent on social studies and moral education. In the third year of the lower secondary school the balance is weighted even further against social studies and moral education, the figures being 50 and 13 per cent respectively. These figures imply that, compared with the situation when the influence of the occupying powers was still strong, in independent Japan there has been a return to basic subjects. What are these? And how far is the criticism that curricula are inflexible and do not adequately take into account the mental, moral, aesthetic and physical needs of individual children justified?

The Reform Council, pointing to widespread violence and bullying in schools, referred to the need to strengthen 'morals' education. As a subject it occupies one lesson a week in both the elementary and lower secondary school. However, at least in some private schools great attention is given to the moral education of pupils and indeed informs the whole ethos of the school. Interpretations of moral education are, perhaps, uniquely Japanese, and find expression in demands that pupils should be polite, punctual and neat in appearance and obey traditional rituals. In one school visited pupils are expected to clean their classrooms regularly to develop a sense of community responsibility. In another, great emphasis is placed on regular attendance.

Individual and class prizes are awarded to pupils who are never absent. In another school great emphasis is given to preparing young women to be good mothers. In these and other ways the moral development of children is emphasized. The Institute of Moralogy, which has a university and a high school within the same complex, has under the leadership of the grandson of the founder of 'moralogy' C. Hiroike an ongoing and active research programme dealing with the international aspects of the science of morals. In many ways the institute is unique and through its supporters played an important role in the earlier debates about 'morals' education.

Now while the teachers' unions concern themselves principally with salaries and conditions of service the final report of the National Council for Educational Reform came in for considerable criticism from union leaders on the grounds that it was reactionary and might well lead to a revival of militarism. The old feuds clearly have not entirely disappeared. On other curriculum issues a balance has been reached between American and continental European models. At all levels of education, including the course of general education provided in the first year of university courses, components from the language arts, the social sciences and the natural sciences are included in curricula. This broad fields model reflects US curriculum theory. In addition music, the fine arts, physical education and home-making find a place in what are essentially encyclopaedic European-like curricula in the elementary and lower secondary schools. Over the six years of elementary schooling the number of class 'hours' allocated to the various subjects varies, as does the total number of 45-minute lessons in a year – from 850 in the first grade to 1,015 in the fourth, fifth and sixth grades. In all six grades Japanese language, social studies, arithmetic, science, music, drawing and handicrafts, physical education and one lesson a week of moral education constitute the curriculum laid down in Monbusho national guidelines. Two lessons a week of home-making are included in the fifth and sixth years. In the first three years one lesson a week can be devoted to locally determined special activities and in the last three years the number of such lessons is increased to two. Compared with 'The percentage distribution of school hours in a typical elementary school' in the 1956 issue of *Education in Japan*, which groups Japanese language and mathematics together, social studies and science, music, drawing and handicraft into very broad areas for which the time allocations varied each year from 15 per cent to 45 per cent, the curriculum of the 1980s is indeed less flexible than that in operation shortly after the end of the occupation. Again in 1956 the total number of school hours per year throughout the elementary school was 870 compared with the variable number in 1986. Moral education as a subject was, of course, missing from the 1956 curriculum.

So it was from the 1956 lower secondary school curriculum which included a foreign language, vocational study, home-making and 'others' as options which constituted between 7 and 15 per cent of the annual school timetable. In 1986 the flexibility had been reduced to three (first and second grade) or four (third grade) elective subjects which may be used for increasing special activities which are allocated two lessons a week throughout the three years. Of the four lessons devoted to elective subjects in the third grade one is taken from either music, arts, health and physical education, or industrial arts and home-making. There are three foreign language lessons in each of the lower secondary school grades and one lesson a week of 'other subjects specially required'. The room for manoeuvre is consequently strictly limited compared with the freedom given to teachers, schools and local authorities in the mid-1950s.

Throughout the period considerable attention has been given to English. It is a required subject in lower secondary and upper secondary schools and a required element in all university courses. It should be said, however, that except by comparison with curricula in England and Wales, before the introduction of a national curriculum in 1988, and in the USA, the curricula in Japanese schools are not markedly different from those found in schools in other industrialized countries.

Perhaps because of the university examinations the upper secondary school curriculum is the subject of most discussion and even criticism. The principle of choices made by individual schools and local authorities is nevertheless retained at this level of education. Monbusho guidelines allow for differentiation in terms of pupil interests and gender. An American-style 'credit' system provides flexibility. To obtain a 'credit' in any subject at least one lesson a week (35 in a school year) is taken in it. Thus 35 units of school time, each lasting 50 minutes, make up one credit. In order to graduate from a high school pupils have to complete at least 80 'credit' hours over the three-year course, or about 27 'credits' each year. This implies a school week of 27 lessons. Over the years debate has turned on the proportion of credits, out of

Japan's curricula

the 80, which should be required and how many should be optional.

Under the occupation in 1951, in a 'Tentative course of study for upper secondary schools', the number of 'required' credits was set at 38 out of a total of 85 necessary for high school graduation. As Monbusho regained more control after the occupation the number of required credits was raised. In the 1960 course of study 68 credits in specified subjects were required out of the 85 needed to graduate. The course of study was revised again during a period when reforms in education were again under consideration. In the 1970 revised course of study the number of credits in required subjects was decreased to 47. In the course of study prepared in 1978 and introduced in 1982 the total number of credits needed for graduation was reduced to 80. Of these 32 had to be taken in specified subjects. In 1988 this course of study was still operating. It emerged from the request by the Ministry of Education, Science and Culture that the Curriculum Council should consider (1) the content of education in the light of the expansion of upper secondary school enrolments, (2) how a balance between elementary, lower secondary and upper secondary levels of education could be maintained under these circumstances and (3) what could be done to alleviate the burden of work expected of pupils and students while strengthening the teaching of basic subjects.

The 1982 course of study was based on the view that the autonomy of individual schools should be respected so that ministry guidelines could be applied more flexibly. Traditionally Monbusho set rigid curriculum requirements and teachers had to teach exactly what was required from prescribed textbooks. The result was that all students reached on average a higher level of academic achievement than probably anywhere else in the world. It also realized substantial equality of provision for all. The National Council on Educational Reform, however, reported that many students were unable to cope with the demands of such exacting standards and reported on increases in truancy. Prior to their final report it was held that while compulsory schooling should provide a common base of knowledge the upper secondary school should provide curricula which would be meaningful and useful in the future life of individual students by meeting their diverse abilities and aptitudes under local conditions. The Reform Council reiterated in its final report the need to conduct education in accordance with the needs and abilities of individual students. In effect it supported the view that 'cramming' should be abolished yet the content of education should be sufficiently substantial to prepare students adequately for higher education and the world of work.

Since 134 credits in a wide range of general and vocational subjects are approved by the ministry and only 30 required credits chosen from the language arts, the social sciences and the natural sciences are needed in order to graduate, it is possible for schools and local authorities to offer in effect a range of semi-specialized high school courses. Several private schools visited early in 1988 were taking advantage of this freedom by offering either different courses in general upper secondary schools, or courses in which at least 30 credits were devoted to specialized vocational studies in technical high schools.

There is no doubt that university entrance examinations have a profound influence on the kind of curriculum most upper secondary schools offer. For students wishing to enter a university the pattern of credit hours in Table 9.1 would most likely to be followed.

A typical pattern of elective subjects taken by students intending to specialize in science at university would include science I, 4 credits; science II, 2 credits; physics, 4 credits; chemistry, 4 credits; biology, 4 credits; earth sciences, 4 credits. In addition home-room and additional credits adding up to 5 might be taken to give a total of 102 credit hours.

Students might specialize in technical-vocational subjects. For such students 51 credit hours have to be completed in the same broad fields of knowledge as in the general university-orientated courses. A pattern in a specialized field might include the credits given in Table 9.2.

Other main vocational courses are business studies, agriculture and horticulture. In business studies the total number of credits in general subjects is about 57 for boys and 61 for girls with 38–42 devoted to specialized vocational courses. The balance in agri-culture is about 48 (boys) and 52 (girls) in general subjects and 46 (boys) and 42 (girls) in agricultural subjects. Roughly half the curriculum is therefore devoted to general subjects and the other half to vocational subjects.

It should be said that in at least two private vocational high schools visited in 1988 great emphasis was placed on 'moral' education. In the Chikushi Technical High School for boys in Dazaifu, Kyushu, politeness, punctuality and regular attendance

Table 9.1 University entrance studies in a Senior High School

	First year	Second year	Third year	
Japanese language	5	5	5	15
Social studies		7	8	15
Mathematics	6	5	3	14
Science	6	5	3	14
Health & physical education				
Boys	5	5	3	13
Girls	3	3	3	9
			Total	80

Table 9.2 Specialized industrial subjects in a Senior High School

Subjects	Credits (1st–3rd years)
Machine shop practice	14
Mechanical drawing	9
Machine design	7
Machine shop theory	6
Prime mover	3
Industrial measurement automatic control	2
Materials for:	2–7
Machine works	
or Industrial management	
or General electricity	
or Industrial English	
Total	43–48

gave meaning to the ethos of the school which was designed to develop a spirit of co-operation and 'guts' in boys whose training enabled many of them to enter the Honda car factory as technicians. In a secondary girls' high school (Fukuoka Minami Girls High School) while technical business skills were taught the main aim of the founder principal was to prepare her girls to be good mothers.

Diversity within university entrance courses is also possible. Bunri High School, located in an affluent new suburb of Tokyo and established eight years ago as a private school, provides three somewhat specialized courses. The balance of credit hours taken in the general course between the humanities, the social sciences and the natural sciences does not allow for specialization and a majority of students enrol on this course. Students on the mathematics and science course can take more credit hours in these subjects during the second and third years than they would in a general course. On the third course – English – students take more 'credits' in English than is expected of students on the general course. The academic aim of this school, with about 1,900 students, is to prepare students for well-known universities. It hopes in the future to develop close links with some high-status universities and that some of its graduates will return to teach in the school when they have studied in a university and received a certificate to teach in an upper secondary school.

Undoubtedly the private schools add variety in a system in which the emphasis is on equality of provision rather than diversity on the basis of the different abilities of individual children. There is, however, evidence that public schools can also innovate. In the Gifu Prefecture, for example, an elementary school has been lavishly equipped with computers on the initiative of the local mayor. A great deal of software has been made on the premises and pupils cheerfully and actively learn a number of school subjects with the aid of these computers.

In its Occasional Paper 02/86, *New Upper Secondary School Education in Japan*, the National Institute for Educational Research of Japan reports on the diversification of the school curriculum. The 1982 course of study gave upper secondary schools an opportunity to prepare their own curricula. In that year the Ministry of Education, Science and Culture conducted a nation-wide survey with the help of prefectural boards of education on how the new guidelines were to be implemented. The results of the first survey showed that about a quarter of the public upper secondary schools offered more than 25 credits, out of the minimum of 80, on elective subjects. In the second survey the proportion of schools taking advantage of the freedom granted by Monbusho's guidelines had increased to 42 per cent. There is evidence that the new course encouraged diversification. Two surveys in Hyogo Prefecture reveal how wide was the choice of electives among students on the general course. Indeed the largest proportion of the upper secondary school students chose vocational subjects such as art, industry, commerce, home-making, and hygiene and nursing. Language electives included German, French, Spanish, Chinese and Korean. The surveys in

Hyogo showed that although university entrance examination subjects – mathematics, the Japanese language, science, English and social studies – were selected by many students a great many other subjects were selected in accordance with the interests and inclinations of individual students.

Further evidence that attempts were being made to meet the needs of individual pupils is that streaming in English and mathematics has increased in recent years. The organization of classes in terms of the ability of students to master the subject–matter is flexible and does not apply to all subjects in the curriculum.

From 1975 on, new upper secondary school curriculum models were introduced in some prefectures round the big cities of Tokyo and Osaka. The ministry gave maximum support to these initiatives. It has also helped by allowing prefectures to increase the size of upper secondary schools. In the Chiba prefecture, for example, three upper secondary schools were opened on the same site and joint operations were planned although each school had its own facilities. In Saitama Prefecture three upper secondary schools were combined to be run as a single unit with an estimated 3,240 students. Its size makes it possible for it to offer 150 different subjects. To prevent a breakdown in human relationships six student guidance units were set up, each with a vice-principal in charge of 540 students. While having a general course the school offers eight areas of study in the humanities, science and mathematics, languages, art, technology, physical education, home-making and commerce.

While such schools might be regarded as experimental it is nevertheless difficult to justify the criticism made of present Ministry of Education, Science and Culture officials that they impose regulations which make it impossible for schools to meet the varied aspirations of pupils. Curricula throughout the compulsory stage of education leave rather little room for the individualization of content – at the same time they meet the need to ensure equality of provision: one of the requirements which motivated reform movements in Western Europe after 1945. At the upper secondary level of education, ministry guidelines make it possible for schools and local authorities to provide individual pupils with choices. Even the national university entrance examination is less restrictive than many of the examinations set by high-prestige private universities.

It is unlikely, however, that the present emphasis on university entrance subjects will change until big corporations adopt new or different recruitment policies. At the moment what is important to them is the university from which a potential employee has graduated not what he or she has learned during the four-year undergraduate course. It may also be necessary for upper secondary schools, universities and employers to take more account in their selection processes of qualities of character and to pay less attention to examination successes. The frequently heard statement that 'It is difficult to get into a university but easy to get out' can hardly be sustained when in one famous private university students are required to take an entrance examination in order to attend the seminars of a senior and famous professor in the subject of their choice.

The National Council on Education Reform identified as the major problem facing educators changes in the economy which had not been matched by changes in the educational system. It is certainly the case that since 1945 curriculum debate has covered at regular intervals much the same ground. Pressure to reduce the power of Monbusho to prescribe the content of education and the textbooks which must be followed faithfully has ebbed and flowed.

Members of the national council rehearsed many of the arguments which have been used both by educators and members of the public who favoured the proposals made by the United States Education Mission and by those who opposed them. The lack of consensus in the council's report makes it possible for members of both sides to claim that the report favours their position. Meanwhile, parents, teachers, employers and even students appear to be reasonably satisfied that examinations serve a useful purpose and prevent the abuse of nepotism in a society based on family relationships and obligations. Japan's economic success makes it difficult to accept that if education necessarily plays a major role in economic development the content of education in Japan, which is selected on criteria drawn from continental European and American models, is inappropriate. On the other hand the slowness with which, under considerable pressure from the Americans, curricula in Japan have changed since 1945 admirably illustrates the power of teachers to prevent reform and their unwillingness and indeed inability to make the psychological changes needed if the content of education is to be radically revised. Teachers, including university academics, may be more responsible than officials in the Ministry of Education,

Science and Culture for the failure of the Japanese system of education adequately to respond to changes in the economic life of a dynamic society.

Further Reading

Aso, Makoto, and Amano, Ikuo, *Education and Japan's Modernization* (London: Japan Information Centre, Embassy of Japan, 1978).

Beasley, W. G. (ed.), *Modern Japan: Aspects of History, Literature and Society* (London: Allen & Unwin, 1975).

Dore, R. P., *Education in Tokugawa Japan* (London: Routledge, 1965).

Dore, Ronald, *British Factory – Japanese Factory: The Origins of National Diversity in Industrial Relations* (London: Allen & Unwin, 1973).

Duke, Benjamin C., *Japan's Militant Teachers: A History of the Left-Wing Teachers' Movement* (Honolulu, Hawaii: University Press of Hawaii, 1973).

Duke, Benjamin C., *The Japanese School: Lessons for Industrial America* (New York: Praeger, 1986).

Hall, Robert King, *Education for a New Japan* (New Haven, Conn.: Yale University Press, 1949).

Hiroike, Chikuro, *The Characteristics of Moralogy and Supreme Moralogy* (Tokyo: Institute of Moralogy, 1966).

Holmes, Brian, 'Individual freedom and social responsibility', in *Problems in Education* (London: Routledge, 1965).

Holmes, Brian, 'Education in Japan', in *The Yearbook of World Affairs, 1979* (London: Stevens, 1979).

Institute of Moralogy, *An Outline of Moralogy: A New Approach to Moral Science* (Tokyo: Institute of Moralogy, 1987).

Krauss, Ellis, S., *Japanese Radicals Revisited: Student Protest in Postwar Japan*, (Berkeley, Calif.: University of California Press, 1974).

Ministry of Education, Science and Culture (Monbusho), *Education in Japan: A Brief Outline* (Tokyo: Ministry of Education, Science and Culture, 1986); and *Annual Report* of the ministry (annually).

Ministry of Education, Science and Culture (Monbusho), *Education in Japan: A Graphic Presentation* (Tokyo: Ministry of Education, Science and Culture, 1959, 1971, 1982).

National Council on Educational Reform, Japan *National Council on Educational Reform: Final Report* (Tokyo: Ministry of Education, Science and Culture, 1988).

Reischauer, Craig, and Albert M., *Japan: Tradition and Transformation* (London: Allen & Unwin, 1979).

Rohlen, Thomas P., *Japan's High Schools* (Berkeley, Calif.: University of California Press, 1983).

Stoetzel, Jean, *Without the Chrysanthemum and the Sword: A Study of the Attitudes of Youth in Post-War Japan* (London/Paris: Heinemann/ Unesco, 1955).

Suzuki, D. T., *Zen and Japanese Culture* (London: Routledge, 1959).

White, Merry, *The Japanese Educational Challenge: A Commitment to Children* (London: The Free Press, Collier Macmillan, 1987).

Chapter Ten

Voluntary transfer – the People's Republic of China

China has never been completely occupied by a foreign power. During the nineteenth century competition between the Europeans, Americans and Japanese helped to prevent overt colonization. Throughout the period Chinese officials remained hostile to 'foreign devils' and refused to grant their representatives diplomatic rights. This traditional approach to foreigners was sustained by Chinese confidence in a long cultural heritage. It was enhanced when European governments recognizing the value of Chinese methods of selecting scholar-officials to serve the emperor introduced competitive examinations to appoint civil servants. The Chinese had reason to be proud of their system of education and the high status and vicarious political power it gave to teachers. Pride in their cultural heritage and confidence in the value of education have not changed.

On the other hand, the Chinese have always been willing to learn from other countries. Thus prior to 1949 when the communists took power, French, English, German, American and Japanese influences had helped to shape the school and higher educational systems of China. For example, during the earliest attempts to create a national system of modern education a Japanese model, which owed much to Western theory and practice, was adopted almost completely.

American influence was considerable but short-lived. During the first quarter of the twentieth century American educators including John Dewey, Paul Monroe and Helen Parkhurst visited China. An American 6–3–3 system of education was established by legislation in 1922 and curricula became less academic. A credit

215

system allowed for greater diversity and the integration of vocational studies into the curriculum. At the college level, pragmatism interested many Chinese philosophers and courses which broke away from traditional subjects were introduced. Under the Guomindang, which came to power in 1927–8, Chinese leaders looked to the more centralized European systems for inspiration and the American influence declined.

In the event, according to *Achievement of Education in China* published by the Department of Planning, Ministry of Education of the People's Republic of China, the communist government inherited a very underdeveloped system of education. Some 80 per cent of the population was illiterate and the enrolment ratio of school-age children was 20 per cent. Even in 1983 there were 230 million illiterates. Pre-school education and provision for handicapped children were even more backward. There were very few schools in the rural areas and in the hinterland inhabited by national minorities. Institutions of higher education and specialized secondary schools were, for the most part, located in large towns and cities. A tiny educated elite ruled over a vast semi-feudal and partially colonized country of largely illiterate farmers. The elimination of illiteracy, the expansion of education and its more equal distribution remain high on the list of Communist Party objectives.

To eliminate illiteracy in China is complicated. The number of characters which have to be memorized if even simple texts are to be read run into the thousands (some authorities claim that 1,800 have to be known). A written language makes national communication possible in a country where many different languages meet the needs of largely rural populations. In the USSR literacy in one of the many mother tongues is a constitutional right granted to parents. Pride in Chinese scholarship probably re-enforced political reasons for rejecting occidental scripts. Recently a new common language called Putonghua has replaced Mandarin as the medium of instruction except in designated areas where non-Han linguistic minorities live. On the other hand the authorities did not face the dilemma created in many colonized countries by the existence of an alternative international foreign language, such as Spanish, French, or English, as a competitor to one of the indigenous languages. When Soviet influence was strong, Russian was the most popular foreign language. To make modern scientific knowledge more widely available much technical Russian literature was translated into Chinese. Since Mao's death English has become the medium of communication with the outside world and modern science.

The modernization of curricula has been constrained by Chinese traditions of scholarship which run extremely deep. The content of pre-1949 education was enshrined in the Confucian classics which dealt with family relationships and by extension human relationships throughout the whole empire. In these terms the principles of good government were central to the education of potential scholar-officials who were selected on the basis of a series of competitive examinations conducted at county, prefectural, provincial and national levels. Candidates who succeeded in examinations held in the capital could expect to be appointed to the highest positions in the imperial civil service. Until 1905 when it was abolished, the imperial examination system determined the content of education in China. Since then the ideals which informed it have continued to make curriculum reform difficult. Indeed conflicts since 1949 over curricula can be seen as fundamentally between those scholars and teachers who continued to believe in the virtues and high standards of Chinese scholarship and those who wished to introduce Marxist-Leninist theory and practices imported from the Soviet Union. A pragmatic acceptance of the value of Western scientific knowledge and technological know-how has created a context in which the debate has been conducted.

Who shall be educated?

In practice, since 1949, the argument, at times violent, has turned on the organization of the school system. Should it be differentiated and selective or unified? As in the USSR where Marxist-Leninist doctrines inform educational debate, so in China it has been conducted in terms of the rhetoric of Mao Zedong, who while rejecting Khrushchev as a revisionist 'wearing the cloak of Marxism-Leninism' remained a follower of Marx and Lenin. In his *Little Red Book* or 'Red Guards Handbook' he frequently justified his advice by reference to them. In practice during the first period of educational reconstruction contacts between China and the rest of the world were restricted to socialist countries and particularly the Soviet Union. Thousands of undergraduates were sent to the USSR and Eastern Europe. Over 600 students from these countries were sent to China.

In 1949 Mao's stated commitment was to establish contact with foreign friends. It meant that Soviet experts were invited to work in the Ministry of Education in Beijing but less than 10 per cent of the Soviet experts were educationists. Before relationships between the two countries deteriorated in 1960 many delegations from China visited the USSR. A conscious attempt was made by leaders in China voluntarily to learn from Soviet experience. Apart from the books which were translated from Russian there is little to suggest that during the period of overt co-operation between the two countries Soviet practice made a vast difference to the Chinese school system. Paradoxically, during the Cultural Revolution between 1966 and 1976 policies were much nearer than those in the 1950s to the principles of policy espoused in the Soviet Union.

Clearly, however, after 1949, the government of the People's Republic of China made strenuous efforts to extend education by restructuring higher education; by reforming teaching; by setting up second-level schools for children of workers and farmers; by developing adult education; and by providing scholarships for needy students. But at first the expansion took place within the twelve-year structure which had been established in the 1920s – six years primary, three years lower secondary, three years upper secondary and four years university. In this American-type structure, however, the Chinese differentiated between school types and curricula. Prior to the Cultural Revolution distinctions were made between 'keypoint' and other secondary schools which allowed some secondary schools to send most of their students to prestige universities.

One of the first tasks undertaken by the new government was to rebuild and reopen many schools after the devastation caused by foreign and civil wars. It also took into public ownership all schools and institutions and recovered from foreigners the schools run by them. Between 1949 and 1952 policies were designed to reduce the differences in provision between rural and urban areas and between workers and peasants. People-operated schools in local communities and worker-peasant schools were set up. Some spare-time adult educational facilities were established for urban workers. Higher education was expanded but polytechnical universities were separated from liberal arts and composite universities. As a result the second and third levels of education remained differentiated in ways which did not do violence to Chinese traditions or Soviet practice.

Between 1953 and 1958, under the influence of Soviet advisers, emphasis was given to quality and high standards of achievement particularly at the third level of education in urban areas. This policy was in line with the attention given in the USSR to the maintenance of academic standards in large urban universities such as the State University of Moscow.

Mao's 'Great Leap Forward' movement, initiated in 1957, meant, however, that expansion was encouraged by introducing half-work, half-study schools for a vast number of illiterate adults. Open door policies were advocated and agricultural middle schools were set up. Emphasis was still on urban schools: under the slogan 'walking on two legs' (a policy initiated in 1955–7) high-standard urban schools were supported by the state and rural schools were financed and run by members of the local communities.

Prior to 1966, then, expansion took place within a selective two-track system. In urban areas regular secondary schools prepared youngsters for higher education. In the other track specialist technical schools trained middle-level professional workers such as nurses. Training schools for workers prepared middle-level personnel such as carpenters and welders. Between 1958 and 1960 the number of schools categorized as specialized secondary schools more than doubled. Of these the proportion of secondary technical schools amounted to about two thirds of all schools. School curricula were very closely related to school type in this diversified system.

Paradoxically, after 1962 and during the Cultural Revolution the number of specialized secondary schools declined and after the break with the Soviet Union Chinese leaders introduced policies legitimized by the principles of Marx and Lenin and not by Soviet practice. In June 1966 most of China's schools were shut down as students divided into competing groups. When in 1968 schools started to reopen, a different kind of secondary school structure began to emerge which was designed to remove the inequalities of the two-track system and the distinction drawn between urban and rural schools.

Primary schools were unified into five-year schools in which pupils in rural and urban areas were to be educated in exactly the same way. Distinctions between existing types of secondary schools were abolished. The authorities were particularly anxious to eliminate the 'keypoint' schools in which financial and peda-gogical resources were concentrated. During the Cultural

Revolution these highly academic selective schools were transformed into ordinary secondary schools with lower and upper sections. The distinction between work-study and full-time schools was abolished. A vast number of formal and non-formal educational institutions was set up in the rural areas. Entrance examinations to secondary schools (and indeed to universities) were abandoned. Streaming in secondary schools was not allowed and no pupil was either held back or allowed to skip a class.

These moves were designed to remove the advantages previously enjoyed by children from the middle class and the intelligentsia. Admission policies were introduced which gave workers and peasants with practical experience an advantage. Many of them were admitted by 'three in one' committees of workers, peasants and soldiers to study not only in secondary schools but in universities. In fact the recommendation of a party official played a major role in the admission of students to a university. The abolition of entrance examinations and the two-year work experience requirement made it impossible for administrators any longer to rank-order their schools. Not surprisingly, according to not necessarily very reliable statistics, the number of pupils enrolled in secondary schools shot up from 14.4 million in 1965 to 68.5 million in 1977.

In summary, during the Great Proletarian Revolution a powerful group within the Communist Party, perhaps with the blessing of Mao, accepted Marxist-Leninist educational principles far more wholeheartedly than before. Its members tried to unify basic first- and second-level education by admitting everybody to schools at these levels regardless of place of residence, social class position and academic achievement. Academic learning was, by intention, closely associated with productive labour and intending students were required to work in industry or on a farm for two years before entering university. In short, the policies proposed in the USSR under the Khrushchev reforms of 1958 to bring education nearer to life were copied in China during the Cultural Revolution. They failed in the USSR and were to fail in China.

By 1975 criticism of these policies was widespread. Academic standards were criticized. In a paper prepared by Huang Shiqi for *Achievement of Education in China – Statistics 1949–1983* a devastating critique is made of the damage done to education during the Cultural Revolution. He states that 'this decade of internal turmoil seriously disrupted the functioning of, and inflicted heavy losses on, the educational enterprise'. Normal instruction was in some cases suspended for four years. Schools were closed. Teaching staff suffered and many schools were occupied. 'Not only a whole generation of youth became the victims of this turmoil, but also the quality of teaching in various types of schools deteriorated seriously.' The consequence was, according to Huang Shiqi, that the country 'now suffers from a shortage of qualified manpower on every front and an abnormal age structure of her professional personnel'.

The dispute was apparently among party members. The death of Mao and the liquidation of the 'Gang of Four' made it possible for the party under Hua Guefong to rectify what had gone wrong. So in 1977 college entrance examinations were reintroduced. In 1978 revised versions of the regulations issued in the early 1960s were published under *Provisional Regulations on Higher, Secondary and Primary Schools*. Good order was gradually re-established. After 1979, in accordance with decisions taken by the Central Committee of the Chinese Communist Party, the status of education in the process of socialist modernization was raised. These measures culminated at the 12th National Congress in 1982 in a number of educational policies.

These included (1) speeding up the development of higher education; (2) accelerating the training of postgraduates; and (3) changing the irrational structure of secondary education. The policies imply a return to a more selective system based upon the right and duty of every citizen laid down in the 1982 constitution to receive education. Some idea of the success with which 'education for all' has been achieved can be gleaned from Chinese statistics.

In 1983, 94 per cent of school-age children were enrolled in first-level schools but almost 20 per cent of them were over age. A majority of children was in rural primary schools. About 67 per cent of all primary school pupils went on to lower secondary schools and of these not more than 36 per cent entered senior secondary schools. Only 33 per cent of pupils in general secondary schools were in rural areas. Less than 45 per cent of the children in primary schools and 40 per cent of the pupils in general secondary schools were girls (1983).

Since 1976 many specialized secondary, agricultural and vocational schools have been restored and new ones opened. Admission to 'keypoint' schools is now based on merit rather than parental position. Between 1978 and 1983 the number of higher educational institutions increased by 207 and the number of students has grown by 14 per cent. In 1985, at the request of the Chinese authorities, a Unesco conference was held in Shanghai to discuss the development of 'key' universities.

In May 1985 the Central Committee of the party and the State Council resolved to reform the educational system. The reform set out to make education a strategic focal point in the socialist modernization of China; gradually to implement a nine-year compulsory system; to boost technical and vocational education; and to reform the administration of higher education. Debates about, and criticism of, the privileged position of the 'keypoint' high school continue but it is clear that in the interests of modernization the abandonment of a unified school structure and the elimination of curriculum differentiation have been post-poned.

The determination of the Chinese authorities to provide 'education for all' has been maintained against formidable odds. Trad-itional attitudes towards the education of girls have had to be overcome. Differences between rural and urban areas have created problems. The constraints placed on modernization by deeply held Confucian beliefs are considerable. Finally it is not clear how equal education can be provided for everyone in common schools while ensuring that vocational and technical schools promote industrial modernization.

What knowledge is of most worth?

As in Western Europe major debate in China turned on access to education and the kind of institutions in which it should be provided. In China control of the curriculum also raised ques-tions about the relative merits of Confucianism informed by occidental innovations and views of knowledge legitimized by Marx and Soviet educationists. In this conflict during the Cultural Revolution Chinese academics suffered greatly. Many of them were dismissed and made to undertake menial unskilled jobs like sweeping the streets. Political committees of workers, soldiers and peasants made it impossible for teachers to regulate admis-sions to schools and institutions of higher learning. Only after the death of Mao were the more old-fashioned teachers able to regain some of their former status and power based on their role in the life of imperial China.

This power had been retained by pragmatic teachers who between 1860 and 1905 had paid considerable attention to Western knowledge. This knowledge came in part from Japan where, after the Meiji Restoration, modern scientific knowledge and a Western system of education had been introduced to modernize the country. After the 1911 revolution, some elements of Chinese classical learning were removed from school curricula and emphasis was placed on moral, utilitarian, military and aesthetic education. The content of education was centrally determined along Japanese lines and consisted of the classics, history, geography, morals and the sciences – a pattern not vastly different from those in European schools at the time. When in 1915 relations with Japan became strained, Chinese educationists turned to the USA for inspiration.

During this period the primary school curriculum was encyclopaedic – consisting of conversation, reading, composition, penmanship, arithmetic, hygiene, citizenship, history, geography, nature study, gardening, industrial arts, imaginative arts, music and physical education. At the second level, vocational studies were introduced for the majority of students who were not destined to go on to higher education. New textbooks were prepared which paid attention to the development of individual children and experimental methods of teaching included project method and Dalton-plan techniques. In colleges new courses in librarianship and a wider range of professional subjects were introduced on an experimental basis.

American curriculum models became less popular when the Guomindang came to power in 1927–8 but Western influences were not eliminated. The fragmentation of knowledge implied by the US credit system was rejected in favour of consolidated academic subject knowledge. These subjects, taught with examinations in mind, dominated curricula although along with Chinese literature, mathematics, physics, chemistry, biology, history, geography and foreign languages, citizenship was included in the upper secondary school curriculum. Vocational schools with more restricted curricula were set up for the less academically gifted.

Soviet advisers confirmed the need for encyclopaedic curricula on the authority of Lenin's views. In spite of the view taken by Cai Yuanpei in the 1930s when the Nationalists were in power that a distinction should be drawn between academic affairs and the political manipulation of students by political parties, after 1949

223

the government of the People's Republic of China was committed to the politicization and polytechnicalization of the curriculum. The communist authorities welcomed student activism since it had contributed to the success of the revolution. Indeed Mao was determined that the political training of the young should not go by default and political education was included as a separate core subject in first-level schools. Mao's quotations were carefully studied. Revolutionary songs were sung. These and other activities were intended to erase bourgeois tendencies and to develop an appropriate socialist or communist consciousness.

In curriculum terms the relationship between political consciousness and professional competence is encapsulated in the slogan 'red and expert'. It lies at the heart of attempts made in China to interpret the historical experience of mankind in ways which will promote communist ideals. Although R. F. Price (1977) writes that it is a mistake to regard Soviet polytechnical theory as the same as Mao's insistence that theory should always be related to practice, and that there is no Chinese term for polytechnical education, the ideas expressed by Marx, Lenin, Krupskaya and Mao are sufficiently similar to justify the claim that central to Chinese assumptions about worthwhile knowledge is the view that it should be related to productive life in a socialist society. Theory and practice should be closely linked and education should be brought nearer to life.

Mao illustrated his commitment to polytechnical curriculum theory by stating that 'natural science is man's weapon in his fight for freedom' (*Mao's Thoughts*, p. 205). For him dialectical materialism has two characteristics. It is based on an analysis of 'class' and the dependence of theory on practice (ibid. p. 206). If man is to succeed in his work he has to 'bring his ideas into correspondence with the laws of the objective external world' (ibid.).

Attempts were made during the Cultural Revolution to realize this theory in practice. It runs counter to the traditional assumptions of teachers. Most of them see worthwhile knowledge as that encapsulated in abstract principles and universal propositions *per se*. They are reluctant, and frequently do not have the experience, to relate their knowledge to the worlds of industry and commerce. Evidently some Chinese commentators thought it was foolish to try. In 1985 a senior ministry official wrote that much time had been wasted teaching physics by reference to its applications in steam and other engines. In this remark his acceptance of the intrinsic value of scientific principles as such is very apparent. As in the Soviet Union the polytechnicalization of knowledge is viewed with suspicion in China and few teachers know what it means.

Curricula in the 1980s

Everywhere the primary school curriculum is the same for all pupils. At the second level the content of education depends very much on the type of school attended. Attempts to unify second-level education have had considerable implications for curricula which were not recognized for more than a decade in many countries. The dilemma is as apparent in China as elsewhere.

Pre- and post-Cultural Revolution school curricula showed these characteristics. Data for the period 1966 to 1976 are not available but implicit in the rhetoric of the Red Guards is the view that differentiation of school types and curricula should be reduced or eliminated. Policy decisions in 1985 confirmed the view that differentiation at the second level of education was necessary if modernization is to succeed.

(1) PRIMARY SCHOOL CURRICULA

Since 1977 primary schools have been expected to raise the cultural and scientific level of young people and train them to realize the aims of modernization. Literacy is fundamental to the tasks of supplying second- and third-level institutions with well-qualified students and literate workers. Urban schools meet the first objective; rural schools the second. Curricula, which in theory allow for local variations, are academic. A majority of parents who see no prospect that their children will move on to higher education withdraw them from school before the end of the primary stage. The authorities have talked about designing programmes for rural schools but thus far local variations turn on levels of achievement expected of pupils following an academic curriculum.

The emphasis in this curriculum is on language, mathematics and moral training. When in 1980 Beijing lengthened the period of primary education from five to six years it set a trend. Ethics replaced politics in the curriculum and history and geography were reintroduced. The curriculum is encyclopaedic. The teaching plan in Table 10.1 is taken from an article by Billie L. C. Lo in *Contemporary Chinese Education* edited by Ruth Hayhoe.

Table 10.1 Teaching plan for full-time five-year primary schools, 1982

Subjects	First grade	Second grade	Third grade	Fourth grade	Fifth grade	Total class hours	%
Ideological and moral education	1	1	1	1	1	180	3.9
NATIONAL LANGUAGE TOTAL	11	12	11	9	9	1,872	40.3
Speaking and reading	10	11	8	6	6		
Composition			2	2	2		
Writing	1	1	1	1	1		
Mathematics	6	6	6	7	7	1,152	24.8
Foreign language*				(3)	(3)	(216)	
Natural science			2	2	2	216	4.7
Geography				2		72	1.6
History					2	72	1.6
Physical education	2	2	2	2	2	360	7.8
Music	2	2	2	2	2	360	7.8
Art	2	2	2	1	1	288	6.2
Labour				1	1	72	1.6
TOTAL Class hours per week	24	25	26	27	27	4,644	
EXTRA-CURRICULAR ACTIVITY							
Self-study	2	2	2	2	2		
Scientific, technological & recreational activities	2	2	2	2	2		
Sports activities	2	2	2	2	2		
Class meetings & group activities	1	1	1	1	1		
TOTAL School Hrs/W.	31	32	33	34	34		

* A foreign language is offered only in schools with the necessary resources.

Source: This teaching plan has been translated from an official document issued in January 1982. I am grateful to Lau Wing Fong of the Chinese University of Hong Kong and Professor Stan Rosen of the University of Southern California for providing this document.

The total number of class hours increases as the child moves up through the school. The number of extra-curricular class hours, which include self-study, science and technology, sport and class meetings, remains the same. In the regular programme considerable attention is paid to physical education, art and music. The position of a modern foreign language in the curriculum reflects differences between primary schools. These differences, exemplified by the differences between 'key' schools and others and between 'key' schools themselves, are still debated in the light of the previously enunciated principle that provision should be equalized.

(2) SECONDARY SCHOOL CURRICULA

In 'Chinese educators on Chinese education' edited by Ruth Hayhoe, Qian Jingfang and Huang Kexiao write: '"The Cultural Revolution" of 1966–1976 was a catastrophe, which destroyed secondary education entirely ... most of the agricultural secondary schools and vocational secondary schools were either closed or transformed into general high schools; secondary education consisted in only one type of school, that was the general high school. The quality of secondary schooling declined severely' (p. 88). The authors continue: 'The absolute uniformity of secondary schooling is a cancer brought about by the "Cultural Revolution"' (p. 89). The reforms of 1985 were designed to develop technical and vocational secondary schools and to establish vocational classes in general high schools. There is disagreement over the reforms but the authors think that equal stress should be laid on vocational education in general and that in general secondary schools courses involving manual labour and technology should be strengthened and improved. Labour skills should be introduced into the curriculum of general schools; options in the upper classes of the upper secondary schools should allow students to specialize either in the arts or sciences; and in order to develop modern science and technology textbooks from abroad in mathematics, physics, chemistry, biology and foreign languages should be referred to.

The teaching plans provided by Stanley Rosen in Hayhoe's *Contemporary Chinese Education* and confirmed in *Achievement of Education in China – Statistics 1949–1983* indicate (Table 10.2) how courses in the two final years of 'keypoint' upper secondary schools are differentiated into liberal arts and science and how (Table 10.3) the curriculum in 'keypoint' schools differs from curricula in ordinary and agricultural/vocational schools. Labour training in the 'keypoint' schools accounts for the smaller number of class hours per week in them compared with other types of school.

Table 10.2 Teaching plan for full-day six-year keypoint secondary schools (Working Draft, January 1982 – Guangzhou)

Course	Lower secondary (hours/week in class)			Upper secondary					Total time in class programme	
	1	2	3	1	2A	2B	3A	3B	A	B
Politics	2	2	2	2	2	2	2	2	384	384
Chinese language	6	6	6	5	7	4	8	4	1,208	1,000
Mathematics	5	6	6	5	3	6	3	6	906	1,086
Foreign language	5	5	5	5	5	5	5	4	960	932
Physics		2	3	4		4		5	292	560
Chemistry			3	3	3	4		4	288	432
History	3	2		3				3	350	266
Geography	3	2			2	2	3		328	234
Biology	2	2			2			2	200	192
Hygiene			2						64	64
Physical education	2	2	2	2	2	2	2	2	384	384
Music	1	1	1						100	100
Fine art	1	1	1						100	100
Hours/week in class	30	31	31	29	26	29	26	29	5,554	5,734
Labour training	2 weeks			4 weeks					576	

Note:

(a) Programme A in Upper Secondary 2 and 3 is for those who select a liberal arts speciality; Programme B is for those who select a science speciality.

(b) During the labour training period, there are 4 classes per day in Lower Secondary and 6 per day in Upper Secondary.

Since 1976 there has been a decline in the number of students in general upper secondary schools and a rise in the number in specialist and vocational schools. The significance of these changes lies in the number and proportion of students who follow vocationally biased courses in which history and geography are omitted. On the other hand it should be noted that six hours a week are devoted to vocational studies in ordinary upper secondary schools.

In spite of the degree of specialization allowed in 'keypoint' upper secondary schools, curricula in lower and upper 'keypoint' schools are encyclopaedic – the arts/science distinction is one of emphasis only. In the lower secondary school attention is paid to Chinese language, mathematics, a foreign language and the natural sciences. The pattern is not dissimilar to that in continental European schools (and in English schools after the 1988

228

Table 10.3 Teaching plans for various kinds of upper secondary schools (Working Draft, January 1982 – Guangzhou)

	Keypoint schools								(hours/week in class)				
	(hours/week in class)												
	Classrooms not divided by course-work			Classrooms divided into arts & science students					Ordinary schools		Vocational and agric. schools		
Course	1	2	3	1	2A	2B	3A	3B	1	2	1	2	3
Politics	2	2	2	2	2	2	2	2	2	2	2	2	2
Chinese language	5	4	4	5	7	4	8	4	4	4	5	4	4
Mathematics	5	5	5	5	3	6	3	6	6	6	5	5	5
Foreign language	5	5	4	5	5	5	5	4	3	3	2	2	2
Physics	4	3	4	4		4		5	4	4	4	4	
Chemistry	3	3	3	3	3	4		4	3	3	3	3	
History	3			3			3		2				
Geography		2			2	2	3			2			
Physical education	2	2	2	2	2	2	2	2	2	2	2	2	2
Biology			2		2			2					
Elective courses		4	4										
Vocational classes									6	6			
Specialized technical courses											8	8	16
Labour training	4 WEEKS			4 WEEKS					2	2	2	2	2
Hours/week in class	29	30	30	29	26	29	26	29	34	34	33	32	33

Notes:

(a) Programme A in Upper Secondary 2 and 3 is for those who select a liberal arts speciality; programme B is geared for those who select a science speciality.

(b) During the labour training period, there are 6 classes per day in keypoint schools; ordinary and vocational schools can arrange labour training in accordance with their regular vocational or specialized courses.

(c) The physics and chemistry textbooks for vocational schools are geared to a 2-year programme, and are the less rigorous of the two levels of textbook available.

Education Bill is implemented) except that labour training has its place in all secondary schools. As an isolated activity in the curriculum, labour training is unlikely to transform, as a poly-technical curriculum is intended to do, the nature of general education. In China the attempts made during the Cultural Revolution to break down the dichotomy between liberal education and vocational training by 'polytechnicalizing' every subject have been abandoned in the interests of gearing education to industrial modernization.

In neither the USSR nor China has it been possible to prevent teachers from paying special attention to 'high-flyers' who are able without difficulty to tackle academic subjects which will prepare them for university admission. By the same token, in practice curricula in technical and vocational schools are designed to prepare students for specific occupations. It has not been possible to devise curricula which will at one and the same time provide all students with a broad and generous education and train many of them to meet specific manpower needs.

(3) HIGHER EDUCATION

The expansion of higher education since 1947, when there were 207 institutions of higher education, to 1983, when there were 805 (with increased enrolments from 154,612 to 1,206,823), has not taken place without the debate reflected in the 'two-line struggle'. According to the 1978 constitution education was given the task of training 'red and expert' intellectuals who could promote socialism and a Marxist-Leninist-Maoist ideology and offer party leadership. Educationally the four principles of modernization implied the training of scientists, technologists and economic administrators. The technical and scientific levels of working people had to be raised, culture developed and economic construction stepped up.

After the disruption of the universities during the Cultural Revolution instruction in the most up-to-date science and technology by strengthening international science exchanges became the cornerstone of policy. College entrance examinations were reintroduced. Higher education was expanded and diversified. Curricula were reformed. Administrative reforms were proposed and a new concept of higher education planning was introduced. Yet by 1985, when a decision was taken to reform education, there was room for improvement according to some Chinese commentators.

For example, the training in regular university courses of highly specialized personnel had far outpaced training in short-cycle institutions. A ratio of more than three to one caused a serious imbalance in the composition of the workforce so that senior technical personnel had to do lower-level work. Curriculum biases toward science and engineering and against the humanities and social sciences meant that in 1983 only 5.9 per cent of all those enrolled majored in finance and economics and only 1.5 per cent majored in political science and law. Most students were studying basic rather than applied subjects. Too many students chose heavy industrial specialities and too few chose to study light industrial specialities. It was necessary to increase enrolments in the social sciences including business management, add courses in new aspects of science and create interdisciplinary fields. Criticism was also made of teaching methods which encouraged rote learning and book knowledge but failed to prepare students to face real problems analytically. Students lacked the ability to undertake worthwhile research on their own and to explore new domains of knowledge.

Official statistics only partially confirm these criticisms. These statistics show in historical perspective how students were distributed among the different kinds of higher education institutions. For example, throughout the period 1949–83 twelve major types of institutions are listed – comprehensive, engineering, agriculture, forestry, medicine and pharmacy, teacher training, language and literature, finance and economics, political science and law, physical culture, art and other universities. The number of students following engineering courses has led the field consistently since 1949; in that year the percentage was 26, in 1983 it was 34.7. The percentage of students following teacher-training courses was 10.3 in 1949; in 1983 it was 26. The proportion of students studying medicine and pharmacy dropped by 2 per cent over this period. The overall numbers studying political science and law dropped from 37,682 in 1947 to 18,286 in 1983. The percentage of students studying the humanities dropped from 10.2 in 1949 to 5.6 in 1983. During this period the proportion of students of agriculture dropped from 8.4 per cent to 5.7 per cent.

Engineering, teacher training, and medicine and pharmacy have not suffered. Enrolments in the humanities have always been somewhat less than in medicine and pharmacy and not much higher than in the natural sciences. In short, in spite of fluctuations in stated policy, in practice the emphasis on professional rather than 'pure' subjects has remained a feature of higher education in China. The Cultural Revolution was an aberration remedied by the forces of conservatism after Mao's death and the elimination of the Gang of Four.

Statistics suggest, however, that enrolments in engineering have followed technological change. The percentage of students enrolled in radio and electronics shot up from 3.4 per cent in

231

1959 to 18.8 per cent in 1983. Mechanical engineering attracted 29 per cent of students in 1983 compared with 17.2 in 1952. Major losses occurred in civil engineering, architecture, power engineering and transportation.

These changes would not be unusual in any highly industrialized society since they reflect a shift from traditional extractive industries to new industries which need experts in electronics and mechanical engineering. Whether the changes have been sufficient or the overall expansion great enough to meet the needs of modernization is doubtful. There are less than 1.25 million students in a population of more than a billion. Compared with the number of students in Japan, the USA, Western Europe and the USSR the number of university and higher education students in China per thousand of population is small and probably accounts in part for the difficulties the authorities face in modernizing the country.

Certainly, according to Huang Shiqi, director of the Information and Documentation Unit of the Ministry of Education of the People's Republic, there are too few students enrolled on undergraduate courses in the humanities and the social sciences to meet the needs of the economy. It is proposed that a number of engineering students should undertake management courses. In engineering, in spite of what statistics tell us, serious imbalances are to be corrected. There are too few undergraduates preparing for light industry. More dentists are needed for the health services. Given the specialized nature of higher education courses the authorities are faced with the task of readjusting the proportion of students in the various fields to meet what they regard as manpower needs.

A second task has been to introduce an integrated degree structure into Chinese higher education. Abortive attempts were made in the mid-1950s and early 1960s to introduce academic degrees along lines followed in many countries. This task was taken up again in 1979 under the Minister of Education, Jiang Nanxiang. Regulations were promulgated in February 1980 and came into effect on 1 January 1981. Under these regulations students in higher education may receive bachelors', masters' and doctors' degrees in accordance with their study programmes. By early 1983, however, only eighteen doctorate degrees had been conferred.

The need to increase the number of postgraduate students is apparent. At present the number is too small to meet high-level professional manpower requirements. Their distribution is unsatisfactory. In 1983 more than 45 per cent of students admitted to masters' courses were in engineering; 25 per cent went into the natural sciences and 10 per cent were in medicine. It will take some time for the traditional distribution of students to be brought into line with what the authorities think is needed if the economy is to be modernized.

To hasten the preparation of suitably qualified postgraduates more and more students have been sent abroad to study (1986), many of them for doctoral degrees. Between 1979 and 1983 more than 11,700 students went abroad, a number equal to the total studying overseas between 1949 and 1978. In 1983 9,000 students were in the USA; in 1982 1,393 in Germany and some 570 in France. It is clear that in learning as much as they can from foreign countries the Chinese will introduce curriculum innovations from a number of industrialized countries rather than from one.

The introduction of 'key' universities will have a profound influence on what is taught, how it is taught and to whom. Entrance examinations have been reintroduced making achievement rather than social position the criterion for admission. In most European countries the highest status would be restricted to the older general humanistic universities. In China there are such institutions. Fudan University in Shanghai and Beijing University are examples of this type and have been named as 'key' universities. However, more specialized institutions including former technical and teacher-training colleges have also been nominated as 'key' universities. They are distributed round the country so that very able students can find a place in one of them fairly near to their home. The introduction of these high-status universities, whose future was discussed at an international conference in November 1985 sponsored by Unesco in Shanghai at the request of the Chinese authorities, reflects the importance placed on the preparation of highly qualified experts in a wide range of subjects. In the past, as previously mentioned, too much importance was placed on technology as the key to industrial modernization. Attention is now focused on producing more social scientists and arts graduates. At the same time the presence among the 'key' universities of those which specialize in professional subjects points to the realism with which the authorities are planning the content of higher education in the light of manpower needs in a modernized industry.

The expansion of university education is still urgently needed if

China is to modernize. To increase opportunities the Central Radio and TV University was established by the Ministry of Education in co-operation with the Ministry of Radio and Television in 1979. It was quickly followed by twenty-eight provincial radio and TV universities; nearly 1.2 million students have enrolled since it was founded. Courses include Chinese, English, physics, electronics, basic mechanical engineering, economics and management science. Self-study courses have also been introduced. More than fifty short-cycle (two-year courses) vocational universities have been established in large and medium-size cities. The courses offered are closely related to local needs for secretaries, accountants and so on. The students from these institutions will be assigned jobs on completion of their studies.

Somewhat less overt attention to the expansion of university education as a human right and in accordance with the wishes of students is given in China than in many other countries. As in Japan expansion has been accompanied by a high level of competition. At the point of entry to university selection has been made stiffer by the introduction of a unified national college entrance examination. It serves the purpose of allocating students to universities and courses in accordance with their achievements and in part in accordance with their aspirations. However, its introduction has been criticized because it takes account of examination results without paying attention to the school records of applicants. Critics suggest that it will encourage students to learn by heart school texts in ways that inhibit creative thinking, an ability to solve problems and independent judgement. Competition for places, particularly in the 'key' universities, will, it is argued, place undue constraints on school curricula which will once again become exclusively examination-orientated. The influence is on 'keypoint' secondary schools, which are intended to qualify workers for industry and prepare students to enter higher education. Critics argue that they are fulfilling only the second of these tasks. They also recognize that highly selective institutions are not democratic. Nevertheless they do no violence to Chinese traditions and may well serve the immediate needs of modernization.

The dilemma in China faces educationists everywhere. It is difficult to reconcile societal needs and the freely expressed wishes of students. Even in mass systems of education such as those of the USA and Japan the dilemma has not been resolved if criticisms of the systems in these countries are to be taken seriously. To balance the search for and promotion of gifted students with the need to provide an education for all raises fundamental questions. Traditional systems made it possible to draw a distinction between education and training. Curricula were designed to educate a small minority of students in high-prestige institutions and to train a majority of them in specialized institutions. Real curriculum difficulties arise when attempts are made to accommodate all pupils and students in unified schools and institutions of higher education. Then there is need for a curriculum which will serve both purposes, namely to train young people for industry and commerce and to prepare them for the next stage of education.

Since 1949 policy changes in China reflect the extent to which attempts to unify the structure of the educational system have failed. Failure to create a system of unified secondary schools and comprehensive universities has resulted in the maintenance of a differentiated system and different curricula. Each type of institution has its own curriculum. For many years ideological arguments have influenced the growth of professional subjects and science.

Present policies retain selection and different types of institutions. The protection of subjects in the field of humanities and the promotion of the social sciences against the powerful competition of engineering subjects is something which concerns educationists in China.

At the same time it is clear that as before the Chinese are anxious to learn from other countries. The USSR is no longer the country to which they most readily and frequently turn. It seems likely that pragmatically they will incorporate into their curricula whatever they think will advance their intention to modernize their economy. It is unlikely that the people of China will readily abandon their time-honoured history, ancient civilization and glorious tradition in education. The rehabilitation of scholars to their former position will undoubtedly make curriculum changes and reforms in the methods of instruction difficult to achieve. It is unlikely that selective examinations will be abolished. Their retention is virtually sure to mean that the content of secondary school education will almost certainly be dominated by examination requirements. China is a classic example of the power of teachers, even against extremely determined politicians, to decide who shall be educated and what knowledge is of most worth.

235

Further reading

Becker, C. H., *et al.*, *The Reorganization of Education in China* (Cambridge, Mass.: Harvard University Press, 1932).

Chan, Pauline, 'Education in the People's Republic of China', in Brian Holmes (ed.), *Equality and Freedom in Education* (London: Allen & Unwin, 1985).

Cleverley, John, *The Schooling of China* (London: Allen & Unwin, 1985).

Fingar, Thomas (ed.), *China's Quest for Independence: Policy Evolution in the 1970s* (Boulder, Colo: Westview Press, 1980).

Franke, Wolfgang, *The Reform and Abolition of the Traditional Chinese Examination System* (Cambridge, Mass.: Harvard University Press, 1960).

Fraser, Stewart (ed.), *Chinese Communist Education: Records of the First Decade* (Nashville, Tenn.: Vanderbilt University Press, 1965).

Galt, Howard, *A History of Chinese Educational Institutions* (London: Arthur Probsthain, 1951).

Hawkins, John, *Mao Tse-Tung and Education: His Thoughts and Teachings* (Hamden Connecticut: The Shoe String Press 1974).

Hawkins, John N., 'Chinese education' in Edward Ignas and Raymond J. Corsini (eds), *Comparative Education Systems* (Itasca, Ill.: F. E. Peacock, 1981), pp. 91–134.

Hawkins, John N., *Education and Social Change in the People's Republic of China* (New York: Praeger, 1983).

Hayhoe, Ruth (ed.), *Contemporary Chinese Education* (London: Croom Helm, 1984).

Hayhoe, Ruth (ed.) 'Chinese educators on Chinese education', *Canadian and International Education*, special issue, vol. 16, no. 1 (1987).

Hayhoe, Ruth and Bastid, Marianne (eds), *China's Education and the Industrialized World* (London: Sharpe, 1987).

Huang Shiqi, 'On some vital issues in the development and reform of higher education in the People's Republic of China', unpublished paper presented at the Vth World Congress of Comparative Education Societies in Paris (2–6 July 1984).

Huang Shiqi, 'An outline of the development of education in China during the past thirty-five years', published in *Achievement of Education in China – Statistics 1949–1983* (from an unpublished paper, Beijing: People's Education Press (1984)).

Huang Shiqi, 'On some vital issues in the development and reform of higher education', in *Higher Education in Europe*, vol. 10, no. 3 (1985), pp. 63–75.

Kiu Wenxiu, 'Developments and interrelationships of higher education in new China' (unpublished paper, Hebei University, the People's Republic of China, June 1984).

Lo, Billie L.C., 'Primary Education: a two-track system for dual tasks', in Ruth Hayhoe (ed.), *Contemporary Chinese Education* (London: Croom Helm, 1984).

Ma Ji-xiong, 'On the universal primary education in China' (unpublished paper, the People's Republic of China, June 1984).

Mao Tse-Tung, *Mao Tse-Tung's Quotations: The Red Guard's Handbook*, introduction by Stewart Fraser (Nashville, Tenn: George Peabody College for Teachers, 1967).

Ministry of Education, *Achievement of Education in China: Statistics, 1949–1983* (Department of Planning, Ministry of Education, People's Republic of China, 1983).

Needham, Joseph, *The Shorter Science and Civilisation in China*, ed. Colin Ronan (Cambridge: Cambridge University Press, 1978).

Orleans, Leo A., *Manpower for Science and Engineering in China* (Washington DC: Committee for Science and Technology, US House of Representatives, 1980).

Orleans, Leo A., *Science in Contemporary China* (Stanford, Calif.: Stanford University Press, 1980).

Price, Ronald, *Education in Communist China* (New York: Praeger, 1970).

Price, R. F., *Marxism and Education in China and Russia* (London: Croom Helm, 1977).

Purcell, Victor, *Problems of Chinese Education* (London: Kegan, Paul, Trench, Trubner, 1936).

Rosen, Stanley, 'New directions in secondary education', in Ruth Hayhoe (ed.), *Contemporary Chinese Education* (London: Croom Helm, 1984).

Taylor, Robert, *China's Intellectual Dilemma: Politics and University Enrollment* (Vancouver, BC: University of British Columbia Press, 1981).

Unger, Jonathan, *Education under Mao: Class and Competition in Canton Schools 1960–1980* (New York: Columbia University Press, 1982).

Index

'A' levels (*see* General Certificate of Education)

'AS' level (*see* General Certificate of Education)

Academy of Sciences (USSR) 104

Academy of Pedagogical Sciences (USSR) 19, 102, 108, 113, 118

Adult Education Act 1966 (USA) 94

activités d'éveil (France) 57, 78

Africa 122, 123, 124, 125, 131, 132, 136, 138, 142, 170, 174

agrégés, professeurs (France) 62
societé des 20, 71

Aid for International Development (AID) 127

algebra (*see also* mathematics) 93, 117

All India Council for Technical Education 163

Alliance for Progress 1961 190

American Association for the Advancement of Sciences 85

Aquinas, Thomas 10

Arabic 65, 160

architecture 150

Argentina 170, 175, 178, 181, 182, 183, 185

Aristotle 8, 9, 25, 28, 83, 90

arithmetic (*see also* mathematics) 34–5, 117, 205

Arnold, Thomas 26

art 12, 27, 38, 54, 66, 77, 78, 116, 159, 211

Asia 7, 122, 170, 174

Asquith report 1945 (Britain) 123

Assessment of Performance Unit (APU) (England and Wales) 40

Association of Southeast Asian Nations (ASEAN) 18

Astier Law 1919 (France) 63, 73

attainment targets 38, 45, 57

Australia 124, 136

Ayacucho Foundation (Venezuela) 187

bachillerato (Latin-America) 180

baccalauréat (France) 59, 62, 63, 77
de technicien 62, 77

Bacon, Francis 28, 83

Bagley, W. C. 82, 89

Baker, Kenneth 38

Balliol College 26

Bangkok 18

Bantock, G. H. 36

basic education 136, 147, 148, 149, 153, 156–7, 161, 166, 179, 180, 186, 189, 190

Basque 65

behavioural objectives 87, 88, 172, 173–4

Bengali 160

Bennett, Neville 38–9

Berger, Peter 131

Bestor, A. E. 90

Bible 7

biological sciences (*see also* science) 12, 63, 77, 89, 92, 113, 116, 117, 191, 208, 223

Biological Sciences Curriculum Study (BSCS) 1959 (USA) 92

Bloom, Benjamin 87, 173

Bode, Boyd H. 96

Bolivia 175

Bourdieu, Pierre 71

Brazil 170, 171, 175, 178, 179, 181, 185, 186, 187

brahmins 6, 149

Breton 65

brevet d'enseignement professionel (BEP) (France) 62, 77

Britain (*see also* England and Wales) 10, 12, 19, 21, 122, 123–4, 127, 128, 177
influence on other countries 123–4, 130, 134–5, 136, 137, 142, 146–8, 166

Broudy, H. S. 87